THE NUCLEAR WEAPONS FREEZE AND ARMS CONTROL

Edited by
STEVEN E. MILLER

BALLINGER PUBLISHING COMPANY
Cambridge, Massachusetts
A Subsidiary of Harper & Row, Publishers, Inc.

International Standard Book Number: 0-88730-010-3

Library of Congress Catalog Card Number: 84-6162

Printed in the United States of America

Library of Congress Cataloging in Publication Data

Main entry under title:

The Nuclear weapons freeze and arms control.

Papers presented at a conference held Jan. 13-15, 1983 at the American Academy of Arts and Sciences, Boston, organized by the Academy and the Center for Science and International Affairs, Harvard University.
    1. Atomic weapons and disarmament—Congresses. 2. Arms control—Congresses. I. Miller, Steven E. II. American Academy of Arts and Sciences. III. John F. Kennedy School of Government. Center for Science and International Affairs.
JX1974.7.N865   1984   327.1'74   84-6162
ISBN 0-88730-010-3

Contents

7 Preface
   Paul Doty

10 What Now for Arms Control?
   Paul Doty

NUCLEAR FREEZES

13 Arms Control and the Nuclear Weapons Freeze
   Jan H. Kalicki

17 The Freeze and Beyond
   Henry W. Kendall

22 A Rapidly Negotiable, First-Stage Nuclear Freeze
   Franklin A. Long

25 Conceptual Foundations of a Comprehensive Nuclear Freeze
   Christopher E. Paine

30 Exploring the Feasibility of a Ban on Warhead Production
   Jane M.O. Sharp

37 Soviet Diversion of Plutonium under IAEA Safeguards
   An Exchange between Frank von Hippel and Joseph S. Nye

PUBLIC OPINION AND THE FREEZE MOVEMENT

39 Public Attitudes Toward the Freeze
   Louis Harris

41 Learning from the P.S.R.: Successful Methods for Major Impact
   H. Jack Geiger

44 The Freeze in Political Context
   Jonathan Moore

47 The Impact of the Nuclear Freeze Movement on Congress
   Douglas C. Waller

CRITIQUES OF FREEZES AS INSTRUMENTS OF
ARMS CONTROL

53 The Freeze: Near-Term Issues and Near-Term Approaches
   The Honorable Albert Gore

57 Why We Should Freeze Total Deployed Nuclear Weapons
   Jan M. Lodal

60 Perspectives on the Freeze
   Roger C. Molander

65 Arms Control vs. the Freeze
   Christopher M. Lehman

ASSESSING FREEZES:
COVERAGE, VERIFICATION, TIMING

73 Verification of a Nuclear Freeze
   William E. Colby

75 First Steps Toward a Freeze
   Herbert Scoville, Jr.

80 Verification and Negotiation
   Walter Slocombe

88 Judging the Freeze: The Inevitable Trade-offs
   Leon Sloss

DO FREEZES SATISFY ETHICAL CRITERIA?

95 Ethical Dimensions of the Nuclear Danger
   Sister Mary Hennessey

100 The Freeze Movement as an Ethical Achievement
   Rev. Jack Mendelsohn

103 Acceptable Deterrence and the Freeze
   Bruce Martin Russett

109 Ethical Aspects of Nuclear Freeze Proposals
   Charles H. Fairbanks, Jr.

SOVIET INTERESTS AND INITIATIVES

117 Moscow's Arms Control Agenda
   Stephen J. Flanagan

124 Soviet Military Programs and the Freeze
   Stephen M. Meyer

134 Why Andropov Would Reject a Bilateral Freeze
   Dimitri Simes

CONSEQUENCES OF A FREEZE

137 The Political Importance of the Freeze
   Richard J. Barnet

140 Western Europe and the Freeze
   William E. Griffith

144 The Economic Impact of a Bilateral Nuclear Weapons Freeze
   David Gold

151 The European Perspective on the Concept of a Nuclear Freeze
   Johan Jørgen Holst

POLITICAL PERSPECTIVES

159 Fire and Ice
   The Honorable Charles McC. Mathias, Jr.

163 Public Support for the Freeze: The People Speak
   The Honorable Edward J. Markey

WHERE DO WE GO FROM HERE?

165 Nuclear Arms Control: Nothing Until Everything?
   McGeorge Bundy

170 Stopping the Nuclear Arms Race: Defining the Possible
   Randall Forsberg

177 Avoiding Nuclear Sectarianism:
   Toward a Compromise
   Joseph S. Nye

182 Avoiding Nuclear War: Can the Freeze Help?
   Graham T. Allison

186 Legislating Bilateral Freeze Restraints and Mandating
   Negotiations on the Freeze
   Jeremy J. Stone

EXECUTIVE SUMMARY

197 A Nuclear Freeze Reprise
   Steven E. Miller

Preface

The conference which is reported in these pages had its origins in the divergence that was clearly taking place in 1982 between the traditional arms control community and the freeze movement. Much of the arms control community has viewed the freeze movement with skepticism, criticizing its shifting definitions of a freeze, and insisting that what is proposed to be negotiated will require many years at best, thereby robbing the freeze supporters of the expectation of quick and visible results which fires their movement.

At the same time, the freeze movement continues to display its broad public support. While this support may not be highly focused on a precisely defined version of a freeze, it is important to reach clearer views of what can reasonably be expected in the time scale of the present Administration as well as the one that follows in 1985.

It is in this context that the Center for Science and International Affairs and the American Academy of Arts and Sciences planned this conference. By bringing together freeze proponents, arms control specialists, government officials, and public interest group leaders, it was hoped that some differences could be resolved, the essential issues identified, and an agenda of work to be done formulated. The papers which make up this volume, all of which were revised following the conference, show substantial progress in these three directions, and this is elaborated in Steven Miller's summary of the conference.

It may be of help to record the charge that was put to the conference. It was as follows:

"This past year has seen the rapid growth of a grass-roots movement and of sizeable Congressional sentiment in support of various forms of the proposition that Soviet and American nuclear weapons development, production, and deployment ought to be frozen at current levels and in a verifiable manner, until more permanent arrangements can be negotiated to reduce substantially the nuclear arsenals of the superpowers. The movement reflects not only public frustration with a perceived lack of progress on arms control, but is inspired by a more profound disillusionment with traditional approaches. It has triggered the largest outpouring of public interest in the United States in the brief span of the nuclear age. And, it is credited with forcing the Administration to accelerate the development and presentation of its plans at Geneva. On the other hand, the Administration's approach sees freezes as a delay to its plans to negotiate reductions directly, and many arms control specialists see its expectations as being far from attainable.

"Reactions to the freeze have been largely visceral, not analytical. In the current debate, several fundamental questions have gone largely unanswered:

1. What are the essential features of those freezes that should be examined in detail?
2. Would such freezes be verifiable?
3. Would such freezes be negotiable with the Soviet Union?
4. To what extent would such freezes preserve imbalances that would remove incentives to negotiate reductions?
5. What are the broader political and economic costs and benefits of such freezes? And of the absence of such freezes?
6. Should such freezes include intermediate-range missiles, on which negotiations began in January 1982?
7. On balance, should such freezes be designed to promote the START and INF negotiations or to stand in place should these negotiations not succeed?

"A key consideration in the discussion of these questions is what a balanced nuclear weapons moratorium would look like. A nuclear weapons moratorium could be configured in a number of ways, depending on the desired scope, duration, and relationship to formal arms control talks. In terms of scope, a moratorium could apply to some or all strategic weapons, to medium-range "theatre" weapons as well, or even to naval weaponry and battlefield weapons (artillery shells, depth charges, surface-to-air missiles). It could apply to the development of some or all delivery systems, to the production of weapons-grade fissile material as well as bombs and warheads and testing, or to all of the above plus design and development. Each of these stages would have different implications for the monitoring of compliance, and would pose problems of different political and technical complexity. Indeed, the conflicting requirements of prompt negotiability, broad coverage, and adequate verification may exclude many otherwise attractive approaches unless inventiveness comes to the rescue.

"The continuation of the freeze could be tied explicitly to, associated tacitly with, or be independent from progress in arms reduction negotiations. Though intended to encourage the first step toward reductions, it could complicate or inhibit their achievement, if one side saw greater merit in an existing freeze than in future arms reductions, and equally, if one side saw its programs to correct imbalances blocked.

"Finally, there is the challenge of finding how to merge the spontaneous enthusiasm that freeze proposals have unleashed with workable specific programs for reducing the risks of nuclear war. Some success in this direction is needed in order to avoid the risks of polarization within the broad interested public and the disappointment that comes from expectations not grounded in what is really possible."

There remains to be recorded the debt that is owed to those who made it possible to hold this conference on very short notice. The intellectual debt is to the Steering Committee that I chaired—Albert Carnesale, Fen Hampson, Steven Miller, Michael Nacht, Joseph Nye, George Rathjens, and Dorothy Zinberg. Fen Hampson, aided by Christine Lundblad, carried out the difficult organizational assignment with great skill. And Steven Miller has shaped the documents into a coherent report and captured the essence of the conference in his summary—all in record time. Lynn Whittaker deserves special thanks for her countless hours of effort in overseeing the production of this volume. We appreciate as well the willingness of so many to participate, especially Senator Mathias, Congressman Gore, Congressman Markey, and Charles Fairbanks and Christopher Lehman of the Department of State for their role in linking our deliberations to the political nerve center.

The financing of the conference was made possible by a number of contributions all made possible on short notice. Without these, and the confidence that they would be forthcoming when the planning was being done in late 1982, the conference could not have been held. They are as follows: the W. Alton Jones Foundation, the Ploughshares Fund, the Rockefeller Brothers Fund, the Rockefeller Family Fund, Mortimer Zuckerman, as well as others who wish to remain anonymous.

Paul Doty
April 12, 1983
Cambridge, Massachusetts

What Now for Arms Control?

Paul Doty

For all those for whom meaningful arms control is preferable to an unrestrained competition in nuclear arms, some serious stocktaking is in order. Compare the decade that began in 1963 with the one that followed. In the 1963 decade 10 agreements and treaties of an arms control nature were made and ratified between the Soviet Union and the United States and, in some cases, many other countries. In the decade of 1973 to the present none of any significance have been ratified. Arms control and disarmament have come to a full stop. We wish well for the negotiations in Geneva but expectations are not running high. Therefore, all who have concern and involvement over our nuclear futures have some obligation to examine the ways in which the process can be started again, to invent new approaches, and to test those against such experience as we have.

Many of the obstacles that held up progress after 1973 are still with us. One is the very poor state of relations with the Soviet Union. This slows negotiations because distrust and the near absence of dialogue prevent the rapid exploration of possibilities that might lead to agreement. This situation seems unlikely to change soon. A mighty obstacle, homegrown, is the two-thirds Senate vote needed for ratification. So far as we know, no other industrialized democracy has more than a majority requirement for ratification. Given the present composition of the Senate and its slow rate of change, this obstacle too seems unlikely to change. A third obstacle is the long tradition of slow and deliberate negotiation. There was one exception, when Harriman and Khrushchev negotiated the Limited Test Ban Treaty in 13 days. But, otherwise, the heavy tradition of nonurgency has taken its toll. Wars are not fought on such timetables: the effort to prevent war deserves better. But, here too, there seems little hope for change. Much of the procrastination follows from the four-year cycle of changes in our executive branch and the year lost when each new administration must reassess and relearn. This too is unlikely to change.

One can always hope that the next administration will find ways to overcome all these obstacles, and that the Soviets will be ready and eager to negotiate. But, we know it cannot be this easy.

To overcome these obstacles, to reach agreements that greatly lower the risk of nuclear war, requires nothing less than a thoroughly aroused and informed public, a bipartisan commitment to seek these ends, and a well-thought-out and tested arms control program that will win enthusiastic support that will last the course.

This is a tough set of conditions to meet. But they have been met for other causes in the past: for women's suffrage, for winning World War II, for civil rights, for ending the Vietnam War, for the environment. No one would argue that preventing nuclear

Paul Doty *is Director of the Center for Science and International Affairs at Harvard University, Cambridge, Massachusetts.*

war would not dwarf these other virtuous causes. But that may overstate the case. In these causes there was always a clear, positive goal and even though the country did not always get there all the way, as with civil rights, there was a visible change, a smell of victory. With the nuclear issue it could never be claimed that a certain course of action prevented nuclear war. At best, success can be judged indirectly by public opinion, aided perhaps by diminished numbers of weapons and strategic budgets. Thus our task is even harder.

Over these last three disappointing years there has been a major change—the arousal of public concern. It is widely believed to be a change that is unlikely to be reversed, although ups and downs can be expected as other issues, such as the recession, compete for public interest. In the United States, the idea of a freeze in nuclear weapons has been at the center of this arousal of public involvement. It is, therefore, of importance to all who labor anywhere in this broad vineyard of national security, arms control, and disarmament to learn about this development. Then one must ask how the public arsenal can be maintained and lead to a better informed public, how informed publics can promote bipartisan support, and what specific programs are politically possible and consistent with preserving and indeed improving our security.

It is in this sense that the committee has organized this conference. We have sought to bring together a wide representation of persons involved in the freeze movements and those who have worked long in more traditional arms control proposals. Our hope is to promote mutual understanding, to examine specifics and help in the development of a rough consensus of what program or programs will:

—gain wide public support,
—inform the public to discern what is most promising and do-able,
—regain bilateral support,
—relate arms control to sensible military choices—ones that are more secure and stable in crises,
—repair relations with the Soviet Union so that meaningful discourse is possible and prompt.

There is no hidden agenda; the Committee has no positions of its own to advance, nor is this a forum to promote any single point of view to the exclusion of others. This is a forum which we hope will help sift the chaff from the wheat. While the emphasis is on the freeze, we have invited others who focus on somewhat different approaches. They will not have comparable time but we thought it important to become acquainted with these—to see if they are compatible or not with various freezes.

This may not satisfy all the passions which this important subject has aroused. To those who are convinced that a particular form of the freeze is the only key, I must remind them that freezes and moratoria have come and gone. If now this seems like a more fruitful path, a more enduring process, test it and hone it so that it is given the best possible chance of persuading the American public and its government. For those of more traditional arms control outlook, I point to the failure of SALT II ratification. Why did this treaty not fire public support? That would have made the difference. It would not be an idle exercise to assume that wide-scale public support is essential to the success of any arms control measure. Then how would you recast your ideas and reshape your approaches?

So, let us begin. We have much to learn from each other. Don't let pride or rigidity get in the way. Our common goals are too important.

*　　*　　*

Nuclear Freezes

Arms Control and the Nuclear Weapons Freeze

Jan H. Kalicki

On January 25, Senator Kennedy and Senator Hatfield reintroduced their nuclear weapons freeze and reduction resolution in the Senate. The identical resolution has already been introduced in the House of Representatives under the leadership of Congressmen Markey and Conte.

In our view, the nuclear freeze initiative is the most powerful grass roots movement in America since the Vietnam War; it ranks with the greatest popular movements in our history. In a sense, it is a 20th century counterpart of the great Abolition Movement of the last century. And just as Massachusetts was in the forefront of that movement a century ago, Senator Kennedy is proud of the role of Massachusetts today at the forefront of the movement for the abolition of nuclear weapons.

All of us in Congress who are concerned about nuclear arms control and who support the freeze give great credit to Randall Forsberg of Cambridge, Randall Kehler of Deerfield, and to many others in many other states who have had the courage to challenge conventional thinking on strategic arms, and to insist that there must be a better answer to this fundamental issue of our time, and indeed of all time—the prevention of nuclear war.

The nuclear freeze initiative comes at an important turning point in the history of the nuclear arms race and in the politics of nuclear arms control. While in the past, there were significant differences in the strategic power of the United States and the Soviet Union, today we and the Soviets have come the closest to overall nuclear equivalence that we have achieved since World War II—and that we may ever achieve in the nuclear age.

While in the past, political support for arms control was diffuse, today American people are informed and are mobilized as never before in support of a serious effort to halt and reverse the nuclear arms race.

The dangers of failure at this important turning point are clear. In the past, the advent of the nuclear bomb, the intercontinental missile, and the multiple warhead each presented a new challenge to stability; but in this decade we risk an even more deadly combination of extremely high accuracy, destructive power, and reduced warning

Jan H. Kalicki *is Foreign Policy Adviser to Senator Edward Kennedy, U.S. Congress, Washington, D.C.*

time for nuclear attack. In the past, strategic analysts could agree on the need for both mutual deterrence and mutual arms control, but in this decade, we risk not only division amongst ourselves but erosion of the essential popular consensus for both effective arms control and a prudent national defense.

The Reagan Administration appears willing to take these risks. But are we? Despite its protests to the contrary, it is clear that the Administration has done more than any of its predecessors to pursue a nuclear war-fighting capability, while using the charade of arms control negotiations largely as a public relations ploy for its rearmament program. Our government is committed to a doctrine of surviving and prevailing in a nuclear war—even though nuclear survival and victory are meaningless by any acceptable standard. Our government is also committed to dubious positions in INF and START, while abandoning the trilateral negotiations for a CTB. These positions represent failures in the critical effort to reduce the risk of nuclear war, and these failures threaten the cohesion of our alliances and the respect of our nation around the world.

It would be easy for arms control supporters to blame the present Administration for this sorry state of affairs. But the broader truth is that arms control concepts have become drafted into the service of the nuclear arms race. To be sure, initial quantitative limits were negotiated—but our search for qualitative improvements in the name of stability became subsumed in deadlier rounds of nuclear competition, from the MIRVs of the 1970s to the MXs and perhaps the ABMs of the 1980s. We codified mutual vulnerability in SALT I and essential equivalence in SALT II, only to forfeit any serious debate over the alleged window of vulnerability and to permit advocates of new land-based missiles to mislead us as to the overall balance and its overall stability. We abandoned a properly limited view of nuclear deterrence—a sure second-strike capability which prevents the use of nuclear weapons—and accepted a dangerously unlimited view of deterrence which called for matching each other's counterforce and ultimately war-fighting capabilities, and led once again to new spirals of the nuclear arms race, toward rather than away from a third and final world war.

In this situation, there is a solid, practical case for a nuclear freeze—it can be negotiated, verified, and applied mutually to nuclear testing, production, and deployment by the United States and the Soviet Union. But it is crucial for arms control experts, committed as we are to the prevention of nuclear war, to understand the broader philosophical and political importance of the nuclear freeze initiative—and the unique opportunity before us.

In sharp contrast to the traditional presumption that a specific improvement in nuclear capability should be pursued if it contributes to stability, the freeze offers the opposite presumption that it is no longer adequate simply to manage the arms race, and that the time has come to stop it and run it in reverse. In so doing, the freeze offers us a major opportunity to return to a more limited and prudent definition of deterrence, to recognize and maintain the present situation of nuclear equivalence, and to reject the Siren lure of just one more quick nuclear fix—which will inevitably be matched by the other side and propel rather than reverse the nuclear competition.

I also want to emphasize that the freeze we favor goes hand-in-hand with reductions in the level of nuclear weapons. Both the nuclear freeze campaign and its congressional supporters call for an immediate, mutual, and comprehensive nuclear weapons freeze, followed by major and stabilizing reductions in the nuclear arsenals of both the United States and the Soviet Union.

It is misleading to speak of "freezes" in the plural. Of course, there are others who have applied the label of the "freeze" to their own separate ideas on nuclear arms control. But you have to read their fine print carefully. They are either partial freezes or deferred freezes. Sometimes, they are little more than a pretext for a further buildup of nuclear arms.

The reason that the freeze represents a major opportunity is, again, the status of both the nuclear arms race and the politics of nuclear arms control. We have the chance to prevent major new nuclear weapons systems from being deployed by both the Soviet Union and the United States—beginning with new generations of mobile ICBMs. We also have a resounding expression of support for the nuclear freeze from the American people: over 11.5 million Americans in 45 out of 48 cities, counties, and states voted in favor of the freeze initiative last fall.

Our congressional resolution proposes an immediate nuclear freeze—the sooner and the more comprehensive the better—provided that it is both mutual and verifiable. If the Administration ignores the will of the people and fails to propose a nuclear freeze at the bargaining table, then our objective would be to change the government and put forward a U.S. nuclear freeze proposal in the spring of 1985.

The next two years thus provide a major political opportunity for nuclear arms control in the form of the nuclear freeze. But they also pose a challenge to the arms control community, represented so impressively at this conference. Will arms control experts focus their intellectual resources on helping to translate the nuclear freeze initiative into political reality—or will they become distracted by secondary or tertiary arguments about technical issues, which are really at the margins of the fundamental policy decision to propose a nuclear freeze?

Important voices in the expert community recognize that it is now possible to translate the freeze into reality; that we are tapping important new sources of political support for nuclear arms control across the country; and that the appropriate response is to consider not how little arms control, but how much arms control and disarmament we can secure. They recognize that even the SALT II agreement without loopholes for MX and Trident II plus a CTB agreement without loopholes for low-threshold nuclear testing or "peaceful" nuclear explosions add up to a freeze on wide margins of deployment and testing. These elements of a comprehensive freeze have already been negotiated and found to be both verifiable and in our national security interest by intelligence, defense, and arms control authorities inside and outside of government. They further recognize that we have similar capacity to achieve and verify a freeze on nuclear production—as well as remaining testing and deployment—based on standing U.S. and Soviet proposals and the kinds of on-site inspection opportunities already attained in the CTB negotiations under the Carter Administration. As Paul Nitze himself has pointed out, verification must only be adequate over *militarily significant* numbers of weapons. Thus the production of marginal numbers of additional nuclear warheads would have no impact on a nuclear balance governed by 50,000 warheads in U.S. and Soviet hands today.

All this is to suggest that indeed a freeze can be achieved in short order—through a number of approaches ranging from a negotiators' pause to more formal agreements—if arms controllers will rise to the opportunity for truly ending the nuclear arms race. That opportunity may not return again in our generation.

There are those in the expert community who disagree with this analysis, who believe that the technical problems are not secondary but primary, or who believe that a comprehensive nuclear freeze is politically unattainable. But many of those who worried about the verifiability of SALT II before 1980 have come to embrace its verifiability today, or even assert the verifiability of the present U.S. proposals for START. To some extent, the objections being raised to the freeze are less technical than political, devices to forestall acceptance of a new strategic concept. In our view, the benefits of a comprehensive halt to the nuclear arms race, at this time of essential strategic equivalence, outweigh any possible risks of freezing nuclear weapons systems on both sides.

It is even more curious for opponents of the nuclear freeze to claim that it is not politically feasible. We should frankly recall that not many experts thought that a nuclear test ban could be attained in the early 1960s—until a major national and international movement was organized against nuclear testing and radioactive contamination from the atmosphere. Not many thought that we could prohibit antiballistic missiles—until major public protests appeared against inviting nuclear attacks on our cities and towns. And not many thought in 1980 or 1981 that a major new movement could achieve the spectacular political results that we have seen in 1982 and we can expect to see in 1983 and 1984.

So the challenge for this conference should be to respond openly to the clear and strong public support for serious arms control and reductions, beginning with the most comprehensive freeze that we can achieve.

Whatever their position on a nuclear freeze, there is no division among serious arms control supporters about the need and the importance of pursuing nuclear reductions while increasing stability. This conference should focus on the precise terms of the freeze as a first and essential step to these stabilizing reductions. But in so doing, we must not lose sight of the broader strategic importance of the freeze concept. It offers a new approach to strategic arms control, one which allows us to reverse rather than propel the nuclear arms race.

In 1981 and 1982, enormous energy was devoted across the nation—and in the legislative branch—to shift the presumption of our nation's strategic policy decisively from fine-tuning the nuclear arms race to actually halting and reversing it.

In 1980, such a transformation was surely inconceivable to most assembled here today. Now, in 1983, it is not. The American people have spoken out eloquently and persuasively for this transformation. The Congress is responding to the people. The critical issue for us in this conference at this time is this: Will the arms control community embrace the opportunity for a major firebreak against a new round of the arms race, giving us the time and the chance to negotiate the stabilizing reductions we all desire? Or will we proceed with business as usual, in which arms control becomes the handmaiden, witting or unwitting, of a continuing military buildup that means less, not more, security for all?

* * *

The Freeze and Beyond

Henry W. Kendall

It is now widely appreciated that a general nuclear war involving the two superpower nations would result in unprecedented destruction that would be inconsistent with the national objectives of the two countries. Such a nuclear conflict might well start in Europe and would then result in great damage to most of that continent. Yet the seemingly endless friction between the Soviet Union and the United States has spawned and sustained a continuing, very vigorous, and highly dangerous nuclear arms race. In this arms race, the immense common interest in avoiding the ruin and desolation of nuclear war has been largely lost from view.

The offspring of this somber contest have been new technologies and new weapons for fighting nuclear war. When deployed, many of these new weapons can be easily concealed and therefore impossible to count and verify so to place their control beyond the grasp of arms control agreements. The accuracy and the weapons yield of many weapons of this new generation will, as George Kennan has said, generate "fears, temptations, and compulsions" that might precipitate a nuclear first strike. The risk of nuclear war is now real and is growing, a fact not lost on the American and European publics. Within the last year or so the perceived risk of nuclear war has generated pressure for its reduction.

In the United States this pressure is most powerfully expressed in widespread public support for a halt in the nuclear arms race: "a mutual and verifiable freeze on the testing, production, and further deployment of nuclear warheads, missiles, and other delivery systems." This call has engendered much controversy so that two quite different bills in the Congress have resulted.

It is impossible not to recognize that the risk of nuclear war has many roots; so in consequence many diverse actions are required to abate that risk. In particular, the threat is not solely a product of weapons procurement decisions, however threatening these have frequently appeared to be. The threat is enhanced as well by employment plans—most notably by the U.S. and NATO doctrine of nuclear first-use (should circumstances demand), as well as by deployment modes such as highly ac-

Henry W. Kendall is Director of the Union of Concerned Scientists, Cambridge, Massachusetts.

curate, land-based MIRVed missiles, possibly vulnerable to preemptive attack, or forward-based tactical nuclear weapons subject to "use them or lose them." Taken together, these elements have combined to make possible an inadvertent, accidental nuclear war whose scale could not, in all probability, be controlled.

A nuclear freeze should be understood as only one of several necessary approaches to solving the underlying problem. A freeze, if well implemented, would largely halt the upward spiral of the nuclear arms race and beneficially affect the now badly strained relations between the superpowers. But because a freeze would address neither the sizes of the now swollen inventories of weapons nor nuclear doctrine it could form, by itself, no more than an incomplete basis for national security policy. A freeze would focus primarily on policies, procurement, and procedures, including the testing of new systems.

Building a broad base of political support is a critical component not only of successful arms control but the success of other measures to reduce the risk of war. The failure of SALT II is one recent example where this need was neglected and one which was not lost on SALT advocates. But creating and sustaining the needed political support must deal with some deeply seated political realities. The public is clearly deeply concerned about the nuclear arms race and the risk of nuclear war. It is also deeply concerned about the persistent threat posed by the Soviet Union and the claims by some that that nation strives for, and may achieve, nuclear superiority. A solution that reduces the anxieties over the risk of war but does not satisfactorily comprehend the Soviet threat is no solution. What must be sought is a national policy which preserves, and, indeed, enhances the security of the United States and its allies, and from which develops a marked reduction of the nuclear risks. Only by this means can public support be sustained and long-term solutions achieved.

The freeze proposal has become a unique vehicle for expressing the great public anxieties over nuclear risks. For this reason, as well as for its other merits, it is the key element in generating public support. However, an informed and powerful constituency will increasingly be required for those other steps, supplementing a freeze, needed to provide adequately for U.S. and NATO security. The public must have assurance that the twin concerns, nuclear and Soviet, are at the same time accommodated.

In the winter and spring of 1982, the Union of Concerned Scientists (UCS) reviewed the various means by which the risk of nuclear war might be abated. UCS benefited by aid and advice from military and defense experts from the U.S. and abroad. We wished to identify those steps which together could form the basis for a new national security policy dedicated to preventing the use of any and all nuclear weapons and reducing drastically their aggregate destructive power.

These recommendations are now supported by over 5,000 American scientists, engineers, and medical experts, as well as by over a third of the membership of the National Academy of Scientists and a number of senior, retired military officers.

The recommendations USC has proposed are as follows:[1]

    1.   The NATO alliance should, at this time, announce its intention to adopt a

policy of No-First-Use of nuclear weapons in Europe. This will necessitate the development, over several years, of conventional strength so that a non-nuclear attack by the Soviet Union can be repelled without reliance on nuclear weapons. While strengthening its forces, NATO should withdraw forward-based tactical nuclear weapons. The Soviet Union should withdraw its own tactical nuclear weapons as well.

2. The United States should announce its intention to adopt a policy of No-First-Use of nuclear weapons elsewhere in the world. As in Europe, such a policy will be contingent on the development of adequate conventional strength.

3. The U.S. and the U.S.S.R. should immediately begin negotiations covering strategic and medium-range nuclear forces. These should aim for greatly reduced arsenals by the end of the decade, attained by continued and verifiable reductions. Massive cuts can be made which would still leave each side with adequate retaliatory strength. Negotiations on the tactical nuclear forces are important as well.

4. In order to provide an environment conducive to successful negotiations, the U.S. should, at this time:
   i) announce its readiness to engage in an intermediate bilateral freeze on the buildup of strategic nuclear weapons, and on the flight testing of new strategic missiles; and
   ii) announce its intention to renew negotiations leading to a Comprehensive Test Ban Treaty covering all nuclear explosions.

5. The U.S. and the U.S.S.R. should develop and implement a joint program to curtail the spread of nuclear weapons. Such efforts will lack credibility if the two superpowers fail to curtail their own arms race.

The fourth recommendation is a statement of the freeze that we believe it is practical to implement. It is important to emphasize its importance in producing an environment conducive to successful negotiations as well as halting the nuclear arms spiral.

The third recommendation is, in essence, a restatement of the call for deep cuts in the strategic arsenals first set forth by former Ambassador George Kennan.

The first of these recommendations, the call for a move by the NATO allies towards a policy of No-First-Use of nuclear weapons, is similar to a proposal prepared independently of UCS by McGeorge Bundy, George F. Kennan, Robert S. McNamara, and Gerard C. Smith, found in the Spring 1982 *Foreign Affairs* article, "No-First-Use and the Atlantic Alliance."

The second of these recommendations reflects the UCS view that a No-First-Use policy on the part of the United States is important, not only in Europe, but elsewhere in the world as well.

The freeze proposal, the deep-cuts recommendation, and a number of treaties that have been proposed or negotiated (SALT I, SALT II, ABM, and others) would eliminate specific weapons, reduce the numbers of weapons, or establish nuclear-free or nuclear-restricted zones. They are invaluable steps in bringing the nuclear threat under control. Yet not one of them directly addresses the way in which nuclear weapons would be used in combat. That is, not one challenges that set of doctrines and plans that could so easily convert a conventional conflict into a nuclear one. And this is an important gap. Even if the most extensive deep cuts that have been proposed were negotiated, the superpowers would retain arsenals of immense destructive capability. A No-First-Use declaration would complement a freeze by substantially reducing the risk that remaining nuclear weapons would be used.[2]

In summary, there are several necessary elements to a comprehensive program that seeks to abate the risks of nuclear war. A freeze is an important component and one which should have an early and high priority. Such a program should include, we believe, steps toward adoption of a policy of No-First-Use of nuclear weapons as well as moves towards deep cuts and increasingly effective curbs on nuclear weapons proliferation.

---

1. The full text of the USC statement is appended to this paper.
2. *No-First-Use: A Report by the Union of Concerned Scientists*, published February 1, 1983, sets out the arguments for a No-First-Use policy and identifies those elements that must be improved so as to make feasible its adoption.

Union of Concerned Scientists
A Framework for a New National Security Policy

Since 1945, the superpowers have pursued a grotesque nuclear arms race. Each builds two to three nuclear weapons daily. Today, their arsenals have the explosive power of well over one million Hiroshima bombs. Nuclear superiority is a meaningless goal when so many thousands of weapons are already in existence.

All attempts by the superpowers to enhance their security through accelerating the nuclear arms race have, inexorably, diminished that security. The probability of nuclear annihilation is increasing, whether one lives in the United States, the Soviet Union, or Europe.

If this trend is to be reversed—if the security of the Western Alliance is to be enhanced—a comprehensive new policy must be adopted by the United States. This must take the following realities into account:

1. The U.S. now has 9,500 strategic nuclear weapons and the U.S.S.R. has 7,000. There is rough equity between their strategic arsenals. No defense against these weapons exists. Neither side, now or in the forseeable future, can disarm the other in a successful first strike.

2. At present, NATO doctrine includes the use of tactical nuclear weapons to repel a non-nuclear attack. The use of such weapons on the battlefield can swiftly escalate to all-out nuclear war which would devastate much of the northern hemisphere. Therefore nuclear weapons can serve no rational military purpose in conflict between the superpowers.

3. The NATO Alliance has the manpower, economic wealth, and technological prowess to mount an adequate conventional defense against a non-nuclear attack by the Soviet Union.

4. A nuclear war is most likely to begin as an outgrowth of conventional war, through miscalculation, or as an act of desperation.

5. The advent of new nuclear weapons that are more threatening heightens the risk of an attempted pre-emptive attack. Many are less verifiable than those now deployed, making arms control treaties more difficult to achieve.

In light of these facts, it is clear that we must have a new national security policy dedicated to:

- preventing the use of any and all nuclear weapons;
- reducing drastically the destructive power that threatens our existence.

After a careful review of the available options, we conclude that the following coordinated initiatives are urgently needed to enhance the security of the U.S. and its allies:

1. The NATO Alliance should, at this time, announce its intention to adopt a policy of No First Use of Nuclear Weapons in Europe. This will necessitate the development, over several years, of conventional strength so that a non-nuclear attack by the Soviet Union can be repelled without reliance on nuclear weapons. While strengthening its forces, NATO should withdraw forward-based tactical nuclear weapons. The Soviet Union should withdraw its own tactical nuclear weapons as well.

2. The United States should announce its intention to adopt a policy of No First Use of Nuclear Weapons elsewhere in the world. As in Europe, such a policy will be contingent on the development of adequate conventional strength.

3. The U.S. and the U.S.S.R. should immediately begin negotiations covering strategic and medium-range nuclear forces. These should aim for greatly reduced arsenals by the end of the decade, attained by continued and verifiable reductions. Massive cuts can be made which would still leave each side with adequate retaliatory strength. Negotiations on the tactical nuclear forces are important as well.

4. In order to provide an environment conducive to successful negotiations, the U.S. should, at this time:
   i) announce its readiness to engage in an intermediate bilateral freeze on the build-up of strategic nuclear weapons, and on the flight testing of new strategic missiles; and
   ii) announce its intention to renew negotiations leading to a Comprehensive Test Ban Treaty covering all nuclear explosions.

5. The U.S. and the U.S.S.R. should develop and implement a joint program for curtailing the spread of nuclear weapons. Such efforts will lack credibility if the two superpowers fail to curtail their own arms race.

* * *

A Rapidly Negotiable First-Stage Nuclear Freeze

Franklin A. Long

The objective of a nuclear freeze is to slow down or stop the so-far inexorable development and deployment of more and more (read destructive and deadly) nuclear warheads. The essential notion is not new. The proposed treaty for a Comprehensive Ban on Nuclear Tests that was very nearly negotiated in 1959 was perhaps the first serious effort to obtain a nuclear freeze, albeit a partial one. Growing concern about the nuclear arms race has led to greatly increased interest in much broader and more effective freezes. A comprehensive nuclear freeze, one that would stop all stages in the manufacture, testing, and deployment of nuclear warheads, would clearly be very desirable and have a great impact. It would not, however, deal with the other worrisome aspect of nuclear weapons, which is the very large number of such weapons that already exist.

Hence many U.S. citizens who support a bilateral comprehensive nuclear freeze between the U.S. and the U.S.S.R. also wish to see prompt movement by the two countries towards substantial reductions in numbers of nuclear warheads and weapons systems for their delivery. A frequent concern is that negotiation toward a complete nuclear freeze may be so difficult and lengthy as seriously to interfere with efforts for other desirable arms control measures. The question then becomes: are there useful and desirable nuclear freeze proposals with characteristics that lend themselves to rapid successful negotiation?

Since a freeze that is simple and rapidly negotiable, but that is also verifiable, will almost surely be a partial freeze, it makes sense to offer it as a first-stage freeze, i.e., one that appropriately could be followed by additional, more comprehensive freezes, or alternatively by substantial arms reductions. This analysis deals with the general characteristics of a first-stage nuclear freeze, and proposes a specific one as an example.

Adequate verifiability will be a major requirement if a freeze is substantive enough as to impose genuine and significant constraints on the nuclear weapons programs of the parties to a freeze treaty. If negotiation is to be rapid, this need for verification virtually demands that both the U.S. and the U.S.S.R. be able to verify a particular freeze by "national technical means," where the explicit meaning of this is that the monitoring of an agreed freeze will not require on-site inspection. Fortunately, the implications of monitoring by national technical means are well understood by both the U.S. and the U.S.S.R., since this type of verification has been the agreed procedure for a number of negotiated arms control measures. Fundamentally, it involves inspection by photographic and other types of earth-orbiting satellites using tech-

Franklin A. Long *is Professor Emeritus of Chemistry, Science and Society at Cornell University, Ithaca, New York.*

niques that are already employed by the intelligence-seeking organizations of the two countries.

There are a variety of nuclear freeze proposals for which this sort of national monitoring should be mutually acceptable. Consider the following as one example of a freeze that should be valuable in its own right, and also an attractive preliminary to further negotiations on arms control:

A freeze by the U.S. and the U.S.S.R. on the testing and the deployment of all long-range nuclear weapons systems, where long-range is defined as maximum ranges of over 1000 kilometers.

A treaty embodying this could be monitored by national technical means. The necessary capabilities should already exist in both the U.S. and the U.S.S.R., since monitoring of testing and deployment of long-range nuclear weapons has been carried out for many years by both nations.

This proposed freeze would be an important first step. It would put a halt to deployment of new and improved strategic nuclear weapons, as well as intermediate-range nuclear weapons. The freeze on *testing* would constrain, and, over time, halt the continued improvement in accuracy of these weapons. The resulting halt in weapons development and deployment could be enormously helpful for follow-on negotiations on arms reductions.

Even with this fairly simple freeze, there would be a variety of elements where negotiation would be needed. Just what weapons are covered? Would, for example, long-range bombers be included? What about other dual-purpose weapons? None of these areas of uncertainty seems an insuperable obstacle, but they and others would need to be addressed, with agreement on the joint positions.

A different point is the likely requirement for a limited number of "proof tests" of existing nuclear weapons systems. This would become the more important if the freeze were scheduled to be of indefinite or comparatively lengthy duration. Both sides would probably want some proof tests but would also want assurances that only proof testing was being carried out. There would be conflicts between those who would want proof tests to be restricted to very small numbers, and those who would seek ample assurance with, therefore, considerable proof testing. But there is no obvious reason why these conflicts could not be resolved.

A basic decision would be what sort of agreement is to embody the components of the freeze. The most obvious to contemplate is a formal treaty between the U.S. and the U.S.S.R. Even better would be an agreed treaty between these nations to which other nations could signify their acceptance by signing. This is the character of the influential 1963 partial test ban treaty which has been signed by 125 nations. However, the problems in negotiating a formal treaty, and then of getting it ratified, could slow down what otherwise might be a fairly rapid negotiation.

An alternative worth considering is to obtain the desired nuclear freeze by separate but simultaneously announced moratoria by means of which the U.S. and the U.S.S.R. would each commit themselves to a moratorium on testing and deployment of agreed categories of nuclear weapons systems (subject, again, to possible provision for proof testing). A moratorium could be for an agreed period, e.g., five years, with extension a possibility. The U.S. has had experience on moratoria with the U.S.S.R. on arms and testing limitations, and the resulting knowledge would be useful in developing with the U.S.S.R. mutually acceptable components of a nuclear freeze.

There are pros and cons for a moratorium versus a treaty. However, for a comparatively straightforward and simple freeze agreement, one that can be monitored by national technical means, a moratorium seems appropriate. This is especially so if a principal objective of a first-stage freeze is to accelerate the processes whereby the U.S. and U.S.S.R. brings about more wide-ranging, substantive arms control measures such as deep cuts in numbers of nuclear warheads and delivery systems, or more extensive freezes, including restrictions on production of fissionable isotopes and nuclear warheads.

If the idea of a rapidly negotiable first-stage nuclear freeze finds supporters, it would be desirable for groups within the arms control community to explore the proposal in considerably more depth. The analyses would need to consider carefully the alternative freezes that might be entered into. Even with the requirement that the verification be by national technical means or be of a character that is rapidly negotiable, there are several interesting partial freezes that could serve as a useful first step. Detailed analysis could be made of three or four of the most promising of these. This would permit answers to what might appropriately be included in particular freezes. Possible "sticking points" in the different proposals should be sought out and then examined as to possible responses. The comparative virtues and drawbacks of a moratorium with Soviet colleagues interested in arms control might be initiated to see whether they would also involve themselves in in-depth exploration of nuclear freezes that would be interesting and appealing to them.

* * *

Conceptual Foundations of a Comprehensive Nuclear Freeze

Christopher E. Paine

It has been my experience, since becoming involved in the nuclear freeze issue several years ago, that opponents and indeed many proponents of significant progress in nuclear arms control often make the mistake of transforming questions of *political possibility* and *strategic desirability* into questions of *technical feasibility*. Much government, as well as non-government, expert commentary on the freeze suffers from this deficiency.

Consider, for example, the question of freeze verification. Despite frequent official and unofficial off-the-cuff assertions as to its "unverifiability," it is well understood within the intelligence community, and I hope among most arms controllers, that one simply cannot make meaningful judgments about the verifiability of a freeze without specifying *what Soviet activity is being monitored*, for compliance with *which provision* of a freeze agreement, using *what combination of monitoring systems, cooperative measures, and on-site inspections*, over *what period of time*, and to produce *what desired level of monitoring confidence?*

Similarly, a freeze is opposed on the allegedly "technical" basis that many of our weapons are aging and in need of "modernization," which the freeze would prohibit. But "modernization" is not the same as "replacement," which could be permitted for delivery vehicles of the *same type*, and this requirement must in turn be distinguished from "maintenance" of existing weapons until they are removed by a deliberate process of reductions.

In point of fact, the current arsenal can be maintained without "modernization" or "production for replacement" until at least the year 2000. The Air Force, for example, recently testified that the Minuteman originally "had a design life of three years and a design goal of ten years. The Minuteman is fully capable now and should continue to be an effective weapons system through the year 2000, if not indefinitely." The Air Force says this could be accomplished through a periodic depot maintenance program to correct normal aging problems at a cost of about $150 million for each three-year-cycle!

While there are many such technical issues regarding the design and verification of a comprehensive freeze which remain to be fleshed out, the current *lack* of such detail in certain areas should not be taken as *prima facie* evidence of technical infeasibility. On the contrary, what has been accomplished so far in the ABM, SALT, and test ban negotiations supports the opposite presumption — that much *more* is indeed possible.

Christopher E. Paine is Staff Assistant for Arms Control at the Federation of American Scientists, Washington, D.C.

In the 10 minutes allotted, there isn't time to address all these specific issues fully here; I have tried to address some of them in articles which I would be pleased to provide to anyone who would like a copy. But I do not believe that these technical issues—which are quite clearly resolvable, given adequate information and analysis—are really what is at the heart of the current administration's, and at least some arms controllers', opposition to the comprehensive freeze approach. While there is a substantial overlap in the *goals* of both the freeze and the more traditional arms control agenda, the underlying concept of a nuclear freeze differs significantly from the more cautious, piecemeal approach which has characterized the arms control enterprise over the last quarter century. In a most fundamental and important sense, the freeze represents a shift in the *operative* presumptions about the nature of arms control.

It presumes shifting from a process which has sought and obtained partial limitations on those weapons most susceptible to agreement—most often at the price of legitimizing others as necessary instruments for maintaining "equivalence" and "stability"—to a process which would permit new weapons to be built *only* as the reluctant consequence of the failure of determined efforts to *preclude* them by agreement.

It is, in one respect, regrettable that one needs to highlight such a shift in presumption at all, since the freeze concept, directed at reducing the risk of nuclear war by *ending* the Soviet–American competition in nuclear arms, is the natural goal of arms control efforts. Interpreting the term "control" as a license for the management of an ongoing nuclear arms race is a perversion of the concept. The National Center for Disease Control in Atlanta, for example, does not interpret its mission as mandating the introduction and controlled spread of new forms of disease! In the international body politic as well, the notion of "controlling" pathological developments logically subsumes the notion of *precluding* them altogether. And the nuclear arms race is indeed an extremely virulent form of social pathology, no matter how hard some people who call themselves arms controllers may strive to forget this fact.

Thus the appropriate question is not, why does the freeze movement think it can accomplish so much, but rather, why has the arms control community been willing to settle for so little? Posing this question is by no means an attempt to belittle the accomplishments of this community to date. Certainly, twenty years ago the very notion of binding agreements between strong ideological and military adversaries did not go down easily with the Congress and the military establishment. And the ABM Treaty, is, in effect, a freeze of indefinite duration on a potentially very significant part of the nuclear arms race.

But increasingly, in my view, the dominant conventional wisdom in arms control is becoming the tangled product of an ongoing and debilitating Faustian bargain with the national security establishment. At the risk of oversimplification, let me nevertheless characterize this bargain as follows: It appears to have sought "stability" in the strategic military relationship between the two superpowers by establishing limitations on strategic offensive nuclear weapons, both as a means of restraining future demand for such weapons (arms race stability) and as a means of diminishing pressures and nominal "incentives" for swift use of these weapons in a crisis (crisis stability).

The price paid for getting the powers-that-be to entertain such notions was, and continues to be, passive acquiescence in the very doctrines, strategies, and nuclear forces for "extended deterrence" which are driving the arms race forward, thereby guaranteeing that arms control has become an exercise in *managing* rather than *ending* the nuclear arms race.

The military doctrine of "first use" of nuclear weapons which purports to buttress U.S. global security commitments wherever U.S. conventional forces are thinly deployed or seriously challenged poses serious obstacles to arms control. The demands of a military establishment, built around the strategy of "escalation dominance" across the "full spectrum of conflict," cannot easily be reconciled with a negotiating posture based on the willingness to concede "essential equivalence" at the bargaining table. How many promising voyages in arms control have come to grief on the shoals of this particular contradiction in our policy. It constitutes a virtual "Bermuda Triangle" for arms control.

Sustaining the credibility of a national security policy which seeks to "enhance deterrence" by manipulating the threat of nuclear war is no small or easy task. On the *technical-military level*, it requires continuing modernization of U.S. nuclear capability, particularly improving accuracy and weapons "survivability" while reducing undesired "collateral effects," thereby increasing the possibilities for employing these weapons and, hence, their nominal military utility as a "warfighting" deterrent threat.

Thus a continuing nuclear arms race, embracing in particular nuclear warhead and delivery vehicle *characteristics*—flight time, accuracy, reliability, survivability, weapons effects, and so on—as well as numbers and sheer explosive power, is seen as indispensable to the task of "extended" nuclear deterrence.

On a purely *psychological level*, however, any and all nuclear modernization is justified—quite apart from the issue of real military utility (which for nuclear warfare is difficult to assess in any case)—to prevent any "misperception" by opponents, or wavering allies on the brink of "Finlandization," that U.S. leaders have lost their resolve to employ nuclear weapons in defense of American and allied interests.

According to this view, which enjoys widespread acceptance as a kind of subliminal postulate of U.S. defense policy, any significant diminution in the national commitment to nuclear modernization would indicate to the world that the United States is backing away from its first-use nuclear commitments in Europe and elsewhere, a perception which cannot help but lead, we are told, to increased political challenges to U.S. and allied interests, Soviet-supported proxy wars, international crises, and possibly nuclear conflict.

The belief in the mind of a potential enemy that an American president might *irrationally*, or in the case of a non-nuclear enemy, *immorally* pursue nuclear escalation to assert American interests is, we are told, an essential part of the strategy of deterring lesser conventional attacks on those interests.

This is a theory of deterrence based on generating an overwhelming impression of having willfully and systematically deceived ourselves. Given the existence of a nuclear-armed opponent willing to match our every move, the main vehicle for expression of this policy has become a massive and perpetual arms race.

This is the *real* meaning of the oft-stated requirement to maintain "stability." The usual panoply of arms control concerns about stability are, for the most part, socially acceptable second and third order manifestations of this primitive underlying requirement to assert our "nuclearized" national will.

In one of his more reflective moments, Henry Kissinger is reported to have once wondered aloud, "What in God's name is strategic superiority?" Arms controllers would do well to ask themselves a similar question, "What in God's name is strategic stability?" Whatever intellectual currency the concept may have had has now been thoroughly debased by its thoughtless invocation at every turn in the nuclear debate. What manner of weapon can *not* be justified by one or another technological vision of what constitutes "stability."

We are told that it is terribly "destabilizing" if the Soviet Union can launch a successful paper attack on our ICBMs, but "stabilizing" if we can attack theirs, because it forces them to move to a purportedly more survivable basing posture, one which we have been searching for over the last decade and still can't find ourselves! But didn't the Soviets just finish building what *they* thought was a "survivable" basing mode for their ICBMs—namely, hardened silos—and didn't we find that development "destabilizing" because it afforded "sanctuary status" for their ICBM force in scenarios involving limited nuclear attacks in support of conventional and theater nuclear forces? Moreover, the easiest and cheapest response on either side—Launch-Under-Attack—is considered "destabilizing" by some because it places a hair trigger on nuclear war, and "stabilizing" by others because it convincingly reduces whatever "incentives" might exist for launching a surprise attack.

Who's on first in this debate? It's hard to escape the conclusion that the whole enterprise of managing an objectively "stable" balance between the two superpowers, in the context of an ongoing technological arms race, has somehow lost its intellectual rudder. Sometimes it seems we no longer know what we mean when we talk amongst ourselves, much less when we try to address the American people, our allies, or the Russians.

An integrated defense-arms control policy based on this concept of "strategic stability" has reached the condition once encountered by the Ptolemaic system of astronomy. There are now too many epicycles, too many intellectual pirouettes, for the resulting vision to be at all compelling. Thus there is both a political and intellectual need to redefine the nature of the problem.

The political need, as we all know, is well on the way to being met—the nation-wide freeze movement is bringing about significant change in the political context in which negotiated solutions to the problem of nuclear war must necessarily be carried out. Twenty-five years ago SAC could adopt the motto "Peace is Our Profession" with nary a murmur against the idea that peace was being ensured by the threat to incinerate 100 million Russians. Today the President tries to rename the MX the "Peacekeeper," and every one derides him for his clumsy self-serving hypocrisy.

The intellectual need, however, is only just beginning to be met, partly because of the arms control community's natural reluctance to rapidly depreciate a portion of its own intellectual capital, and partly out of pique that the *vox populi* is now being heard in inner sanctums where previously only "experts" dared to tread. I believe the time has come for the arms control community to recover from this fit of pique and grasp the tremendous opportunity represented by the present situation.

Since the previous approach of arranging a stable balance has failed to limit the *demand* for new nuclear weapons, the freeze is very much in step with the times by suggesting, in essence, that we pay special attention to the *supply* side of the equation, an approach which should appeal to the President, but obviously doesn't, perhaps because the freeze emphasis is on *extinguishing* rather than *expanding* the supply of new nuclear weapons. (Expanding the supply of new weapons is obviously quite consistent with the President's professed desire to reduce *existing* weapons.)

Conceptually, "supply-side" arms control has a number of inherent advantages over the present orthodoxy. The freeze takes direct account of the very large component of bureaucratic and military-industrial self-perpetuation involved in the nuclear weapons programs on both sides. It does not rely on the national security establishment to resolve the contradiction between "escalation dominance" and "essential equivalence," because this is usually resolved in favor of new weapons. And in place of the intellectual quagmire surrounding present concepts of "stability," the freeze advances a number of precepts more in accord with current realities:

First, that the nuclear arms race *itself* is a prime source of instability in relations between the two superpowers;

Second, that in view of the huge existing arsenals, new or additional nuclear weapons can no longer be the source of *improvements* to crisis stability, if they ever were.

Third, that the military advantage to be gained from the clandestine development or improvement of weapons under a freeze is small in comparison to the survivable destructive potential already amassed by both sides, suggesting that undetected violations of the freeze are unlikely to affect nuclear deterrence itself.

This approach to the problem of arms control has the fortunate added effect of considerably reducing the pressure for *uniformly high* monitoring confidence for each and every aspect of a treaty, thereby easing the *political* as well as *technical* task of arriving at an "adequately verifiable" agreement, a problem which has bedeviled arms control in the past. In other words, since the country would no longer be fascinated with marginal advantages in strategic arsenals to increase the credibility of our escalation strategy, we wouldn't have to be so preoccupied with *promptly* detecting marginal changes in the Soviet arsenal. Over the longer term, the probability of disclosure for even a modest cheating program is quite high.

Thus I am hopeful that a comprehensive nuclear agreement can be designed which takes into account the security of both sides, and I commend this task to your attention.

The freeze movement has created a context in which arms controllers, if they are serious, will see the opportunity to accomplish most, if not all, of their once cherished goals. I hope we are optimistic enough, and imaginative enough, to take up the challenge. Ultimately, nothing lasting will come of this tremendous outpouring of public concern unless it is embodied in binding agreements which can withstand the pressures generated by the non-nuclear aspects of the Soviet–American competition. The cause of arms control needs the freeze movement. And the freeze needs the skill of sympathetic arms controllers who still believe that an end to the nuclear arms race is possible. Joining forces could make the world a much safer place.

* * *

Exploring the Feasibility of a Ban on Warhead Production

Jane M. O. Sharp

Most of the components of the bilateral nuclear freeze, as originally outlined by Randall Forsberg,[1] are built on long-standing United States arms control objectives which have been thoroughly researched and debated, and for which adequate monitoring schemes have already been worked out. A comprehensive test ban, for example, has been pursued with varying degrees of urgency since the late 1950s until the Carter Administration suspended negotiations when the Soviets invaded Afghanistan.[2] Limits on flight-testing and ceilings on deployed forces are features of existing arms control treaties. A cutoff in weapons-grade fissile material has been a declared objective of the United States since President Eisenhower's Atoms for Peace in 1953, was pursued explicitly by the Johnson and Nixon Administrations, and endorsed, if not pursued with any enthusiasm, by the Carter Administration as part of the Final Document of the first UN Special Session on Disarmament in 1978.[3]

The important new feature of the comprehensive freeze proposal, around which such impressive political support has rallied over the past two years, is a ban on the assembly of new warheads. This warhead ban has two objectives—one qualitative and one quantitative. First, it seeks to curb the qualitative aspect of the nuclear arms competition by preventing further technological innovations in warheads innovations which in recent years have been in the direction of smaller "cleaner" and therefore more "usable" munitions. Second, it seeks to impose quantitative ceilings on Soviet and American nuclear weapons stockpiles both to halt the pernicious practice of acquiring extra weapons as bargaining chips in current negotiations, and to prevent the further accumulation of systems which are neither limited by existing treaties nor being discussed in the current arms control agenda—in particular, to preclude the production of warheads designed for short range weapons and sea-launched cruise missiles currently under development by both sides.

The ban on warheads is at the heart of the freeze and, not surprisingly, is the aspect of the comprehensive package about which the technical community is most skep-

Jane M. O. Sharp is Visiting Scholar at the Peace Studies Program at Cornell University, Ithaca, New York.

tical, in part because some believe that maintaining a technological edge over the Soviets is important for American security, and they are unwilling to relinquish modernization, and in part because of apprehension that such a ban could only be verified by unacceptably intrusive inspections. The fact is that the United States cannot maintain a technological edge over the Soviets indefinitely and the pattern has been for the Soviets to catch up with the latest American innovation in about five years. Indeed one reason that the Russians might be skeptical about a freeze is that they would be frozen in a technologically inferior position.

In order to assess how feasible a warhead ban would be to negotiate and to verify, we need to address at least five questions:

1. Which facilities in the United States and the Soviet Union could be closed down completely under a warhead production ban?
2. Which facilities in both countries would have to be kept open to service existing nuclear systems?
3. What would be the monitoring requirements for adequate verification?
4. How receptive are the Soviets likely to be to a warhead production ban and how cooperative in terms of verification?
5. What should be done about the stockpile of obsolete warheads on each side, and the replacement of deployed weapons?

1. *Nuclear facilities which could be closed down under a warhead freeze.*

The production path of a nuclear warhead is well known. In the United States, weapons-grade fissile material is produced in only a handful of facilities and all nuclear components are shipped along known routes to a single final assembly point. Intelligence professionals have stated that the nuclear weapons production cycle is at least as concentrated in the Soviet Union. Currently, in the United States, all weapons-grade plutonium and tritium is produced in three reactors at the Savannah River plant operated by Dupont, in Aiken, South Carolina, and the N-reactor at Hanford, Washington State, which the Reagan Administration converted to weapons-grade plutonium production in October 1982.[4] Three of these reactors could be closed down if no new warheads were being produced. The plutonium and tritium bombs which act as triggers in thermonuclear warheads are assembled at the Rocky Flats plant operated by Rockwell in Golden, Colorado. Uranium and lithium deuteride components are manufactured at the Y-12 plant operated by Union Carbide at Oak Ridge, Tennessee. These components are shipped from Rocky Flats and Oak Ridge to Amarillo, Texas, for final warhead assembly at the Pantex plant. These American plants, and analogous facilities in the Soviet Union, could all be closed down under a bilateral ban on warhead production.

2. *Nuclear facilities which must be monitored.*

Tritium is used in warhead trigger mechanisms and to boost radiation effects. Since tritium has a half-life of only 12 years, tritium reservoirs in nuclear warheads need replacing periodically. This operation is relatively simple, involving the modular replacement of a cannister of tritium gas, and can be done in the field. It does mean, however, that to maintain an operational nuclear weapons stockpile pending further agreed reduction, at least one reactor would have to be kept active to produce tritium. This could be either the facility currently producing tritium at Savannah River, or a new smaller reactor could be established elsewhere if this were deemed necessary to facilitate monitoring.

Three other facilities—the Portsmouth gaseous diffusion plant in Piketon, Ohio, and the Union Carbide plants in Paducah, Kentucky, and Oak Ridge, Tennessee—produce enriched uranium designated not for warheads (though that from the Portsmouth plant is weapons-grade), but for naval and research reactors. These would have to remain open, as would analogous facilities in the Soviet Union, but verifiable limits could be set for the production of highly enriched uranium.

3. *Monitoring requirements: warhead production and fissile material.*

A Soviet–American ban on warhead production could be initiated by a tacitly agreed moratorium without waiting for the conclusion of a formal agreement. The United States could announce that for a limited period—say 12 months—two of the Savannah River reactors and the N-reactor at Hanford would be deactivated, and the three facilities which between them manufacture and assemble all American nuclear warheads (Rocky Flats, the Y-12 plant at Oak Ridge, and the Pantex plant in Amarillo) could be placed under some kind of caretaker arrangement. The Russians should obviously be invited to reciprocate by announcing the closing down of analogous facilities in the Soviet Union. Cessation of activity on both sides could be monitored by existing national technical means: satellite-based cameras and infra-red sensors.[5]

If after 12 months, the Soviet had neither reciprocated with a similar moratorium nor demonstrated any good faith in negotiating a more permanent agreement, obviously the United States would have to reassess the continuation of its own moratorium. Workers in the affected plants should in any case be guaranteed their incomes at least through the initial moratorium period and every effort made to provide alternative employment in the event of a permanent ban.

One potential snag is the perceived need for routine inspections of weapons in the deployed stockpile. Spokesmen at the Pantex plant claim that a portion of their time is devoted to weapons maintenance, which involves stripping down, checking, and reassembling the electronic and fissile components of the warheads. Estimates vary, but this represents no more than 10 percent of Pantex time which suggests that weapons are only spot checked and that a one year moratorium on all activity at Pantex would mean forgoing maintenance checks on only a very small fraction of the total weapons stockpile of between 20,000 and 30,000 warheads—hardly a major security risk.

Obviously one of the more important issues to negotiate with the Soviets, for the purpose of a long-term agreement, is a more precise definition of which facilities on both sides should be banned, and which must remain open to conduct mutually acceptable weapons maintenance programs, pending agreed reduction.

To remain viable a warhead production ban would need to be supplemented by limits on the production of weapons-grade fissile material. This will require two levels of monitoring. First, it means opening up civilian nuclear plants in the Soviet Union and the United States to inspection by the International Atomic Energy Agency (IAEA) to ensure that fissionable material from nuclear power plants is not being diverted to weapons use. This would put the nuclear weapons powers on the same basis as the non-nuclear weapons states party to the Non-Proliferation Treaty (NPT) and remove one of the most discriminatory aspects of that agreement. At the second United Nations Special Session on Disarmament in June 1982, Soviet Foreign Minister Gromyko agreed to open up Soviet civilian nuclear plants to IAEA safeguards, a gesture which had already been made earlier by Britain, France, and the United States.

As already noted, a nuclear weapons freeze as currently envisaged would not cut off all military use of fissile material since plants would still be permitted to produce tritium for warhead use and enriched uranium for naval and research reactors. A second monitoring task, therefore, would be to reassure other parties to a warhead freeze that fissile material for permitted uses was not being diverted to clandestine warhead production. Some analysts have suggested that this will require qualitatively different and more rigorous inspection techniques than the IAEA has implemented thus far to monitor compliance with the NPT. But others argue the opposite is the case. Wolfgang Panofsky, for example, has noted that:

the standards of safeguarding the nuclear power industry and fuel cycle of the Soviet Union and the United States to prevent significant diversion need not be as stringent as those pertaining to the IAEA regime applied to non-nuclear weapons states. Clearly, the required sensitivity of safeguards is much lower when existing nuclear weapons stockpiles over 10,000 warheads are to be monitored than when diversion leading to the manufacture and test of a single warhead is at issue.[6]

Panofsky goes on to argue that the increase in required IAEA safeguarding is more quantitative than qualitative, but suggests that administratively the IAEA may not be as well suited to monitoring the United States and the Soviet Union as the nationals of the two countries.

Hans Blix, Director General of IAEA, is optimistic that the agency safeguards could be expanded to monitor a nuclear weapons freeze.[7] In 1983, the budget for IAEA safeguards activities was only $34 million so it would not be unreasonable to ask all the industrial countries to increase their contributions to the agency for the purpose of upgrading the inspection teams. It should be noted that there have recently been qualitative improvements in agency monitoring techniques. The agency, in conjunction with the United States Arms Control and Disarmament Agency recently completed an eight-country test—which included Bulgaria—of new tamper-proof monitoring devices to provide remote continuous verification (RECOVER) by means of on-site, yet non-intrusive means.[5] Such devices should help allay the concern that smaller plutonium isotope separation facilities might be used for covert production of small batches of weapons-grade plutonium.

4. *Likely Soviet interest in and compliance with a warhead production ban.*

Reagan Administration statistics notwithstanding, many analysts see the Soviets barely hanging on to nuclear parity in the face of new American weapons programs. It is difficult to imagine, therefore, that the current leadership would not be willing to explore a ban on warhead production as part of a more comprehensive freeze, if offered in the near future. They will be much less interested, however, if the Department of Energy proceeds with Reagan Administration plans to reactivate several nuclear facilities to cope with a projected "fissile materials gap" in connection with proposed new systems; and the opportunity for a bilateral freeze will almost certainly be lost once the United States has deployed its Pershing IIs, GLCMs, SLCMs, MX, and a new Trident missile. The Soviet emphasis then will undoubtedly be on pursuit of parity through counterarmament.[8]

A classic problem in postwar arms control diplomacy has been how to reconcile the Soviet insistence on defining the limits to be imposed before considering methods of verification, with the Western tendency to establish monitoring procedures before committing themselves to limitations, a dilemma currently being played out in exquisite slow motion at the MBFR talks in Vienna. An important confidence-building aspect of an American initiated moratorium, therefore, would be to meet the Soviets half way by accepting some self-imposed limitation before discussing verification in detail.

The Reagan Administration has emphasized the need for more on-site inspections to monitor existing signed, but not yet ratified, treaties and has suggested that it is Soviet recalcitrance on inspections which retards progress in arms control. In fact, the United States military is just as likely to oppose intrusive on-site inspection as is the Soviet Union. Moreover, many weapons and intelligence experts have observed that on-site inspection is a vastly over-rated monitoring tool, useful only in a small number of instances.[10] Nevertheless, the political value of on-site inspection should not be underestimated—both to reassure skeptical legislators and as a powerful deterrent to cheating on either side. For a freeze to be politically acceptable to the United States Congress we do need positive signs of Soviet cooperation in monitoring and more openness with military data. In the early days of SALT the military members of the Soviet delegation were reluctant to share data on strategic forces even with their own civilians. Since then, however, Soviet behavior in a variety of arms control forums has demonstrated a definite trend towards more openness with data and a more cooperative attitude towards all aspects of monitoring compliance with agreements. Let me note several encouraging signs from recent negotiating history:

1. the successful operation, at least through the Carter Administration, of the

bilateral Standing Consultative Commission established to resolve ambiguities about compliance with SALT I;

2. the data exchange at SALT II, which Semyenov said reversed 400 years of Russian history;
3. the cooperative monitoring procedures embodied in the Threshold Test Ban Treaty, the Peaceful Nuclear Explosion Treaty, and the draft Comprehensive Test Ban Treaty;
4. Gromyko's speech at the second United Nations Special Session on Disarmament in June 1982, in which he offered to open Soviet civilian nuclear plants to IAEA inspection, and to accept some form of on-site inspection with respect to a ban on chemical weapons;
5. the data released in connection with the INF talks;
6. the beginnings of disaggregation of Soviet and East European troop data at MBFR;
7. the expressions of willingness, by Brezhnev and others since late 1981, to open up the western military districts of the Soviet Union to create a wider zone for European military confidence-building measures than those currently in effect under the CSCE;
8. the Prague Declaration issued by the Warsaw Pact summit meeting on January 5, 1983, which endorses the concept of "international procedures" as well as national technical means to verify compliance with arms control agreements.

In addition to these examples in connection with specific negotiating forums, the Soviets have recently published extensive data on the East-West military balance in both English and Russian, for Western and Soviet readerships. While much of the material in these pamphlets is Western data re-issued with a Soviet seal of approval, its dissemination suggests a change of policy at high levels and a greater sense of urgency in the Politburo towards arms control. [10]

The United States will obviously require a more extensive exchange of data and more cooperation in monitoring a warhead freeze than has been forthcoming from the Soviets to date. Nevertheless, new leadership in Moscow and the trend towards more openness, especially the positive experience with the SALT SCC, suggest that a similar consultative mechanism—or expansion of the SALT SCC mandate—could resolve ambiguities on both sides about compliance with a bilateral freeze.

5. *Dealing with stockpiles of obsolete warheads and replacements.*

Stockpiles of obsolete warheads are additional sources of fissile material from which warheads might be fabricated. Admiral Noel Gayler and Senator Alan Cranston have endorsed "Deep Cuts" scheme, whereby fissile material would be removed from obsolete warheads and reallocated to peaceful use as fuel in civilian reactors.[12] This was the original idea in Eisenhower's Atoms for Peace proposal in 1953 and was resurrected in Congressional hearings on the first United Nations Special Session on Disarmament in the spring of 1978.

Should one-to-one replacement of weapons be permitted under a freeze, pending reduction negotiations? Some analysts have suggested that public support for a comprehensive freeze could fall off precipitously if nuclear weapons levels are allowed to fall by attrition, perhaps to the point where perceptions of stability are undermined. Others, however, believe that insistence on replacements smacks too much of the force-matching approach which has dogged traditional arms control, and hope that a freeze would indeed lead to "arms control by attrition." Many freeze proponents are still agnostics on the replacement issue, but if the prospect of attrition is broadly perceived as destabilizing, then a long-term freeze would have to be designed to allow for replacements, though exceptions to a complete ban on nuclear production would complicate the verification problem. The best way to circumvent the replacement issue would be to design a freeze in stages of limited duration, which avoid too long a time lag before embarking on reduction negotiations.

In conclusion, a bilateral ban on the production of nuclear warheads is necessary to halt both the qualitative and quantitative aspects of the Soviet–American nuclear arms competition. Such a ban should not be difficult to negotiate since only a handful of facilities on each side would be affected. Verification that production had ceased in closed down plants, and that clandestine production of warheads was not being carried out in those plants remaining open for permitted nuclear activities, could be adequately verified by increasingly sophisticated national technical means. But recent Soviet statements and Soviet behavior in arms control forums since the early 1970s suggest that cooperative monitoring procedures would also be feasible.

To be effective, a warhead ban must be supplemented by provisions for the dismantling of obsolete warheads on each side which, otherwise, could be mined for the production of new warheads and by provisions which specify permissible weapons maintenance and replacement procedures.

---

1. Randall Forsberg, "A Bilateral Nuclear Weapon Freeze," Scientific American, Volume 247, Number 5, (November 1982), pp. 52-61.

2. The Reagan Administration has decided not to re-open the trilateral negotiations towards a Comprehensive Test Ban (CTB) with the Soviet Union and Britain, until verification provisions have been tightened in the as yet unratified 1974 Threshold Test Ban Treaty (TTBT) and the 1976 Peaceful Nuclear Explosion Treaty (PNET). Multilateral discussions about verification of a CTB continue in a working group at the Committee on Disarmament in Geneva. The Arms Control Reporter (Brookline, Mass.: Institute for Defense and Disarmament, 1982), p. 608 A1.

3. For a summary of the history of proposals to cut off the production of weapons grade fissile material, see William Epstein, "The Time Is Ripe to Cut Off the Production of Fissionable Material for Nuclear Weapons," Proceedings of the 30th Pugwash Conference, Breukelin, The Netherlands, August 1980 (London: Taylor and Francis, 1981); and Wolfgang Panofsky, "Constraints on Fissionable Materials for Nuclear Weapons — A Revival of Old Proposals," Loeb Lecture, Harvard University, March 1983.

4. A 4th facility at Savannah River, the L-reactor, is also scheduled to be converted — to produce super grade plutonium — in October 1983.

5. For a survey of monitoring tasks and available techniques, see "Model Freeze," Federation of American Scientists Public Interest Report, Volume 35, Number 7 (Washington, D.C.: F.A.S., September 1982).

6. Panofsky, op. cit.; see also Frank von Hippel's letter to Joseph Nye in this volume.

7. Hans Blix, Statement to the Second Special Session on Disarmament of the United Nations General Assembly (New York: IAEA, June 16, 1982), p. 11.

8. Karl Pieragostini,"Recovering Verification," *Arms Control Today*, Volume 12 (December 11, 1982) at pp. 4-5.

9. See Stephen M. Meyer, "Soviet Military Programs and the Freeze" in this volume.

10. Wolfgang Panofsky, "On-Site Inspection—Cliche or Reality?" Loeb Lecture, Harvard University, March 1983.

11. See, for example, *Whence the Threat*, Soviet Defense Ministry publication, 1981; Soviet Committee for European Security and Cooperation, *The Threat To Europe* (Moscow: Progress Publishers, 1981); V. Boikov and L. Mlechin, editors, "The Arms Race: The Dangers, The Burden, and The Alternative," special issue of *New Times*, Moscow, 1982.

12. Noel Gayler, "How to Break the Momentum of the Nuclear Arms Race," *The New York Times Magazine*, April 25, 1982; see also refinements of the deep cuts proposal in *East-West Outlook*, Vol. 6 (February 1, 1983).

* * *

Soviet Diversion of Plutonium under IAEA Safeguards

Frank von Hippel

In the final session of the Conference, Joseph Nye stated that the Soviet Union could, even with its entire plutonium production system under International Atomic Energy Agency safeguards, still clandestinely divert enough plutonium to produce *50-500 nuclear weapons per year*. This statement gave rise to enough concern among the members of the audience with whom I spoke subsequently to motivate me to try to clarify the matter. That is the purpose of this comment.

As I will show below, my own estimate, using what I believe are worst-case assumptions, is that the undetected leakage of plutonium out of the Soviet nuclear power system during the late 1980s would allow the production of *less than 25 bombs per year*. This is the equivalent of about one thousandth of the existing U.S. stockpile of nuclear weapons and could therefore not be regarded as a major threat to our security over the period of 5–20 years that a freeze agreement might be expected to last before major further developments took place.

I make the following assumptions:

- The amount of fissile plutonium which would be used by a superpower per nuclear weapon is about 4 kilograms;[1]
- The total nuclear generating capacity of the Warsaw Pact nations in the late 1980s will be 40,000 megawatts—more than twice as large as at the end of 1981;[2]

Frank von Hippel *is Senior Research Scientist at the Center for Energy and Environmental Studies at Princeton University, Princeton, New Jersey.*

- These nuclear reactors will operate on average at 70 percent of their rated capacity;[3]
- The spent fuel of these reactors will contain 150 kg of fissile plutonium per 1000 megawatts of capacity per year of operation;[4]
- *All* this fuel will be reprocessed;[5] and
- Diversion of up to 1.5 percent of the plutonium will be undetectable.[6]

Under these worst-case assumptions, Soviet nuclear power reactors would be producing and Soviet reprocessing plants would be separating annually about 6000 kg of fissile plutonium, and at most 90 kg (less than 25 bombs worth) could be siphoned off into their clandestine nuclear weapons production system.

I hope that Professor Nye will be willing to publish in the conference proceedings the basis of his own estimate so that interested readers may be able to understand why we have come to such different conclusions on this important matter.

---

1. This is the average amount in U.S. nuclear weapons based on 100,000 kg of weapons plutonium and 26,000 nuclear warheads. Since the fissile material in a significant fraction of U.S. weapons is highly enriched uranium rather than plutonium, this is a low estimate. The amount of plutonium in the U.S. nuclear weapons stockpile has been estimated to be about 100,000 kg based on the amount of strontium–90 in the high level wastes produced in U.S. military production reactors. Frank von Hippel, "Global Risks from Energy Consumption," Chapter 5, in *Health Risks of Energy Technologies*, Curtis C. Travis and Elizabeth L. Etnier, eds. (Boulder, Colo.: Westview Press, 1983). The number of nuclear warheads in the U.S. stockpile has been estimated to be 26,000. William M. Arkin, Thomas B. Cochran, and Milton M. Hoenig, "The U.S. Nuclear Stockpile," *Arms Control Today*, April 1982, p. 1.

2. "Power Reactors 1982," *Nuclear Engineering International*, August 1982 Supplement, p. 3.

3. This is probably a conservative assumption. The U.N. (*Yearbook of World Energy Statistics*) assumes 51 percent for the U.S.S.R.

4. This would be approximately the nominal annual discharge rate at design burnup of the pressurized water reactors which will make up approximately one half of the Warsaw Pact's generating capacity. It is also approximately the nominal annual discharge rate of a heavy water reactor fueled with slightly (1.2 percent) enriched fuel—the closest analogue I can find to the Soviet graphite moderated channel-type reactors which will make up most of the rest of the Warsaw Pact's nuclear generating capacity. (According to footnote 2, these reactors are typically designed to be fueled with uranium enriched in the range 1.1-1.8 percent.) International Atomic Energy Agency, *International Nuclear Fuel Cycle Evaluation: Advanced Fuel Cycle and Reactor Concepts*, INFCE/PC/2/8, 1980.

5. According to U.S. analyses, it should not be economical to reprocess *any* reactor fuel for civilian purposes until the price of uranium rises to approximately ten times its current level. U.S. Department of Energy, *Nuclear Proliferation and Civilian Nuclear Power: Economics and Systems Analysis*, DOE/NE-0001-5, 1979.

6. Joseph Nye, private communication, January 15, 1983. I agree that this is a reasonable upper bound estimate.

Joseph Nye Replies:

My thanks to Frank von Hippel for the helpful calculations. I have no disagreement with his numbers in relation to the existing Soviet nuclear programs. My 50 to 500 number was related to the future Soviet breeder program and I mentioned that I was thinking about the next decade. I assumed a 1500 tonne reprocessing plant. That explains the 50 opposed to 25 in Frank's calculation—a factor of two for ten years program growth. The factor of ten relates to the question of whether the Soviets could cheat by running a secret reprocessing campaign while temporarily excluding the IAEA inspectors on a pretext of contamination and "repair." Of course there is some risk they would be caught, and suspicions would be aroused. But I am not sure it is an empty set.

Public Opinion and the Freeze Movement

Public Attitudes Toward the Freeze

Louis Harris

American public opinion now is undergoing a series of veritable seismic shocks which are rapidly becoming opposing forces in our politics to what has been hailed as the Reagan mandate of 1980. Specifically, on the subject you all gathered here to discuss, an urgent, dedicated hunger for peace in a nuclear era has overtaken our people. The deep desire for peace has always been there. The urgency of today is precipitated by the dread realization that humanity could well be wiped out in the event of nuclear war, not just at some vague point in the future, but anytime. And anytime could be now.

Triggering this phenomenon is growing public hostility and suspicion of the Soviet Union, on the one hand, and of the Reagan Administration, on the other. Just this past week, the public held the view by 66-31 percent that the President was doing an unsatisfactory job in negotiating a nuclear arms reduction agreement with the Soviets. By 57-59 percent, a sizable majority is worried that he might well get the country into a major nuclear war.

By the same token, an 85-9 percent majority feels the Soviet Union is a hostile power to the U.S. Fully 51 percent see Russia as an outright enemy of this country, the highest recorded since the Cold War days of the late 1950s. Back in 1976, by contrast, public opinon was suspicious of the Soviets, but felt they were hostile toward us by a closer 69-21 percent. By 62-32 percent, a majority believe there is a likelihood that sometime in the next 20 years the Soviet Union will attack the U.S., and by 69-24 percent that they would not hesitate to use nuclear arms, if desperate enough. This antipathy toward the Russians is not basically rooted in the fact that they have a communist government. Indeed, a 70-25 percent majority is convinced that the People's Republic of China is a friendly power towards the United States, a complete turnaround from a 74-17 percent majority who felt the Chinese were hostile back in 1974.

But, does all this mean that the American people now are convinced that the U.S. and the U.S.S.R. are inevitably headed down the road of ultimate confrontation, which in turn would mean our scrambling to underground atomic shelters, learning evacuation routes out of our cities, or paranoically altering our basic life style to accommodate survival in an impending nuclear holocaust?

Louis Harris *is Chairman of the Board of Louis Harris and Associates, New York, N.Y.*

Not at all. Our people are made of sturdier and more intelligent stuff. Instead, they feel deeply that we must now make all-out efforts to try to find those areas of agreement with the Soviet Union, especially in the arms control area, where both sides and the world will benefit from such accords. Thus, by 76-21 percent, a big majority would favor an agreement with the Russians to freeze all nuclear weapons each country can build and keep on hand. In fact, by an even higher, nearly unanimous 92-8 percent, a majority would like to see an end to the production, storage, and testing of all nuclear weapons by all countries on earth. By 80-17 percent, a majority would support agreement with the Soviet Union in the number of nuclear weapons each country has. By 74-21 percent, a majority favor a U.S.-U.S.S.R. accord which would provide for a reduction of U.S. and Russian nuclear installations in Europe. Yet, the quest for agreement goes far beyond the arms area. By 72-18 percent, a majority favors agreement with the Soviets to guarantee free access to oil in the Middle East, by 56-38 percent an accord to exchange scientists and other technical missions, and by a substantial 69-26 percent agreement to expand trade between the U.S. and Russia.

Taken together, it is patently apparent that the American people are ready for going through the arduous and difficult task of negotiating settlements with the Soviet Union, as the immediate threshold alternative to nuclear confrontation. This sentiment is driven even more by deep worries over the perceived deterioriation of relations than by the sweet and glorious taste of peace itself.

But, people are also in a no nonsense mood on the entire subject of nuclear arms control. By 81-16 percent, a big majority wants the U.S. and the Soviets to agree not to produce any new nuclear weapons, provided both countries have a rough equivalence of such weapons today. Indeed, in the nuclear weapons area, a substantial 64-27 percent majority thinks the U.S. is at least equally as strong as the Russians, up from a 53-41 percent majority who felt that way in 1980. The President's claim of U.S. nuclear inferiority simply is not believed.

But the public's thinking goes quite beyond any of the proposals that have been made. By 66-31 percent, a majority feels it is immoral for any country to be producing more nuclear weapons because they can destroy human life on this planet. This can be taken to mean that if an agreement were reached between the two superpowers of the world to freeze or to reduce nuclear weaponry, the public would come right back and ask for further reductions in kind. And then further negotiations beyond that — until the last vestiges of nuclear weaponry are wiped off the face of the earth. This is an incredible phenonemon.

The path people want to go down, however, is decidedly not one of unilateral disarmament. By an overwhelming 82-15 percent, the American public is opposed to that. They want to negotiate from a position of rough parity and want a freeze or reduction of nuclear weapons to leave the two countries in a state of rough parity, until these hated weapons are finally dispersed from the face of the earth.

* * *

Learning from the P.S.R.: Successful Methods for Major Impact

H. Jack Geiger

Let me begin with the task of asking where has public opinion been? Where is it now from the perspective of one organization or one group of people that's been involved in this? Let me begin historically with a set of events which I think has some possible lessons for us now. The Physicians for Social Responsibility (P.S.R.) began in 1959–1960, a time something like the present in a number of characteristics. There were people—Governor Rockefeller, Commissioner Lilly, and others—telling us that you really didn't have to worry about nuclear war, that all you needed was a little fallout shelter in the front yard or the back yard. Edward Teller was saying that a little radiation was probably good for you—it stirred up the genes. An election had just been won in part over allegations of a missile gap, and so on.

A group of physicians almost entirely in Boston, together with biophysicists and other participants, decided to launch a study project to spell out in the best detail possible the medical, environmental, and related consequences of a given thermonuclear weapon on a given city or area. Ultimately, the results were published in the *New England Journal of Medicine* as a series of three long, related articles occupying most of the issue describing the consequences of two ten-megaton blasts in Boston and the consequences for New England. That exercise made something between a very small wave and a big ripple in the New England area in terms of public opinion and understanding and had a very slight effect nationally.

One year later P.S.R. in cooperation with the St. Louis Committee on Nuclear Information conducted a different exercise. I mention this because it is the only precedent I know for the kind of political push that the freeze represents in terms of public opinion with regard to an effect on government policy and legislation. We were concerned about fallout; we were concerned about atmospheric testing. Somebody bright figured out that one of the really easy ways to follow the path of Strontium 90 was into teeth and that one could collect the deciduous teeth of children, baby teeth. That was done in St. Louis on a very large scale. The teeth were analyzed, and we demonstrated the presence of significant amounts of Strontium 90. Within four months from that demonstration, a Limited Test Ban Treaty which had been sitting on desks for two or three years at that point was signed. My interpretation and memory of that event was that in significant numbers the mothers and fathers of this country simply stood up and said, "I do not care what you say about the details of arms control negotiations, the necessity of this kind of testing or the like; you are not putting that stuff in our kids' teeth." And it was done; right or wrong it was extra-

---

H. Jack Geiger *is Arthur C. Logan Professor of Community Medicine at the Sophie Davis School of Biomedical Education of the City College of the City University of New York, New York, N.Y.*

ordinarily effective. Some of the lessons from that, then, are the lessons of immediacy, the lessons of some degree of specific biological understanding as compared to the general proposition that either nuclear weapons are bad or nuclear war would be awful.

These are lessons that were applied in the rebirth of P.S.R. It faded, never having been more than three or four hundred people, maybe a thousand at the outside, in the early 1960s. It was replaced by other concerns and other issues, reborn in 1979 with about two hundred people and has undergone relatively spectacular growth from 1979 to the present; altogether it now has about eighteen thousand members, of whom about fourteen thousand are physicians. What's more important than that growth is, of course, what impact it's had on the public in the strategies it has employed. I'd argue that the evidence is that it's had a major public impact and that it's worth looking at the methods that were used. The methods that were used were, first of all, to instruct the people of Boston but then to have a national series of local symposia. You don't talk about nuclear war being in the abstract an awful thing; you talk about a metagon on St. Louis and Miami and Denver and Chicago and New York and San Francisco, etc., and you do it in those cities on the sensible old journalistic premise that the best news is local news and that people will relate these kinds of phenomena very readily to where they live and where they are. Secondly, in addition to whatever cultural authority physicians possess you cloak this in other kinds of authority. You make them educational exercises for physicians; you have them at medical schools and universities as continuing medical education propositions; you keep clearly in mind the importance of media coverage, of reaching the public, and that the public is one of the major audiences at the same time. We followed in the beginning a medical model, that is, we concentrated on medical effects, details of death and injury, the effects of blast and heat as well as radiation, the impossibility of medical response; but those were always connected with aspects of what would happen to the physical infrastructure of the environment and above all the social fabric. Perhaps more important than that, after the very beginning, we never gave exclusively "medical" symposia; they were always accompanied by speakers from other fields on general scientific aspects and military aspects, on arms control, on conflict resolution, on some of the psychological problems, on pending arms control negotiations, and the like. And that was, up until about half a year or so ago, the fundamental strategy.

In that light, I have some difficulty with the references this morning to talk of consequences as rhetorical. They may be; but they are also, at least as we have attempted to present them, unarguable. Perhaps more important than that is that it is simply not true that people really knew about this subject — not just physicians and scientists, but the public at large. They knew that nuclear war was bad; they knew that nuclear weapons would be bad; they had neither an accurate quantitative nor qualitative concept of what the explosion of thermonuclear weapons, even on a small scale, would mean. And I think the acquisition of that knowledge, breaking through what people have called psychic numbing or whatever, has made a significant difference.

I'll skip over the reasons for why I think we had such an impact at this period in time. Some of them Mr. Harris has already mentioned—actions of the Reagan Administration, increased anxiety. I think physicians were a new voice on the scene. There's some analogy to the role played by the Catholic bishops. We have cultural authority, we have known commitment to preserve life, we are a politically conservative group by history and reputation, we represented a new voice in the proceedings, we contributed a level of scientific detail. Whether deservedly or not, these aspects helped us make a contribution in addition to that which had been attempted for so many years by the atomic scientists and others.

The transition, an important one, occurred about a year ago. To illustrate it, one of our speakers—Irwin Redliner, a physician—was addressing a large church group not long ago in Wilmington, Delaware and doing what we call the "bombing run"—a megaton on Wilmington or wherever—and in the middle of it a lady raised her hand, stopped him in mid-speech, and said, "Dr. Redliner, we know all of that. What we want to know is what are we going to do about it?" A very clear message from the mule in the old saw that said, "Look, you have my attention, stop beating me with a two by four and explain to me what it is that you want to get done."

What we had to do we then realized and have attempted to do in dealing with that frustration and confusion—and that mule was talking about confusion and dissatisfaction with arms control negotiations as well—was try and reduce those feelings to a set of three very simple ideas that relate to both the freeze and arms control in general: the idea that nuclear war is unwinnable; the idea that it is unsurvivable; the idea that there is in no meaningful sense a destructive advantage anymore for one side or another. These ideas found their expression in the freeze very specifically and was one of the reasons P.S.R. decided to endorse the freeze and to speak for it and to it.

Challenging the freeze on the grounds of interference with arms control may indeed have its own validities, but it is done at some risk to the bedrock of support that underlies, in my view, support for both freeze and for a variety of further or alternative arms control measures. People seized on freeze because they had no stomach for the complexities of circular error probables divided by the square root of throwweights. Nor did they have confidence in them, nor do they exclude them subsequently. Our impression is that the question is *not* either freeze or arms control in the long run but that the freeze is seen as the one equivalent of not putting Strontium 90 in kids' teeth *at this point*, a demonstration of specific government action from which further steps can follow.

* * *

The Freeze in Political Context

Jonathan Moore

I will try to take a broader view of the dynamic process which actually translates public opinion and political action into public policy. Let me identify some contextual factors in a quick, speculative inventory of considerations and questions about (a) where we are now, (b) what's ahead, and (c) what choices are faced. This may help frame the remarks made on this panel and in the following discussion to help us comprehend better the relationship between freeze movements and arms control results.

What Is the Situation Now?

1. The freeze movement has remained stronger than many predicted, particularly given a combination of neutralizing factors which include (a) the passage of time, (b) President Reagan's START proposals, and (c) intense public preoccupation with the economy.

2. The freeze was a major issue in the fall 1982 elections, although it is important to keep in mind that it was decisive in very few Congressional races. The number of pro-freeze votes in the House of Representatives was increased significantly. And in referenda engaging 25 percent of the national electorate in eight states, the freeze won by a 3-2 margin.

3. The vitality and momentum of the freeze pressured the Administration to reduce its inflammatory rhetoric and to make its START negotiating position at least appear to be more serious—but this greater political sensitivity to and sophistication about the issue in the White House can be a double-edged sword, so to speak.

4. A number of independent polls demonstrate that public support is very strong for a mutual and verifiable freeze. But public schizophrenia and ambivalence—essentially involving hang-ups about dealing with and relying on the Russians—persist. Unqualified pro-freeze support has not taken off and could be on a plateau. And stubborn economic problems distract attention from the issue.

5. In addition to traditional and predictable categories of support, the main line churches and a large aggregation of citizens more aware of the consequences and scared of the greater risks of nuclear war have added crucial numbers to the movement, but not yet enough. Freeze proponents probably cannot increase their size and broaden their base without sustaining the moderate, non-extremist, and non-unilateral character of the effort.

What Lies Ahead over the Next Two Years?

1. The Administration is now more susceptible to and aware of political pressures

---

Jonathan Moore *is Director of the Institute of Politics at the John F. Kennedy School of Government, Harvard University, Cambridge, Massachusetts.*

and stakes, in terms of: (a) the potential electoral power of freeze sentiment generally; (b) whether the recurrent "leadership" issue will identify with arms control during the '84 Presidential election; (c) no longer being confident of the 1980 "mandate" or the resistance of Presidential popularity to slippage; (d) considerably less strength in the House of Representatives; and (e) not being able to count on a strong economy for the '84 election.

2. We have a President who can get the people to support virtually whatever he might want in the way of serious negotiations with the Russians, who seems quite capable of change in the policy, and who may be looking for a winning issue, so to speak. But there is a big difference between a President who can effectively contain pro-arms control sentiment to keep things roughly as they are without getting into a lot of political trouble and a President who wants to mobilize and exploit pro-arms control sentiment in the country to change the policy.

3. There are some important variables which are difficult to calculate. Does this President get the image as the first since World War II to be against arms control, or not? Does the Administration lose ground and become more vulnerable politically to the freeze merely by looking disorganized and inept, or does it begin to manage the situation more effectively? Does something happen in the way of a scary nuclear weapons-related incident or accident which could galvanize the freeze movement, or do the Russians do something menacing which could give impetus to enhanced militaristic patriotism, or neither?

4. In the relatively short run, there are two main determinants on the American side to serious progress in negotiating arms control agreements: (a) how well our national economy recovers and when, and (b) how effectively the President manages the politics and manipulates the cosmetics of arms control policy. In other words, if we were to make a certain set of assumptions for roughly eighteen months from now—a pretty good or improving economy; the appearance of negotiating progress or activity; no scary galvanizing nuclear weapons incident; and a cut-back on defense spending—then the freeze might not be that big, popular, or decisive in the 1984 elections.

Political and Policy Choices

1. Does the movement push the freeze as a "pure option" or as a means of bringing about some improvement in national policy in overall posture and negotiating position? It is possible that the only way of accomplishing the latter is to continue to push the formulation which has public understanding and support, without sacrificing suppleness or being rigid.

2. Should freeze proponents concentrate on influencing the current Administration to change its position or on attempting to bring about its defeat? Rejecting the former objective in favor of the latter at this point would be to risk political effectiveness and philosophical consistency.

3. Is pro-arms control, anti-arms race activism better off staying the way it is, riding the Congressional freeze resolution and drum-beating the issue into the

1984 election, or changing? It could: (a) become more ideologically pure and intense; (b) invent a "daughter of freeze" by concentrating on a more narrow objective (e.g., measures to avoid accidental war, destabilizing weapons, comprehensive test ban, SALT II); or (c) attack specific targets in Congress such as weapons systems funding, in order to sustain vitality, interest, and momentum by exercising political muscle. A compelling option might be to combine retention of the essential character of the movement along with selective efforts to resist Congressional approval of authorizing and appropriating actions inconsistent with its overall philosophy.

The challenge lies with the two elements in the process—political activists and policy activists—finding convergence and reciprocalness. This requires both integrity and flexibility on both sides, and a recognition of their mutual dependency. The movement has got to strike a balance between sticking to what it's got going for it politically in order not to lose influence, and being responsive to officials and experts shaping the position further so as to affect a more progressive and viable policy. And the traditional arms control elites ought to be careful about trying to manipulate a freeze movement which is both the catalyst for and the product of public attitudes disaffected by substantive policy expertise which perpetually claims complexity and public ignorance and by "arms race business as usual" over the last thirty years. Actually to accomplish desired change in this area requires an active public to be more sophisticated and responsible about the realities of the problem on the one hand, and government officials and their advisers to be guided by what the public wants and is willing to support on the other.

* * *

The Impact of the Nuclear Freeze Movement on Congress

Douglas C. Waller

Introduction

On August 5, 1982, a historic vote was taken in the U.S. House of Representatives. For the previous eight months, a nationwide movement had been gaining momentum in the United States. It was the nuclear freeze movement and in this short period it had accomplished many notable political feats, not the least of which was pushing an Administration with no previous arms control interest or initiative to the negotiating table in Geneva to begin strategic arms talks. The White House hoped that President Reagan's May 9 Eureka College speech, which outlined his START proposal, would go a long way toward diffusing the American freeze movement. After all, it would be argued, the public must stand behind its President and not undercut his negotiators at Geneva. But the freeze supporters, who realized that START still allowed the building of destabilizing weapons by both superpowers, were not persuaded. The movement continued to grow, as did the political pressure on Congress to endorse the freeze concept.

On August 5, the first Congressional test of the freeze came in the House in a vote that its members had come to realize meant a lot. After all, here was one chamber of Congress, that "disintegrated ministry" as Woodrow Wilson once termed it, prepared to cast a vote of no confidence in the President's arms control proposal. Here was the House, which usually defers to a President about to enter into such negotiations, coming within two votes of telling a chief executive in no uncertain terms as he pulls up to the bargaining table what kind of arms control treaty it wants negotiated.

The freeze lost on August 5 by a margin of 204-202. Despite the loss, freeze supporters cheered the House vote. (Two years ago, at the height of the Reagan arms buildup rhetoric, such a resolution would never have even made it to the House floor.) Thus, by anyone's political assessment—be they freezers or anti-freezers—the movement's accomplishments in 1982 were formidable.

This paper examines two questions about the freeze. Congress is largely a stimulus-response institution. Therefore, what has been the stimulus the nationwide freeze movement has provided? And more importantly, what has been the response of Congress to the freeze and what will be its response in the future? In discussing Congress, this paper will limit itself to the House, where support for the freeze is stronger than in the Senate and where there has been more legislative activity on the proposal.

Douglas C. Waller *is Legislative Assistant to Representative Edward J. Markey, U.S. Congress, Washington, D.C.*

The Freeze Stimulus

The freeze coalition and the other arms control groups chalked up a string of political accomplishments during 1982. While Congress was preoccupied in the early part of the year with what it thought would be the major issue of 1982—the battle over the President's budget—the freeze was becoming a major diversion from the battle. On March 10, 1982, Senators Edward M. Kennedy and Mark Hatfield introduced the freeze resolution in the Senate and Congressmen Ed Markey, Silvio Conte, and Jonathan Bingham introduced the same measure in the House. This Congressional involvement with the freeze helped bring more national media attention to the movement. Twenty days later, the House held over 18 hours of special debate on the freeze and arms control in general; such a debate had not occurred in that chamber since the Vietnam War.

By the spring and summer months, a nationwide teach-in on the freeze and the dangers of nuclear war was taking place. During Ground Zero Week, April 18-25, people gathered to talk about life—or the lack of it—after nuclear war. Not only did college campuses begin holding seminars on the arms race and the freeze, but business and community organizations, professional groups, labor leaders, educators, doctors, lawyers, ministers, and scientists organized on the issue. Freeze endorsements poured in from prominent individuals. Publishing houses, magazines, and newspapers began churning out material on nuclear war and arms control. Freeze groups have been formed in every state and practically every Congressional district. More than 500 town meetings, city councils and county commissions have passed freeze resolutions. One hundred and thirty-five Catholic bishops endorsed the freeze. On June 12, almost one million persons gathered in New York to rally against nuclear war.

Presently, freeze leaders estimate that tens of thousands of activists are working on the proposal nationwide. What is noteworthy about the freeze is that it is a predominantly middle-class movement made up of family people, business and professional people, the clergy, educators, and scientists. Unlike the Vietnam protests a decade ago, the freeze movement gained its foothold not on college campuses but in grassroots America—in community centers, town halls, church basements, and living rooms all over the country.

General public support for the freeze has been overwhelming. Most opinion polls have shown respondents backing the freeze by a 3-1 margin. Pollsters and political analysts have questioned what the public is actually saying in these surveys. Everett Carll Ladd concluded in the August/September 1982 issue of *Public Opinion* that "American opinion on nuclear weapons and war has changed scarcely at all over nearly four decades." Current freeze polls show that Americans want to restrict the development of nuclear weapons on both sides; they want to minimize the chance of nuclear war occurring; but they do not trust the Soviets and they do not want a nuclear arms treaty that gives the Soviets a military advantage. These are the same goals that have surfaced in opinion polls dating back to the Hiroshima explosion, Ladd notes. Yet one reason the freeze has caught on nationwide has been the fact that the long-held public goals turn out to be the goals of the present freeze resolution, which (1) calls on both sides to halt the nuclear arms race, (2) wants a treaty that is verifiable so the United States does not have to rely on trust, and (3) recognizes that a freeze now would not leave the Soviets with an overall strategic advantage. Of all the surveys done on the freeze, one of the most revealing of this public sentiment came in an April 1982 *Washington Post*/ABC News Poll. A majority of the people polled did not believe the Soviets could be trusted. A majority agreed that the Soviets would have an advantage over the United States in nuclear weapons if we froze now. But three-fourths said it does not matter if the United States or the Soviet Union is ahead in nuclear weapons because both sides have enough firepower to destroy the other no matter who attacks first. And by a 3-1 margin, the people polled favored an immediate nuclear freeze on both sides.

There have been other factors that have helped build public support for the freeze. Contrary to what Ronald Reagan and *Reader's Digest* may claim, one of the principal instigators of the nuclear freeze does not live in the Kremlin. He lives at 1600 Pennsylvania Avenue. Mr. Reagan as a candidate talked about nuclear proliferation being none of our business and as president about nuclear warning shots. His military advisers talked about fighting, surviving, and winning a nuclear war. Clearly, while the administration had its mind on rearming America, the American people began asking, "Who's thinking about preventing a nuclear war from ever occurring in the first place?"

The freeze has also survived and thrived because not only is it a simple idea, it is also a simple idea that makes good sense. And as Ralph Waldo Emerson once said, "Nothing astonishes men so much as common sense." The freeze recognizes that both sides are at overall nuclear parity. With 50,000 warheads stockpiled by the two superpowers, both sides have the capacity to destroy the other many times over, under any nuclear war-fighting scenario. The freeze recognizes that the problem now with the arms race is the arms race, that the next round of nuclear weapons both sides are deploying or planning to deploy only increases the threat of nuclear war rather than deters it. The freeze resolution thus calls on both sides to halt the arms race and reduce in a way that can be verified. The freeze also *can be implemented*, if there is the political will on both sides to do so. "What possibly can be wrong with heeding the call, stopping the arms race and proceeding with substantial reductions?" former Arms Control and Disarmament Agency Director Paul Warnke has asked. "I haven't yet heard a good answer." Neither have the American people.

Congressional Response to the Freeze

On the surface, Congressional response to the grass-roots call for a freeze has been substantial. It began with the March 10 introduction of the Kennedy-Hatfield/Markey-Conte-Bingham freeze resolution and was followed by the special House debate on the issue. On June 23, the House Foreign Affairs Committee approved the nuclear freeze resolution by a bipartisan 25-8 vote. And, as noted above, the House then came within two votes of passing the nuclear freeze resolution on August 5.

November 2 was the next important date for the freeze. The economy was clearly the number one issue in the mid-term elections. But the freeze did not rank far behind in many Congressional races. In what was the closest this country has ever come to a national plebiscite on arms control, more than one-fourth of the nation's voters cast ballots in state and local freeze referendums. The result was a solid victory: over 11.5 million people, or 60 percent of those voting in the referendums, voted for the freeze.

But perhaps more important to members of Congress was the freeze's political fallout in individual district races. In several House races, candidates who opposed the freeze paid the political piper (the Coyne-Kostmayer race and LeBoutillier-Mrazek race being the most notable examples). In dozens of other races the freeze, even though it took a back seat to the economy, was nevertheless an important issue that either gave a candidate headaches if he opposed it or a welcome boost if he supported it. According to figures compiled by the Council for a Livable World, in 15 key races that organization had been monitoring, pro-freeze challengers had ousted anti-freeze House incumbents; in five open House seats, pro-freeze candidates beat anti-freeze candidates; and in 16 close races, pro-freeze incumbents prevailed over anti-freeze challengers. On the negative side for the freeze, in three races pro-freeze House incumbents lost to anti-freeze candidates; and in six open House seats, anti-freeze candidates beat pro-freeze candidates. Overall, however, the freeze had a net gain of 20 to 30 seats in the House. The percentage of House races where the freeze played a role in electing a candidate was admittedly small. However, an analysis of the effects of the freeze movement on members of Congress would be incomplete if it dwelled solely on the races where a candidate won or lost because of the freeze. Likewise, an analysis would be incomplete if it relied solely on nationwide opinion poll data to assess the effect of the freeze on members of Congress.

Indeed, much of the effect of the freeze movement upon members of Congress is more qualitative than quantitative. To examine this hard-to-measure effect, we must start with the member of Congress. Most likely, he or she enters the job with little military background, except for perhaps a two-year stint in the service after school. Most members of Congress were lawyers, business executives, or local elected officials before they came to Washington. While comfortable with domestic issues, their command of defense issues is minimal. "Neither education nor experience equip a majority [of Congressmen] to match ends with means in ways that consistently maximize U.S. security and minimize U.S. expense," writes Congressional Research Service defense specialist John M. Collins in his latest book, U.S. Defense Planning: A Critique. "Only a few members, including those assigned to Armed Services and Appropriations Committees, ever develop full appreciation for manpower or weapon procurement matters and put them in strategic context." Also, few walk into the job with a full understanding of the arms control impact of their defense votes.

The result: A representative can become easily overwhelmed by the platoons of "experts" from the Pentagon and State Department who are briefing him, or by the hundreds of lobbying groups representing every foreign policy and defense issue imaginable who are flooding his office with mail and phone calls and priming his constituents to contact him.

When the defense bill comes to the floor, the representative becomes somewhat of a broker. On one side of him stands the needs of the administration, the Pentagon, and the defense industry lobby. On the other side of him stands his constituents—the "electoral connection." What kind of lobbying does a representative receive from his constituents on defense manpower, weapons procurement, arms control or other broad strategic questions? Very little. A Congressman will be contacted by businesses with defense contracts in his district. If a member has a military base in his district, decisions on votes that affect those facilities and their jobs will be fairly easy to make—if the member wants to keep his job for longer than two years. But it is on the broader issues of defense management and arms control that the Congressional broker gets little guidance from his constituents.

Along comes the freeze movement. The Congressman is now receiving pressure from his district that he has never seen before. Now he is receiving calls and letters from business executives, housewives, doctors, lawyers, and ministers who are now holding him accountable for the arms control impact of his defense votes. His local city councils are passing freeze resolutions and a freeze coalition is being organized in his district. He is fielding questions in town meetings about whether he supports the freeze.

What effect all this freeze activity in an individual district has on the member's defense votes is difficult for an outsider to measure. As Congressional scholar Richard F. Fenno, Jr. has noted, a member's *perception* of his district is the key ingredient and "the constituency a representative reacts to is the constituency he or she sees." When a Congressman looks at his constituency, Fenno correctly points out that he looks at it not just in terms of his "geographical constituency"—that is, the entire population within the boundaries of his district. The Congressman also looks at his constituency in terms of:

a. his "reelection constituency," those people the Congressman thinks will vote for him;
b. his "primary constituency," those people the Congressman perceives to be his strong supporters, who are very important to him during a party primary;
c. his "personal constituency," made up of his close friends and political confidants.

The freeze movement in any district will likely have the most effect on the member in terms of his perception of his reelection constituency and his primary constituency. All told, the number of freeze activists in any member's district will likely be small. Nevertheless they will be, say, 50 activists who are willing to work for a candidate, or against him if he opposes the freeze. They can become part of his hard-core volunteers who drop leaflets or who each reach several hundred other people in the district for support. And while they will make up a very small percentage of his district, a Congressman realizes that they can be the hard-core supporters that win a primary.

Even an anti-freeze candidate who wins an election over the opposition of his local freeze movement may be influenced by that movement. As Fenno points out, "No matter how secure their electoral circumstances may seem . . . members of Congress can always find reason to feel insecure." A small drop in his vote percentage, which the incumbent perceives to be caused by freeze activists, will be enough to cause him to worry. After all, there is always that hidden opponent in his district who will surface if he thinks the incumbent's support is eroding.

In summary, much of the effect the freeze movement has had or will have on representatives may never show up in polling data. But the stimulus is there and it is certainly not unnoticed by the representative.

Between 1969 and 1975 Congress reorganized and decentralized. Power shifted from the committees to the subcommittees, resulting in more members becoming involved in key legislative decisions. More fingerprints can thus be found on the final defense package Congress passes each year. Twenty years ago the Armed Services Committees simply rubber stamped Pentagon requests. Now we see more members on those committees who are routinely challenging Pentagon requests. The information monopoly the Armed Services panels once had is breaking up. More Congressmen not on the Armed Services Committees, more non-defense related committees, more ad hoc groups and task forces are now participating in the legislative process. Therefore, while the leadership of the Armed Services Committees and the Appropriations Subcommittees on Defense still prevail much of the time, they don't prevail as much as they once did.

The freeze movement will nurture even more Congressional concern about the implications of defense programs for arms control and our national security. The Congressional rejection of the dense pack basing mode for the MX may well be the first evidence of this increasing concern. House sponsors of the nuclear freeze resolution hope to have the resolution before the floor by March. This time, they believe they have the votes to pass it. Over the long run, Congress will see more of its members, who were or would have been outsiders in the defense debate, now entering into it, more members questioning defense policy, more members demanding that it be accountable for its arms control impact, and more members calling for a halt to the arms race. Why? Because the voters back home will be demanding that they become more involved.

* * *

Critiques of Freezes as Instruments of Arms Control

The Freeze: Near-Term Issues and Near-Term Approaches

Congressman Albert Gore

I want to express my appreciation to the organizers of this conference for having invited me here, but I want to also express some apprehension at the prospect of being positioned on a panel charged with critiquing not just "The Freeze," but all the little freezes, too.

My initial plan was to meet this challenge by exercising the well-recognized right of every Congressman to ignore other people's agendas and speak only of their own. In the last year, I have published two very detailed arms control concepts, and am sitting on two more. This would be a wonderful opportunity to launch into them, with a select and captive audience like this.

And I still plan to. But not before I carry out plan "B," which is to be responsive to the topic as defined. I intend to do so, however, by discussing freezes, both big and little, from the perspective of the Congress.

Congress deals with the pressures and forces of public controversy in their most elemental form: struggles to determine the allocation of the nation's resources. In coming months, the Congress faces just such a struggle over funding for nuclear weapons programs: not just the MX, although that is by far the most important weapons issue ahead, but Pershing II—the funds for which were held up by the last Congress; and probably other matters as well, including the scale of the cruise missile program, and so on.

Somewhere along the line, the Congress will also vote again on the nuclear freeze resolution. I have little doubt that it will pass in the House, and wouldn't entirely rule out the Senate, for that matter. But the very probability that this will occur underscores the first major point I want to make. Having passed the freeze, we in the Congress must still deal with yes-or-no votes on the future of various nuclear weapons systems. Yet, the freeze resolution offers no guidance where these votes are concerned.

From the beginning, part of the freeze resolution's strength—its ability to stir popular support in the heartland—has been its insistence that a freeze be mutual:

Albert Gore *is a Congressman (D-Tennessee) in the United States House of Representatives, Washington, D.C.*

negotiated with the Soviet Union and guaranteed by our ability to monitor compliance. Obviously, we have no such agreement and, I hope, it is just as obvious that we are not going to have one during the term of the present Administration. Ronald Reagan cannot by any stretch of the imagination be persuaded to *want* an across-the-board freeze; nor can he be forced to negotiate one.

Those of you who are working the freeze movement are best able to judge what would happen if the movement began to demand that the U.S. *unilaterally* suspend weapons development, production, and deployment. But let me say that, insofar as the Congress is concerned, such a shift, in my opinion, would destroy the freeze's influence. Like the general public, many members of Congress have come to doubt the value of endless numbers of new nuclear weapons, and to fear where the President's ideas of nuclear doctrine are taking us. I cannot imagine, however, a situation in which the Congress would legislate a de facto unilateral freeze.

So, for the near term, the freeze cannot really serve as a guide to the perplexed. And it may well be *in* the near term that the fate of the freeze idea is going to be settled. The freeze is an arms control proposal like any other in that it starts from an assessment of the U.S.–Soviet nuclear balance and recommends a policy based thereon. This means, however, that the freeze—like any other rational proposition—depends upon certain conditions and can be invalidated if those conditions change enough.

It is reasonably clear, I think, that we and the Soviets are at the threshold of a cycle of major, destabilizing weapons deployments: deployments that may create circumstances completely at variance with those on which the freeze was predicated. These are the developments which will be driven in part by how Congress votes on the various nuclear weapons systems over the next two years, and of how the Soviets, absent any new constraints, choose to pursue their own interests. So the fate of the freeze hangs in the balance, but the freeze offers no light to those who must make the choice.

Now, let me turn to all the "little" freezes, of partial scope, limited duration, and the like. It is conceivable that one or several of these have that magic combination of qualities that would make it an enormously persuasive idea, yet within the President's grasp. But it is becoming a new cottage industry. Enormous effort goes into the invention of new proposals, many of them with great technical merit. Unfortunately, arms controllers dwell on their differences over such proposals rather than working out a common political front. With all due respect, the publication of an article on an op-ed page or in a scholarly journal is only enough to register an idea in the minds of a rather select group of readers. It is far from being able to mobilize the public, galvanize a stubborn administration, and help guide debate in a confused Congress.

There are definitely some important differences of view among us here. But it seems to me that these are far less significant than the differences we collectively have with the administration's nuclear policies. Therefore, it is crucial that we find some creative way to deal with our differences: not by glossing over them, but by looking for areas of common agreement that might remedy the weaknesses of the big freeze—its lack of relevance for near-term decisions—and the little freezes—their technicality and lack of political impact.

I believe that it is not only impossible to do this, but that the elements of such a consensus are visible, if we step back far enough from the particulars to get a little perspective. Thinking back on the many articles in the press and in journals, and over comments at this and other meetings, it seems to me that there is a nascent consensus, based on three propositions:

1. That, although SALT II is the best available point of departure for negotiations, SALT II itself offers both sides options for expanding nuclear forces that would be dangerous, if exercised;

2. That preparations to exercise these options are well advanced in both the U.S. and the Soviet Union, and unless some way is found to buy time, these decisions will overtake the effort to negotiate reductions;

3. That reductions themselves need to be organized around some clarifying principle or objective, and that this principle is the need for "strategic stability."

On the first point, we already have had an important victory. The administration did not gladly decide to observe SALT II limitations, but acted only under pressure, and because it discovered no better alternative. But just as clearly, the administration would gladly abandon SALT II if that were possible, and could easily seize upon some rationale for doing so. The tendency of some freeze advocates to denigrate what arms control has accomplished, including SALT II, is harmful. It strengthens the position of those within the administration who believe that the treaty is pernicious, and who welcome criticism of it regardless of source. We cannot afford to be complacent that SALT II limits can be preserved. And if they go, then all bets are off.

On the second point, we must again look first at ourselves and examine the implications of what we decide to do. Assuming that the freeze is completely out of the question for President Reagan, what are the alternatives? Would it be best to try to stalemate the President on every nuclear weapons request, and to paralyze decision-making until the issue can be settled two years from now? Or should a good-faith effort be made to define some initiative of smaller scope, build up coalition politics around that, and offer the President a chance to lead, rather than to fail?

Certainly, there are candidates for such a proposal. Paul Warnke has an idea on theater nuclear forces; Jan Lodal has a proposal for freezing overall warhead totals; Jeremy Stone is writing about a variant of the "mutual restraint" idea. And, if you will sit still for a commercial, I too have a contribution in the form of a "negotiator's pause": specifically, a ban on increasing total warheads deployed on ICBMs, and of constraining further improvements accuracy for those missiles, while we try to negotiate their future.

But it is the last point—the need for an overall principle to guide decisions on force posture, and the conduct of arms control—that I think is the most important. Lay people intuitively understand that if it is dangerous for one side to be able, even theoretically, to threaten the other's nuclear forces, and to be in a position to brood about the advantage of a first strike, it is far more dangerous for *both* sides to be in such circumstances.

Yet, vulnerability to counterforce strikes is the likely outcome of the President's nuclear weapons program and his START proposal. General Rowny recently acknowledged that the administration's design is to make the Soviets just as nervous as we are. Virtually every one of us in this room is opposed to that, and convinced that there is a better way to design nuclear forces, and a better objective for arms control. We should make it our business to drive home that point forcibly, and to advance the concept of eliminating the fear of first strike capabilities to the center of the public debate for the near term. It is a principle common to advocates of the "big" freeze, the "little" freezes, and the many reductions proposals—including my own, which go for the throat of the problem, by calling for the phasing out of MIRVed ICBMs, in favor of much smaller numbers of single warhead variants. And it is this point we should make sure gets across, no matter how vigorously we each set out to promote the details of our personal inventions.

I want to conclude, therefore, by talking to you briefly about an effort some of us have undertaken in the Congress, because I hope you will actively support it.

In the last session of Congress, Les Aspin, Tom Downey, and a courageous Republican moderate, Joel Pritchard, joined me in introducing a resolution centered on the issue of strategic stability. As we began the new session, I reintroduced this resolution, this time adding Lee Hamilton's name to the list of original cosponsors. There are more than thirty other members presently agreeing with the resolution, and indications of growing interest among middle-of-the-road Republicans, who find the President's nuclear policy frightening.

The resolution, whose text I will make available to you, is grounded on two propositions:

- That we "should place the highest priority on efforts to reduce and eliminate the fear by either nation of a nuclear first-strike against it by the other"; and
- That we "should seek a verifiable agreement that produces stability in the strategic relationship between the two nations by ensuring that neither nation possesses capabilities which would confer upon it even the hypothetical advantages of a first strike."

My cosponsors and I did not introduce this resolution as a competitor to the freeze, nor is it having that effect. This is an effort to complement the freeze by articulating an issue that can serve as the organizing factor in Congressional debate over nuclear weapons systems, and in the Congress's effort to influence the administration's approach to arms control, during the near term.

I wouldn't for a moment urge the freeze movement to relax its efforts to create an American consensus about nuclear weapons for the long term. But I hope that the freeze will also recognize that there are issues here and now that must be dealt with, and that efforts to do this will be understood and welcomed. Similarly, I wouldn't consider asking specialists to give up their efforts to craft refined alternatives for arms control, because it takes working models of such alternatives to prove that they exist and are worth struggling for. But I would hope that arms controllers will also begin to give more expression to the idea that they are united on broad principles, even when differing on details, and that they use their influence to help generate politics of consensus, rather than of confrontation. Whether the administration will have this or reject it remains to be seen. I admit that the news of Eugene Rostow's sudden resignation is not encouraging. But we ought to make that effort.

* * *

Why We Should Freeze Total Deployed Nuclear Weapons

Jan M. Lodal

The purpose of this session is to examine why certain freezes are not a good idea and to discuss alternatives that might make more sense. While the main problems with "comprehensive" freezes along the Forsberg-Kennedy-Hatfield line have been widely identified, let me begin with a brief summary, after which I will offer some observations.

1. In many cases, new deployments would enhance prospects for peace and stability, not reduce them. Freezing these would reduce our security. (Trident I is a good example.)
2. Production freezes are impossible to verify.
3. Over time, a comprehensive U.S./U.S.S.R. freeze would raise the attractiveness of proliferation.
4. Our allies would perceive a comprehensive freeze as codifying some Soviet advantages, such as intermediate-range missiles in Europe.
5. The freeze does not directly address nuclear stability, which should be the main criterion by which we judge any arms control approach.
6. A freeze provides no reduction in force levels, nor does it necessarily facilitate reductions.
7. The detailed terms of a comprehensive freeze agreement would be almost impossible to negotiate if a rigorous and verifiable agreement were desired. It is simply too complicated technically.
8. The Russians probably wouldn't agree to it anyway, so we are wasting our time.

Some of these problems are not as important as others. But taken as a whole, I believe that this list of criticisms indicates formidable problems with the approach. While any one difficulty could be overcome, it seems quite unlikely enough could be overcome to result in a consummated agreement.

Before considering alternatives, it is helpful to review what a freeze would ac-

Jan M. Lodal *is Executive Vice President of American Management Systems in Arlington, Virginia.*

complish if it were agreed upon. There is the possible long-term deterioration of older systems that might lead to reduced confidence in first-strike capabilities. But such a result is only hypothetical; it is neither impossible to conceive of technological advances that would offset deterioration, nor it is out of the question that the effects would be perverse rather than helpful. The confidence in deterrence might be the victim, rather than whatever confidence either side might have in a preemptive strike. I do not believe that either side has much confidence in its ability to strike first anyway, so I see the risk to deterrence as the greater effect of a prolonged production and testing freeze.

A more compelling argument for a freeze is that it would break the cycle of the arms race. I believe that this prediction of its efficacy is correct, and that the result would be significant and beneficial. The resulting public perception that the U.S. was no longer building useless "overkill" would have the beneficial effect of solidifying support for sensible defense programs. Between East and West, the cessation of deployments and production would reduce tensions and the risk of conflict.

But a comprehensive freeze is not necessary to achieve these results. And given the list of the problems above, focusing on a comprehensive freeze may well impede the process of obtaining the very results the freeze proponents desire.

As I have suggested elsewhere, I believe that a freeze in the total number of weapons ("nuclear charges") carried on all delivery vehicles with a range greater than approximately 1,000 kilometers achieves almost all the results the more comprehensive freeze would achieve with few of the associated problems.[1]

Let me summarize the arguments for a freeze on deployed weapons:

1. All of the weapons currently under discussion in both INF and START would be covered without the various "boundary" problems that currently exist. It would no longer matter whether Backfires were in START, in INF, or in both. Nor would Soviet complaints about forward-based systems being "strategic" in nature be relevant. Finally, since only the number of nuclear charges would be counted, the many definitional asymmetries amongst the various types of weapons and delivery systems would be set aside.

2. In a comprehensive framework, issues such as allied nuclear forces, Chinese forces, geographical asymmetries, and so forth could be considered second order and dropped from consideration. In the context of intermediate-range missiles in central Europe, British and French forces are not insignificant. But in the larger context I have suggested, they are not very important.

3. With complete freedom to mix, each side's force planning could proceed on its own basis. It seems to me we have demonstrated in thirteen years of formal arms control negotiations that we cannot mutually plan our force structures. We have enough trouble planning our force structure by ourselves, much less doing it jointly with the Soviets. We should give up trying.

4. The effect of a weapons freeze on public perceptions would be almost as dramatic as that of a complete freeze. Each deployment of a new system would be accompanied by destruction of an existing system. This alone would change

the perception of the nuclear arms race completely and have a tremendous political effect, both domestically, in Europe, and between East and West.

5. The total number of weapons is about equal on each side right now; thus the criterion of *de jure* equality could be met.

6. If SALT II counting rules are adopted for counting the weapons, verification becomes no worse than under SALT II. (The possible exception is sea-launched cruise missiles, which are a problem under any proposal.)

The freeze proponents have one point that is absolutely correct: Our past approaches to arms control have been much too complicated. They have taken too long to negotiate, cannot be understood by the public, and cannot be seriously discussed at high levels between governments. The negotiating process is then left to technical experts, and we all know how well bureaucracies negotiate.

The freeze proposal seems simple in its statement, but it would be difficult in implementation. Questions of equality could arise and undercut political support for it. But if the freeze were limited to the number of weapons, the arms race would be cut off, yet each side would remain free to make adjustments necessary to overcome any perceived qualitative asymmetries.

One major difference between the approach I have suggested and a more comprehensive freeze is the inclusion of all nuclear weapons in the comprehensive freeze, whereas I have limited my proposal to intermediate-range and long-range weapons. I believe that several facts argue for this approach:

1. Intermediate-range and long-range weapons are those currently subject to negotiation.

2. We have no concept of how to verify limitations on battlefield-range weapons.

3. Battlefield-range weapons are not the subject of major political pressures, so why should we let them impede other progress in arms control which could be made now?

4. Over time these weapons will diminish in importance militarily, leading each side to reduce their stockpiles anyway.

In summary, we need a simpler approach, but a comprehensive freeze would not be simple to negotiate. We should start with a more limited freeze on the total number of weapons (nuclear charges). Once such a freeze is reached, percentage reductions from equal aggregate numbers could be easily negotiated, even at subsequent summit meetings. Compromises among bureaucracies on specific weapons programs would not have to be reached ahead of time, and U.S. and Soviet leaders could easily understand what they were dealing with. Finally, if the weapons freeze did not serve to start a process of broader East–West accommodation, our security would in no way be threatened by the agreement.

---

1. See my article, "Finishing START," *Foreign Policy*, No. 48, Fall 1982. In the article, I use the terms "weapons" rather than the Soviet term "nuclear charges." However, the term "weapons" is ambiguous since a weapon technically consists of more than the nuclear device. "Warheads" is wrong since gravity bombs are not warheads, but should count. "Nuclear devices" would also be an acceptable term, but "nuclear charges" seems to me to be more descriptive. Perhaps we should be willing to acknowledge an occasional Soviet intellectual advance, even if it is only the creation of a more precise term, and adopt "nuclear charges."

* * *

Perspectives on the Freeze

Roger C. Molander

Structuring the Problem

Before analyzing the freeze as an approach to nuclear arms control, it is important to step back and ask the basic question of what we are trying to do here, anyway. What problems are we trying to solve?

In this context it is clear that *the problem is preventing nuclear war.*

Stopping the nuclear arms race, improving relations between the superpowers, and seeking peace in the Mid-East and other international hot spots all relate to the problem of preventing nuclear war. But they are only parts of the larger problem: How are we going to *prevent* nuclear war—and, most important, how are we going to prevent all-out nuclear war between the United States and the Soviet Union?

How Might Nuclear War Occur

When *the problem* is posed in the manner described above, common sense and logic then dictate the next question: What are the generic paths of events that might culminate in an all-out or "general" nuclear war? Nuclear strategists generally agree that there are six such paths, or "doomsday scenarios":

1. Bolt from the Blue;
2. Escalation in a European Conflict;
3. Escalation in a Third World Conflict;
4. Escalation after a False Alarm;
5. Escalation after Terrorist Use of Nuclear Weapons;
6. Escalation after Accidental or Unauthorized Use of Nuclear Weapons.

Each of these six routes to nuclear war can be considered as independent fuses on a nuclear bomb. Not surprisingly, experts believe that some of the fuses are more easily ignited than others. For instance, most (but not all) experts currently believe that for the foreseeable future—the next decade or so—the most likely of the six generic routes to nuclear war would be a Third World crisis in which the superpowers are gradually drawn into the conflict. On the other hand, it wasn't long ago that there was much more concern about escalation in a European conflict. At the same time, the public is often led by the rhetoric in debates over strategic weapons and strategic arms control to focus concern on the bolt-from-the-blue scenario.

Clearly it is important to try to identify which of the "fuses" is most dangerous so that we can allocate more time and energy to the greatest threat—and to this end both expert *and* public opinion on the most likely route to nuclear war is useful. Since we have no experience on how nuclear war might begin, however, we must view each of the six routes to nuclear war as a very real possibility. Furthermore, the stakes

Roger C. Molander *is Executive Director of Ground Zero, Washington, D.C.*

are so high that we cannot afford to relax our efforts until we are confident that nuclear war cannot occur through *any* of these scenarios.

What Tools Do We Have for Preventing Nuclear War?

Having identified the six generic scenarios by which nuclear war might occur, we must now ask ourselves how we are going to ensure that no one of them ever leads to nuclear war. What are the tools available to us—the policies, practices, weapons agreements, relationships, etc.—that might be employed to prevent the scenarios from starting in the first place or, once started, from escalating to higher and higher levels and eventually reaching general nuclear war?

Using our six-fused nuclear bomb analogy, the challenge we face is to prevent the fuses from being lit, or, if any of them is lit, to ensure that it cannot burn all the way to the bomb. Thus what we seek can be compared to the "firebreaks" used to halt the spread of forest fires. By knocking down a wide area of trees and bulldozing away brush from the path of the forest fire, firefighters seek to prevent the fire from racing totally out of control. In the same manner, we might view nuclear war prevention efforts as attempts to cut effective "firebreaks" along the paths of our six fuses, lest one of these fuses burn all the way down and explode the bomb. With this framework, the resources available to us—the nuclear war "firebreaks"—then fall into the following categories:

- Improved Relations between Countries
- Arms Control Agreements
    Strategic nuclear arms control
    Nuclear arms control in Europe
    Conventional arms control
- Nuclear Nonproliferation
- Improved Conflict Resolution Techniques and Mechanisms
- Improved Crisis Communications

In this context the "freeze" can then be viewed as *one* approach to the "strategic nuclear arms control" and "nuclear arms control in Europe" problems (which will henceforth be labelled the "nuclear arms control" problem).

Approaches to Nuclear Arms Control

While there is a broad spectrum of alternative approaches to "nuclear arms control," most would appear to fall in the following four generic categories:

1. SALT: a step-by-step approach which focuses on closing off individual avenues of nuclear competition starting with long-range systems.
2. START: a "big steps" approach which seeks major reductions in force levels and a restructuring of forces to achieve a more "stable" nuclear balance.
3. Freeze: an approach based on an initial comprehensive freeze on all avenues of the nuclear competition to be followed by reductions and stabilizing measures.
4. Unilateral First Steps: an approach based on a U.S. unilateral first step (e.g., 10 percent reduction in intercontinental missile or nuclear weapon levels) followed by a call for an equal Soviet step, etc.

Obviously one or two additional generic approaches to strategic nuclear arms control might also be identified, but it is neither important nor necessary for the purpose of evaluating strategy alternatives to deal at a finer level of detail (e.g., the Ford vs. Carter approach to SALT).

The "Freeze" Path to Nuclear Arms Control

As described above, the "freeze" approach to nuclear arms control can best be characterized as "freeze now, reduce and restructure later." (While generally posed in terms of a bilateral U.S.-Soviet freeze, almost any freeze proponent would argue that a freeze on French nuclear forces, British nuclear forces, etc. would be desirable and tolerable.) In this sense the freeze approach judges the current composition of U.S. and Soviet nuclear forces to be an acceptable interim state against the alternatives of (1) letting the current U.S.-Soviet nuclear competition continue, or (2) pursuing one of the other strategies.

The freeze approach is *simpler* than the other strategies in the sense of ducking the "reduction" and "restructuring" problems but *more complex* if (repeat *if*) it is applied to all avenues of the nuclear competition. The reason it becomes more complex than the others is that an across-the-board freeze raises verification problems that make most arms controls aficionados shudder. The reason they shudder is not the absence of technical schemes for verifying, for example, a freeze on the production of nuclear-armed torpedoes (inspectors with Geiger counters at all submarine ports would probably do it) but instead the challenge of getting the Soviet Union to accept such schemes.

The Freeze and the Verification Challenge

What about verification of an across-the-board freeze? Is it really necessary that every element of such an agreement be subjected to the same "adequate verification" test which, for example, all of the limits of SALT II were subjected to? It is in answering this question that the freeze approach to nuclear arms control is most controversial within the national security community:

- Some believe that the *individual limitation* of any arms control treaty must meet "adequate verification" criteria comparable to those to which the limitations of the SALT II Treaty were subjected (i.e., no significant military impact if undetected cheating occurs). By such standards, the table on the following pages describes (very roughly) the level of intrusiveness which would probably be required for the limitations of an across-the-board freeze to be judged "adequately verifiable."

- Others believe that the "adequate verification" criteria (no significant military impact if undetected cheating occurs) need only be applied to the *agreement as a whole* rather than the individual limitations.

A representative example of this difference of views can be seen by confronting the freeze on nuclear warhead production. Without highly intrusive verification measures (which probably include shutting down all Soviet plutonium production reactors or "riding the rails" with all Soviet plutonium) there would be almost unbounded uncertainty in Soviet nuclear warhead production. Is that acceptable in light of the other advantages of the freeze? The first group says, "No, you have to shut down the plants or ride the rails." The second group says, "Yes, the military impact of Soviet cheating is negligible."

The ultimate arbiter on this question is, of course, the general public. Polling on this question has been very crude, but would seem to indicate that the public tilts toward the first of the above camps. The summer to November 2 drop in support for the freeze in California against a Reagan Administration raising of the verification (and other) issues would also seem to indicate that the public would opt for the first view.

If one of the criteria for a freeze is to be that each individual avenue of the competition to be frozen must be an "adequate verification" possibility, then the question becomes one of "politicial will":

> How might the Soviet leadership be persuaded to accept more intrusive verification techniques and measures beyond national technical means?

Alternatively the question might be posed in terms of a freeze with stages to it:

> What avenues of competition can be frozen with verification by national technical means? With the addition of "black boxes" (unmanned monitoring devices recording and transmitting information to U.S. satellites) at Soviet test and/or deployment and/or production sites? With U.S. personnel at test and/or deployment and/or production sites?

A First Stage Freeze

If one were to accept the verification challenge as a long-term problem to be worked with the Soviets yet still wanted to maintain the "freeze now, reduce and restructure later" approach to nuclear arms control, the basic question is what should one propose for a stage one freeze. In light of the relative maturity of the SALT/START/INF process in which "national technical means plus a little" is presumed to be the means of verification, one possible stage one freeze would be:

- Freeze on *testing* and *deployment* of all systems covered in SALT I or SALT II, currently under negotiation in the INF and START talks (ABMs, ICBMs, SLBMs, IRBMs, MRBMs, heavy and medium bombers, ground-launched cruise missiles, etc.)

If one wanted to push the Soviets on more intrusive verification procedures, one could expand the above (a good idea for lots of reasons) proposal to include *production*. We certainly need to find out as soon as possible whether we should plan our arms control strategy (and thus our "prevent nuclear war strategy") with the idea that production limits which require on-site inspection for verification are in the cards.

Bottom Line

We need to devise a strategy to obtain more and better information from the American public on these and related issues since for the foreseeable future they will be passing judgment on such issues. Witness the experience of SALT II, MX in Nevada/Utah, civil defense, dense pack, and the comprehensive freeze.

VERIFICATION OF A FREEZE

KEY TO SYMBOLS

SALT: SALT I and II verification techniques (e.g., photo-reconnaissance satellites, unencrypted telemetry, etc.).

OSI-1: Mildly intrusive on-site inspection (e.g., U.S. black boxes on Soviet territory, challenge inspection by third party or U.S. personnel in the event of ambiguous events, etc.).

OSI-2: Very intrusive on-site inspection (e.g., third party or U.S. personnel outside Soviet factories and at Soviet test sites, random inspection at weapon deployment sites, etc.).

OSI-3: Extraordinary on-site inspection (e.g., third party or U.S. personnel inside certain Soviet factories and at certain Soviet military sites at all times, close inspection of satellites, etc.).

	Production	Testing	Deployment
Nuclear Warheads	OSI-3	OSI-1	OSI-2
Ballistic Missiles—Land*			
1. ICBMs (> 5500 km)	OSI-2	SALT	SALT
2. IRBMs (3000-5500 km)	OSI-2	SALT	SALT
3. MRBMs (1000-3000 km)	OSI-2	SALT	SALT
4. SRBMs (0-1000 km)	OSI-2	SALT	SALT
Ballistic Missiles—Submarines			
5. Long range (> 600 km)	OSI-2	SALT	SALT
6. Short range (< 600 km)	OSI-2	OSI-2	OSI-2
Ballistic Missiles—Surface Ships			
7. Long range (> 600 km)	OSI-2	SALT	SALT
8. Short range (< 600 km)	OSI-2	OSI-2	OSI-2
Ballistic Missiles—Aircraft			
9. Long range (> 600 km)	OSI-2	SALT	SALT
10. Short range (< 600 km)	OSI-2	OSI-2	OSI-2
Ballistic Missiles—Misc. (Seabeds, etc.)			
11. Long range (> 600 km)	OSI-2	SALT	SALT
12. Short range (< 600 km)	OSI-2	OSI-2	OSI-2
Cruise Missiles—Land			
13. Long range (> 600 km)	OSI-2	SALT	SALT
14. Short range (> 600 km)	OSI-3	OSI-2	OSI-2
Cruise Missiles—Submarines			
15. Long range (> 600 km)	OSI-2	SALT	SALT
16. Short range (< 600 km)	OSI-3	OSI-2	OSI-2
Cruise Missiles—Surface Ships			
17. Long range (> 600 km)	OSI-2	SALT	SALT
18. Short range (< 600 km)	OSI-3	OSI-2	OSI-2
Cruise Missiles—Bombers			
19. Long range (> 600 km)	OSI-2	SALT	SALT
20. Short range (< 600 km)	OSI-3	OSI-2	OSI-2
Cruise Missiles—Non-Bombers			
21. Long range	OSI-2	SALT	SALT
22. Short range	OSI-3	OSI-2	OSI-2

Cruise Missiles — Misc. (Seabeds, etc.)

23. Long range	OSI-2	SALT	SALT
24. Short range	OSI-3	OSI-2	OSI-2

Bombers

25. Long range (B-52, Bear, etc.)	SALT	SALT	SALT
26. Medium range (FB-111, Backfire, etc.)	SALT	SALT	SALT

Other Aircraft

27. Fighter Bombers	SALT	SALT	SALT
28. Anti-Submarine Warfare Aircraft	SALT	SALT	SALT

Submarines

29. Current types	SALT	SALT	SALT
30. New types	SALT	SALT	SALT

*Assessment applies generally to both missiles and fixed or mobile land-based launchers.

* * *

Arms Control Vs. The Freeze

Christopher M. Lehman

Over the past year, the nuclear freeze movement has brought to the forefront of public discussion a deceptively attractive, simple solution to the arms race—freeze it! Calling for an absolute prohibition on the production, testing, and deployment of nuclear weapons and their delivery systems, advocates argue that a freeze can truly bring about a halt in the arms race and reduce the dangers of nuclear war.

The nuclear freeze has been as popular as it is simple. But is it really a plausible path to meaningful arms control, or is it a distraction that makes genuine arms control far more difficult to achieve?

There has been much debate on this question, and surely there is more to come. However, a serious review of the issue forces the conclusion that the nuclear freeze proposal has serious drawbacks as to make it unsuitable as the basis for meaningful arms control.

The Freeze as Sentiment

The rapid growth of the nuclear freeze movement is a phenomenon which cannot be fully explained. However, it is clear that a number of factors were instrumental in boosting the visibility and the political clout of the freeze movement, and they all have a common element—fear. The fear of nuclear war has once again spawned a

---

Christopher M. Lehman is Director of the Office of Strategic Nuclear Policy, Department of State, Washington, D.C.

movement of concerned men, women, and children who demand that we avoid Armageddon.

The roots of the freeze movement go as far back as we care to look, but its more recent impetus has come from the increased attention to defense issues and the undeniable growth in the Soviet threat. The 1980 election in large part turned on the question of defense, and the Reagan Administration has made the rebuilding of U.S. defenses a central element of its program.

The continuing public focus on threats to U.S. security and the huge defense expenditures necessary to meet those threats have helped to create a backlash or an aversion to matters related to defense. This aversion has been particularly strong with respect to our nuclear arsenal where a major modernization of our nuclear forces has served to rekindle strong anti-nuclear sentiment. Anxieties were boosted even further by several statements by Reagan Administration officials concerning nuclear weapons and nuclear war, and since then some politicians have sought to exploit anti-nuclear sentiment for ballot-box gains, and authors and publishers have cashed in as well.

The fear and anxiety that is so much a part of the nuclear freeze movement is, of course, understandable. There have been dangerous developments in the nuclear balance in recent years, and a nuclear war would most certainly be unimaginably horrible. But it takes more than fear to prevent nuclear war. It takes a dual strategy of deterrence and arms control.

The very foundation of peace in the nuclear age has been America's strategy of deterrence. Since the earliest days of our possession of nuclear weapons, the United States has sought to prevent war by discouraging aggression against the United States and its allies. By threatening any aggressor with the certainty of unacceptable levels of destruction, an uneasy peace has been maintained. The history of the twentieth century makes it sadly clear that peaceful intentions and good motives alone never stop aggressors. Military strength does, and the strategy of deterrence has been highly successful in protecting America's security since the end of World War II.

But America has pursued a dual policy since the end of World War II. In addition to maintaining strong military forces for deterrence, we have also vigorously pursued arms control as a complement to our policy of deterrence.

Thus while anxiety over the threat of nuclear war is well warranted, we cannot let fear dictate our response. The proven course of deterrence and arms control is the best means of preventing nuclear war and preserving the peace. A nuclear freeze would be harmful to deterrence and to meaningful arms control and thus a freeze should be rejected.

The Flaws of the Freeze

The arguments against the nuclear freeze proposal are many and would apply to most, if not all, of the various freeze formulae that have been proposed. The most popular freeze proposal, and the one which has earned *the* nuclear freeze label, is the Congressional Resolution introduced by Senators Kennedy and Hatfield and its companion measure introduced in the House of Representatives. This resolution calls for an immediate mutual and verifiable freeze on production, testing, and deployment of nuclear weapons and their delivery systems. This proposal is surely well intentioned, but it will not help accomplish effective arms control. In fact, if a freeze were to be implemented, it would endanger American security and the security of our allies.

The first, and probably the strongest, argument against the nuclear freeze proposal is that a freeze would preserve the current high level of nuclear forces, and would thus preserve an unequal and unstable strategic balance.

The experts have hotly debated the exact status of the strategic balance for years, but there is no debate that the balance has shifted dramatically in recent years in favor of the Soviet Union. There is debate over whether parity still exists, but there is little opposition to the view that present trends cannot continue without directly harming the security interests of the United States.

As a result of a massive 15-year military buildup, the Soviet Union has now surged ahead of the United States in every static measure of strategic power except one—total strategic warheads. In missile throwweight, missile warheads, ICBMs, SLBMs, and even strategic bombers, the Soviet Union has gained the advantage; and qualitatively the Soviet Union has caught up as well.

TOTAL STRATEGIC MISSILES AND BOMBERS

A. NUMBER OF STRATEGIC DELIVERY VEHICLES

B. TOTAL STRATEGIC DELIVERY VEHICLES BY COMPOSITION

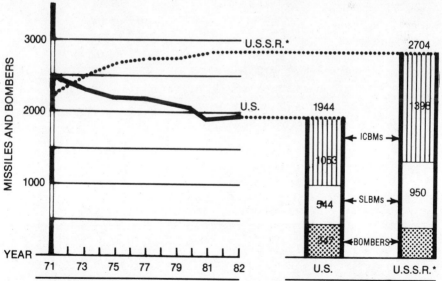

(a) USSR figures include Soviet strategic missiles and BEAR, BISON, and BACKFIRE bombers; the BACKFIRE bomber has been included in this figure because it has an inherent intercontinental capability.

Source: U.S. Department of State

STRATEGIC NUCLEAR BALANCE

U.S.	(Mid-year 1982)		USSR
53	Titan II	580	SS-11
450	Minuteman II	60	SS-13
550	Minuteman III	150	SS-17
1053		308	SS-18
		300	SS-19
		1398	

SLBMs

320	Poseidon		SS-N-6
224	Trident I		SS-N-8
544			SS-N-18
		950	

Bombers

79	B-52D		Bear
172	B-52G		Bison
96	B-52H		Backfire
347		356	

Approximate Totals

	U.S.	USSR
Delivery Vehicles	1944	2704
— missiles	1597	2348
— bombers	347	400
Warheads (missile only)	7200	7500
Missile Throw-Weight	2000 tons	5000 tons

Source: U.S. Department of State

In addition to numerical advantages, the average age of Soviet strategic weapons and their delivery systems has come down considerably while the average age of U.S. systems has gone up. According to U.S. Department of Defense figures, 77 percent of Soviet systems are less than five years old, while 77 percent of U.S. systems are in excess of 15 years of age.

Thus, if a freeze were implemented, the United States would be frozen with aging systems with no opportunity to modernize those forces to ensure a strong and credible deterrent.

Our current strategic weapon systems will also become increasingly vulnerable over time, and a vulnerable deterrent is an invitation to catastrophe. The vulnerability of our land-based missile force is already a matter of major concern. While the freeze would lock us into these and other current systems, the freeze would not prevent advances in conventional air defenses or anti-submarine warfare that could threaten the remaining two elements of our strategic triad. But a freeze would prevent the production of the Stealth bomber and other advances that could counter steadily improving Soviet air defenses. Similarly, the freeze would prevent the production of new Trident submarines and other efforts to stay ahead of advances in anti-submarine warfare.

In short, a nuclear freeze would weaken deterrence over time and thus make nuclear war more rather than less likely.

The present nuclear balance in Europe is also one which should not be frozen in its present state. A freeze now would give the Soviet Union an overwhelming nuclear advantage in intermediate-range nuclear weapons in Europe to the detriment of our own and our allies' security.

A second important argument that flows from the first is that by freezing at today's high and unequal levels a nuclear freeze would undercut our START and INF negotiations and make the prospects for actual arms reductions less likely.

The United States is currently engaged in two separate negotiations with the Soviet Union seeking nuclear arms reductions. In those negotiations, the United States has put forward dramatic reductions proposals: in START, the U.S. is calling for one-third reductions in ballistic missile warheads, and a cut in the number of deployed missiles to about one-half the current U.S. levels. In the INF negotiations, the U.S. has proposed the elimination of a whole category of intermediate-range ballistic missiles. The Soviet Union has responded with counterproposals that also envisage arms reduction. While the Soviet proposals have not been acceptable to the United States, it is important to note that the principle of reductions has been accepted. This is quite significant, especially in view of the fact that the recent SALT II negotiations produced a draft treaty which would have allowed both sides to almost double their nuclear warhead inventory within the terms of the agreement.

Thus, in a very real sense we have already moved far beyond a freeze, and we should not waste the months and years it would take to negotiate the terms of a verifiable nuclear freeze if, in fact, that were possible. Supporters of a freeze may believe that a freeze agreement could be easily arrived at, but experience has shown that any meaningful agreement would require agreed definitions, counting rules, and other details which would unavoidably complicate the implementation of the conceptually simple nuclear freeze proposal.

Aside from the complexities of implementing a freeze, U.S. agreement to a freeze would destroy Soviet incentives for accepting an arms reduction agreement. A freeze at today's force levels would preserve the Soviet Union in a position of relative advantage. The Soviets thus would have every incentive to prolong a freeze and avoid coming to an agreement on arms reductions to lower but equal levels.

Unless the United States and its allies demonstrate their will to take the actions necessary to restore the nuclear balance, the Soviets will have little incentive to agree to reductions in their own forces. Indeed, the Soviet Union initially refused our offers to negotiate on INF systems while they deployed several hundred SS-20 missile systems. They agreed to come to the negotiating table only when it became clear that we and our NATO allies were determined to take steps to counter those SS-20 deployments unless an arms control agreement were reached. A unilateral U.S. withdrawal from the allied "dual track" decision of 1979, which has consistently been endorsed by all NATO governments, would also cause serious doubt on American leadership of NATO and our readiness to fulfill our commitments to the defense of Europe.

Similarly, the freeze would leave the U.S. with a vulnerable land-based missile system, an aging and less credible bomber force, and a submarine fleet which faces block obsolescence in the 1990s. The Soviet Union, on the other hand, would have an arsenal of newer, heavier ICBMs, newer ballistic missile-firing submarines, and over 250 modern Backfire bombers built during the 1970s. Under these circumstances, there would be little reason for the Soviet Union to agree to reductions.

A third important argument against the nuclear freeze is that it is just not verifiable in many important respects. Simply prefacing a freeze proposal with an incantation that it must be mutual and verifiable just doesn't make it so.

As proposed, a freeze would cover production, testing, and deployment of strategic nuclear weapons. However, of those three categories, only deployment is verifiable with high confidence, and there are exceptions to that. Verifying a ban on nuclear testing would be extremely difficult, and the possibility of surreptitious testing at lower-yield levels would be significant. With respect to production of nuclear weapons, however, the task of verifying a freeze becomes unmanageable. Even with on-site inspection, the possibility of detecting the production of nuclear weapons would be low.

Thus inadequate verification alone is sufficient argument against the nuclear freeze as proposed.

The Freeze Ignores Deterrence

There are other arguments against the nuclear freeze, but they are mostly subsidiary to those mentioned here. However, there is one additional criticism of the freeze that needs to be made. The freeze proposal ignores deterrence. It assumes that deterrence is stable and easily maintained no matter what the strategic nuclear balance sheet looks like. It assumes that the vulnerability and looming obsolescence of U.S.

strategic systems will not affect the viability of deterrence. In short, it assumes that the concept of minimum deterrence is valid—that so long as the United States retains the capacity to destroy a few Soviet cities then deterrence will prevail.

This simple view of deterrence has been rejected by every administration since Eisenhower as being inadequate and incredible and therefore dangerous. Deterrence requires capable and survivable nuclear forces on both sides so that neither side can expect advantage under any circumstances by initiating the use of nuclear weapons. Allowing gross imbalances in the level or capabilities of nuclear forces would be destabilizing. Allowing our nuclear forces to be vulnerable to a pre-emptive disarming first strike would only invite attack and greatly increase the probability of war.

These are things we must not allow to happen, yet these are the very things which a nuclear freeze would mandate.

The Freeze Is Bad Arms Control

The arguments against the nuclear freeze are powerful and persuasive. It is a superficially attractive concept, but one which has hidden within it serious flaws that make it unsuitable as the basis for serious arms control. A substantial number of respected arms control experts have supported this view, and even some who support the freeze concept do so as a means of building political pressure in support of arms control while recognizing the internal flaws of the actual nuclear freeze proposal. Respected journals such as the *New York Times*, the *Washington Post*, and the *Wall Street Journal* have all editorialized against the freeze.

Those who support the concept of a nuclear freeze need to stop thinking with their heart and start thinking with their head. We all share the common goal of avoiding the catastrophe of nuclear war. We all share the desire for peace. But we all have a responsibility to work toward practical solutions to man's most serious problem.

The practical solution, in my view, is the proven course of deterrence and arms control. That has been the course adopted by every administration in the postwar era, and it is the course which the Reagan Administration is vigorously pursuing.

We are now engaged in two nuclear arms control negotiations with the Soviet Union—START and INF. The United States has put forward serious arms reduction proposals at the negotiations, and the Soviets have made serious counter-proposals.

It is time for all those who truly desire arms control to support the arms control efforts which the United States is now pursuing. These negotiations seek deep reductions in the levels of nuclear weapons. A freeze at today's high levels of nuclear weapons would be a step backward.

* * *

Assessing Freezes: Coverage, Verification, Timing

Verification of a Nuclear Freeze

William E. Colby

Verification of a nuclear freeze must be first understood as a continuation of normal national intelligence processes. Whether a treaty exists between the U.S.S.R. and the United States restricting nuclear weaponry or not, each nation will develop devices to ensure that it is informed of the weaponry and forces of the other power. While this is obviously a simpler process for the Soviet Union than for the United States, the fact is that we have been able over the past thirty years' development of our modern intelligence system to penetrate the screen of secrecy the Soviets raise around these weapons and forces. The data publicly released by our government plainly shows that the combination of the technique of central intelligence, gathering all facts to a single center for examination and analysis, along with the improvement of our technological capabilities, has opened up subjects which years ago we would have had little hope of learning about.

Thus, the question of verifiability must be seen as applying to our decision-making processes rather than to highly technical measurements of whether particular characteristics of hardware can be positively identified from the sky. We have workable and generally accurate estimates of a wide variety of Soviet weaponry which could not be verified down to the last item. A regular account is kept of Soviet tanks, Soviet aircraft, Soviet artillery, and the forces that man them. Thanks to our capabilities, we discuss in public changes in these weapons a substantial time before we face them, noting in many cases their research prototypes, their testing and development and their production centers, aside from their deployment with units.

In the days before our present capabilities, the world was indeed surprised by the appearance of Sputnik, the earlier than expected detonation of the first Soviet nuclear weaponry, and the secretive smuggling of Soviet nuclear weapons to Cuba. Since that last strategem was penetrated, albeit in its final stages, we have had no surprises of this nature. Our intelligence may well have made errors in some of the more intangible questions it has been faced with, such as Iran. Some of its estimates of the pace of *future* progress of the Soviets have been shown to have been in error by faster than expected movement by the Soviets, such as in improving the accuracy of their missile systems. But our coverage of existing nuclear weaponry has certainly kept

William E. Colby *is an attorney with the law firm Reid and Priest in Washington, D.C.*

even with Soviet progress in these areas and given us ample time to negotiate or to react as we might need to their deployment.

This, then, raises the second major point about verification, that its purpose is not to conduct a legalistic debate over possible breach of contract by the Soviet Union. Its purpose is to maintain the security of the United States. Even if our high degree of confidence of coverage of Soviet weaponry were to be flawed in part, the question is whether a marginal violation which we did not discover would have any importance and whether a violation with strategic potential would inevitably be telegraphed in advance. This brings the obvious corollary that a careful evaluation should be made whether substantial restraint under a treaty in the development of Soviet weaponry would contribute more to our security, even with the chance of marginal violation, than a continuation of unconstrained competition, which we can only watch and match with improved forces on our side.

In this context, the key element of any agreement to restrict nuclear weaponry must be provisions for continuing consultation between the powers with respect to suspected or charged violations. This is the function of the Standing Consultative Committee of the SALT treaties and should certainly be an element of any freeze, limitation, or reduction of nuclear forces. The contribution of this provision to our security can be easily realized by contemplating the likely Soviet reaction to our discovery in some part of the Soviet Union of a new nuclear weapon in the absence of a treaty. We could of course reveal the development, denounce it, and request the Soviets to comment on the matter. The warm and friendly Soviet reaction to such an inquiry would be flat rejection as none of our business. With a treaty, however, and the existence of a Standing Consultative Committee, a procedure exists for the resolution of ambiguities and the settlement of charges or allegations of violation. The SALT I experience indicates that this function provides a degree of communication, modification of behavior, or satisfaction that the suspect violation is not actually one, in effect amplifying the evidence of our intelligence collection facilities.

Beyond this general consideration, of course, there are a number of elements which would be made a part of any treaty with the Soviet Union to facilitate the verification process. Mere hortatory treaties with no machinery for enforcement are worth exactly the value of the paper on which they are written, as there is no way to secure compliance other than repudiating the entire treaty and resuming the arms race. In treaties which have been negotiated with the Soviets, however, a number of cooperative measures and restrictions on secrecy have been accepted by the Soviets when they have been made a condition of our approval and the Soviets themselves wished to complete the treaty. Thus agreements against concealment, declarations of forces, counting rules, test notification requirements, seismic or electronic sensors, and even the inspection team rejected by Stalin in 1946, have all been included in negotiated arrangements, gradually opening the Soviet Union to greater international visibility. The Soviets have not and will not become an open society, but these specific provisions are also subject to the consultation procedures, allowing us to insist on compliance with the behavior required. One additional procedure might be incorporated in future treaties of this nature: a graduated succession of sanctions or procedures for the resolution of differences even after consultation, e.g., through a third party decision, through specified arrangements for retaliatory reaction proportionate to the violation identified, or otherwise.

It is by this approach that I come to the conclusion that a nuclear freeze treaty could be negotiated which would be both mutual and verifiable. The combination of our exceptional intelligence capabilities, cooperative measures or restraints on Soviet behavior, and the consultation process would be adequate to give us ample warning of any substantial program to violate a freeze on the production, development, or deployment of additional nuclear weapons. And Soviet leadership contemplating such high risk treachery would have to weigh the likelihood that some of its own citizen-participants would be sufficiently revolted to ensure that word of it reached the West, resulting in concentration of our intelligence facilities and consultation procedures on the tip given, magnifying the chance that the secrecy screen would be penetrated. Appropriate authorities can certainly debate the details of the verification procedure and capabilities with respect to the production of isolated plants, secret deployment to units, and so forth.

But any major program which would actually have strategic value to the Soviets would be detected well in advance of its reaching operational status.

* * *

First Steps Toward a Freeze

Herbert Scoville, Jr.

The initial step in implementing the freeze concept for controlling the nuclear arms race will be to establish priorities for which nuclear weapons programs should be halted first. Arrangements for stopping in a single agreement all nuclear weapons programs, including delivery vehicles, would be very complicated and almost certainly take so long to negotiate that the arms race would have gotten still further out of control before such a total freeze could, if ever, be put into effect. However, it should be possible to select certain programs for priority effort giving due attention to how easily they can be defined, how well they can be verified, and how critical it is to stop them quickly.

In general the freeze on those programs selected should include testing, production, and deployment even though all of these phases may not be of equal importance or verifiability. Stopping a program entirely, not just a part, decreases the risk of one country gaining an advantage by abrogation of an agreement. Furthermore even though a freeze on one phase of a program may have a relatively low probability of

Herbert Scoville *is President of the Arms Control Association, Washington, D.C.*

being verified, its inclusion in a ban may improve the verifiability of a freeze on the program as a whole.

Highest priority should be given to a freeze of destabilizing strategic weapons systems that threaten a first strike at a major component of the other country's deterrent or its political and military command and control structure. These provide motivations for it to launch a preemptive strike or to adopt a launch-on-warning posture; both make a nuclear conflict more likely. Any weapons systems that produce incentives for the initiative of a nuclear conflict either in a first strike or preemptively deserve first attention in any freeze.

In this category will be the long-range MIRVed ICBMs with larger numbers of warheads per missile, with improved accuracy, and with higher yield. On the Soviet side this would include a halt to further MIRVing of Soviet ICBMs, modernization of their SS-18s and 19s to give them an improved hard target, countersilo capability, and the development of the recently reported new Soviet ICBMs (SS-Xs). On the United States side this would include modification of the additional Minuteman IIIs to provide these missiles with improved guidance systems and higher yield warheads and most importantly stopping the MX program.

Included among such destabilizing weapons should be the most provocative European-based strategic systems. The most dangerous of these are the Pershing II missiles which threaten a surprise attack on the Soviet political and military command and control system and thus create a strong incentive for a Soviet preemptive strike in the event of a crisis in Eastern Europe. While their SS-20s are not quite as provocative, they nevertheless threaten the European-based portion of the Western command structure and nuclear storage sites and should also be included for the sake of balance. In fact efforts should be made to get, as a follow-up to the Andropov offer of December 1982, a reduction of the number of warheads on the SS-20s to at least equivalent levels of British and French strategic warheads as a part of the intermediate range nuclear force INF negotiations.

Verification capabilities for a freeze, and indeed for any arms control measure, should be consistent with the significance of a potential violation. The probability of its detection should be dependent on its security risk, recognizing that there is also a risk from a failure to control at all a given nuclear weapons program. The verification of the testing and deployment phases of the above destabilizing weapons programs has been satisfactorily worked out in connection with SALT II, and this should be even easier for a freeze where the programs would be totally halted. National technical means will quite adequately verify a ban on testing new types of missiles, such as the SS-X and MX; the further MIRVing of existing missiles was also dealt with in this treaty by considering any missile of a type tested with MIRVs as a MIRVed missile. There will be greater difficulty in monitoring the halt to the modification of the existing SS-18s and -19s or Minuteman III where testing of improved guidance systems is already quite complete. But the administration has been reporting regularly on the status of such modernization programs so that any significant change in the status of these programs if the testing, production, and deployment were all halted completely should be verifiable with an acceptable risk to our security. In this connection it is important to recognize that on-site inspections were not needed to monitor SALT and in fact are useful only on rare occasions. In SALT II procedures were worked out to verify limits on MIRVs that were much more satisfactory than the on-site inspections sought unsuccessfully in SALT I.

By agreeing to a complete halt in the further production of the major components of these missile systems, the overall verification capabilities should be enhanced even though the production itself might be the most difficult phase to monitor reliably. One means of improving the verifiability of a production stoppage would be for each side to declare the locations where the major components of each frozen weapons system are produced. This would greatly simplify the ability to verify with national technical means that indeed no further missiles were continuing to be made. The Soviets would make false declarations at great risk of being caught since they do not know exactly how effective our intelligence is. Continued operation of a declared plant in violation of a freeze should be relatively easy to detect, and the conversion of a new plant to produce banned missiles would run a high risk of detection.

A combination of all of these intelligence capabilities and arrangements should make possible quite acceptable verification that the Soviets were not violating a freeze on such programs to the extent that our security would be significantly affected. In this connection it should be recalled that the Soviets already have very large numbers of SS-18s and -19s with relatively good countersilo capabilities so that a significant addition to this stockpile would require a program of sufficient magnitude that it would run a good chance of being detected.

Similar considerations would apply to the European strategic weapons systems. Even though the SS-20 is mobile, the Administration has been able to monitor quite accurately the continuing deployment of these weapons. Any new type of missile in this category would be easily detectable in the testing phase. It might be difficult to verify exactly how many SS-20s would continue to be deployed facing China, but a freeze should ban the movement of the European missiles to the east of the Urals and should halt all production of new missiles since they now have more than enough to deal with potential Chinese targets. The European missiles could be destroyed while under observation by U.S. satellites with arrangement similar to those satisfactorily worked out by the Standing Consultative Commission under SALT I.

A second category of weapons that would require priority action in a freeze are those where verifiability is a vanishing asset. The prime examples in this group are sea- and ground-launched cruise missiles. At the present time neither the United States nor the Soviet Union has any such missiles deployed so that a freeze now would be relatively easy to verify. A program to test, produce, and deploy a significant cruise missile force would have a high probability of being discovered since it would only be necessary to find a single such missile or observe a single such test. However, once such weapons are fully developed and tested and deployed in appreciable numbers, then a freeze would be much more difficult to monitor.

While cruise missiles do have the accuracy and yield to threaten very hard targets such as missile silos and command shelters, current designs are not seriously destabilizing threats to the deterrent since the missiles travel at subsonic speeds. The several hours required for them to reach their targets is too long for a truly threatening first strike system. However, they are small, require limited logistic support, and thus are hard to verify, so they should be controlled quickly because they open up a whole new channel for the arms race. This could negate the gains made in controlling ballistic missile systems.

While the U.S. is now ahead of the U.S.S.R. in cruise missile development, Secretary Weinberger recently warned that the Soviets had extensive programs for ground-, sea-, and air-launched cruise missiles. Thus the U.S. could come to regret its failure to control such weapons much as it now regrets its failure to control MIRVs in 1970.

Air-launched cruise missiles do not require the same priority since arrangements were worked out in SALT II for their verification by limiting the aircraft demonstrably modified for delivering them. Their ability to overwhelm anti-aircraft defenses could improve the reliability of the aircraft leg of the strategic deterrent and thus they could even be a stabilizing factor. It must be recognized, however, that unlimited production and procurement of air-launched cruise missiles could provide an avenue for the development of ground- and sea-launched versions which would make the verification of these more difficult.

Those elements of a freeze that can make the control of the spread of nuclear weapons to other nations or groups easier also deserve high priority. Unless the two large nuclear powers, the United States and U.S.S.R., exercise some restraint on their nuclear programs, the climate will never be conducive for getting potential third countries to give up the option to have nuclear weapons for themselves. The most important measure which could create an appropriate climate for limiting further proliferation would be a Comprehensive Test Ban Treaty ending all nuclear tests. This is looked on worldwide as a key demonstration by the nuclear powers of their sincerity in trying to end the nuclear arms race. As long as the U.S. and the U.S.S.R. are unwilling to stop testing, even though they have carried out more than 1000 nuclear tests, then the other countries can with justice claim they must keep open their option to test as well. It is also a useful element in the bilateral freeze between the United States and the Soviet Union since it would stop once and for all any further refinements in nuclear explosives.

During the Carter Administration, trilateral negotiations among the U.S., U.K., and the U.S.S.R. had achieved wide agreement on the basic elements of a verifiable Comprehensive Test Ban Treaty. The only thing that was lacking to achieve a final treaty was the political will to end all nuclear testing. Unfortunately since then the Reagan Administration has backed off from negotiations on a Comprehensive Test Ban Treaty, and this has sent a bad, negative signal around the world. It is important to reverse directions again and recommence serious negotiations leading to a formal treaty in the very near future. Verification arrangements, which include challenge inspections and unmanned seismic stations in the Soviet Union, were agreed to in the previous negotiations, and these are quite satisfactory for tests down to about a kiloton or even less. Any risks from cheating below this level are minor and are certainly less than the risks of continued testing and unrestricted proliferation of nuclear weapons.

Finally, priority attention should be given to a halt to the production of fissionable materials for weapons purposes. This will then freeze the amount of material available for new warheads and thus stabilize weapons stockpiles where they are now. By itself it will not stop the conversion of existing types of weapons to new models, but it is an important first step in this direction.

The verification of a cutoff of fissionable material production for weapons by the U.S. and the Soviet Union is comparatively easy. First it must be remembered that both sides already have large stockpiles of both plutonium and uranium 235 so that a secret production capacity must be large to be of any security significance. A plant which can produce significant quantities of plutonium or enriched uranium 235 would of necessity be large and could not possibly escape detection by our national intelligence. Existing weapons production plants in the Soviet Union are well known, and it would be obvious were they continued in operation. Building new plants would also be easily spotted.

Diversion of plutonium produced in nuclear power plants could not provide a significant addition to existing stockpiles for many years. IAEA safeguards could very easily detect the diversion of enough material to be important to the U.S.S.R. or the U.S. even though it might be difficult for them to detect diversion of enough material for a single weapon by a non-nuclear nation. The United States has already agreed to accept such safeguards on its peaceful programs, and if the Soviet Union could be persuaded to accept similar safeguards, it would also be a useful precedent for establishing the proper climate for halting proliferation. Gromyko has already expressed publicly a willingness to move in this direction. Since some continued production of weapons-grade, enriched uranium 235 might be required for nuclear powered submarines or other ships, arrangements would have to be made to allow the production of approximately that needed for such propulsion reactors. Some uncertainty on this amount would not be serious since it must be remembered that both the U.S. and U.S.S.R. already have more than 100,000 kg of weapons-grade U-235.

The timing of any freeze is very critical. Delay could easily negate its value in reducing the dangers from the continued arms race. A freeze on counter-deterrent weapons five to ten years from now might not be very effective in making the outbreak of a nuclear conflict less likely. Furthermore, once weapons are tested, available, and deployed, it is always much more difficult to get rid of them than it is to prevent their procurement in the first place. As mentioned earlier verification will become harder rather than easier as time passes.

Therefore speed in working out arrangements for a mutual freeze is essential. Since it is often a slow process to negotiate a formal treaty with all provisions carefully spelled out and then to get it ratified, it may be desirable to start the freeze process through a series of reciprocal national steps. This procedure, which would maintain the bilateral nature of the freeze, has proven effective in the past. Once programs are stopped, it may then be easier to translate these actions into longer lasting treaty restrictions. Simplicity, even at the expense of some loss of perfection, may produce greater effectiveness. It must never be forgotten that the objective of the freeze exercise is to reduce the risk of a nuclear catastrophe, not to obtain some classic arms control treaty.

* * *

Verification and Negotiation

Walter Slocombe

I come to this panel as a person whose current real life role is being a tax lawyer. Arms control, like tax law, has the characteristic that the technical world and the political world tend to meet and overlap in complicated ways—and ways that make the results complicated—and that there is a great deal of interest in evasion and monitoring compliance.

The general topic assigned this panel—issues of scope, timing, and verification of alternative freeze proposals—embraces, in many respects, the full range of arms control, and indeed, of security, issues. So I will confine myself to a few summary comments on the overall topic and then focus on a particular issue—the impact of verification requirements on negotiation and timing.

General Observations

Verification is a special case of general strategic intelligence. From the point of view of what can, in principle, be verified, I agree broadly with what's already been said by Mr. Colby and Mr. Scoville. From the monitoring point of view, verification is identical to intelligence—the same questions, the same ways of answering them, and the same uncertainties—and the same risks associated with those uncertainties. Our intelligence system is vastly better in meeting the monitoring requirements for verification than much of the public debate gives it credit for. The reason for this is simple: Our capacity to monitor for arms control verification is as good as it is because the information we need for arms control verification is the same information we need for general strategic intelligence purposes. As Mr. Colby says, we don't lose interest in some part of the Russian strategic nuclear program simply because we don't have an agreement about it. We may be even more interested in the parts of their force that they won't agree to limit. In theory, there could be a difference in the risks associated with monitoring uncertainties in the arms control case if it were the fact that when the Soviets have agreed not to do something, we were less inclined to credit evidence that they have done it. In practice, however, the record so far is that we are as a country far quicker to get excited over dubious claims of Soviet cheating

Walter Slocombe *is an attorney with the law firm Caplin and Drysdale in Washington, D.C.*

on agreements than over clear evidence of dangerous, if perfectly legal, overt Soviet military developments.

Cheating is not pointless, but to gain advantage. Second, it is important to be clear why, ultimately, it is necessary to verify treaty compliance. Fundamentally, we want to be sure the Soviets don't use a treaty as a cover to gain some secret military or political advantage. We do, to be sure, care about the principle that agreements with the U.S. must be adhered to, so any cheating is unacceptable, and we are rightly concerned at the political and diplomatic significance of a Soviet violation of a solemn obligation. But even those concerns are, fundamentally, related to our interest in prevention of a Soviet advantage: We should not tolerate non-adherence in small things lest we lose our credibility in insisting on adherence in large. But in terms of the *danger* of cheating, the standard for verification is not perfect information, but high confidence that any Soviet violation would be detected in time for us to react before any militarily significant advantage could be gained. (And I include in militarily significant advantages those which carry a substantial political weight.)

In this connection, it is a critical—but less discussed—aspect of the interrelation of verification of arms control and general intelligence that, if there is some great advantage to be gained from the concealment of Soviet strategic programs, they don't need a treaty to violate in order to gain that advantage. If there is some major way in which they can steal a march on us by concealing a program (as they tried to in 1962 in Cuba) they have every incentive to do that even without a treaty forbidding them to do it, and we have every incentive to find out about it.

Beware of advantages obtainable without cheating. Third, it is usually the case—and this is certainly true of the freeze—that the hard questions about a postulated arms control agreement have to do more with what happens if the Soviets seek vigorously to obtain advantages *without* violations than with verification problems. For example, a long-term freeze that stops all kinds of modernization of offensive systems but fails to limit air and anti-submarine defenses and accepts ICBM vulnerability from the outset may be less useful for reducing the risk of nuclear war (as contrasted to merely reducing the cost and numbers of nuclear offensive systems) than an agreement which permits programs to maintain survivability in areas where it doesn't limit threats to survivability.

Detailed unclassified verification analysis is hard. Nonetheless, verifiability is a criterion for any arms control agreement, including a freeze. Not only is it a domestic political necessity, but there is sound reason to assume the Soviets would violate the agreement if they believed they could gain an advantage by doing so. Therefore, a comprehensive review of the impact of verification concerns on the feasibility and security acceptability of a general freeze (at least one that is intended as more than a brief "negotiators' pause") has to look step by step at each provision, and assess the ways the Soviets could cheat and at the significance of possible violations. Such an analysis must consider the possibility of increased Soviet concealment efforts—the infamous "altered practices"—and, what usually gets ignored, the costs in technical and operational effectiveness and confidence from heroic concealment measures. Such an analysis is extraordinarily difficult to undertake on an unclassified basis, since—appearances to the contrary not withstanding—we still manage to keep secret a good deal of the most interesting information about the strengths and weaknesses of our intelligence systems.

Negotiation for Verifiability

Partly for that reason, and partly because of the limited time and space available, it seems to me most useful, rather than to try to evaluate the specific verification problems of particular proposals, to address here the issue of the degree to which the desired scope of an agreement and verification requirements affects the complexity and duration of negotiating an agreement. That is, rather than talk about the details of how we find out things, I want to talk about the negotiating aspect of verification.

To say we can verify an agreement adequately means, as discussed above, that the U.S. could discover a Soviet violation and take necessary reactive action (which could be either preventative—stopping the violation before a danger arose—or offsetting—negating the advantage by action of our own) before the Soviet Union could, by its violation, secure a significant advantage. Assessing the verifiability of a treaty, by that standard, involves at least two steps, each of which affects the negotiating process:

The first is considering how we can observe Soviet behavior so as to find out what they are doing (taking account of how they could make observation even harder). The intelligence community customarily refers to this as the "monitoring" function. During the negotiation of an agreement, these monitoring requirements are relevant because it may be necessary to seek Soviet agreement on provisions that will enhance—or make possible—sufficiently accurate and complete gathering of information for monitoring.

The second step is determining whether the behavior observed is or is not consistent with the treaty. (The intelligence community traditionally likes to reserve the term "verification" for this judgmental step.) The negotiating phase is obviously critical to this part of verification, for it gives the best opportunity to define with precision and clarity what the treaty permits and what it forbids.

Agreement on What an Agreement Means

Agreeing with the Soviets on provisions governing both these aspects of verification is a major element of the negotiation of an effective, useful, and politically viable agreement. Much discussion of verification and negotiation focuses on the first aspect: Having decided the information we would need, will the Soviets agree to special cooperative provisions that may be necessary to ensure we get it. But the second element of negotiating for verification puts, I would assert, an at least equally severe limit on hopes for a freeze that is both verifiable and promptly negotiated.

This second aspect—clearly defining the rules—reflects that for both national security and domestic political reasons it is not enough merely to agree with the U.S.S.R. on broad general propositions—"no new ICBMs will be tested," "no additional bombers primarily designed for nuclear attack will be built." After agreeing on such basic rules, their precise meaning has to be detailed before we really have an agreement.

This will necessarily be a complex process. The complexity of arms control agreements is like the complexity of the tax system: the complexity results not from a desire to complicate, but from the fact that interests clash and from the fact that the subject concerned is inherently complex. Because nuclear weapons are complex—and because actions with respect to them are so multi-faceted, and because limits always impact the two sides somewhat differently—there is no way to reach a simple agreement concerning nuclear arms. Simplicity in *concept* is definitely a virtue in arms control: the freeze, the Zero Option, a common weapons ceiling—all these have the great advantage over conceptually complicated rules in that they can be easily explained and understood. But even simple concepts must be implemented by clear and precise provisions. For example, the *concept*, in the SALT II agreement, of limiting each side to one new type of ICBM is simplicity itself. Yet months of negotiation and scores of words of treaty text of mind-bending intricacy were required to translate that general concept into operational rules conduct.

If one wants an agreement that *can* be abided by, one must have the patience for this effort. The more comprehensive an agreement—the more subjects it covers—the more complex it will prove to be. For an agreement to be verifiable *even in principle*, i.e., for it to be clear what actions are consistent with it, each topic must be spelled out in adequate detail. It is simply not prudent—it is not even plausible—in dealing with the U.S.S.R. to hope that they will naturally share our understanding of general terms, and even less likely that we can expect them to abide by our understanding of the "spirit" of an agreement. In arms control, as in a lot of other things that involve conflicting interests (including tax law) what you see is what you get: The parties will operate on the principle that you cannot do what is not permitted but you can do what is permitted, and within that framework you are free to act in ways that you think serve your interest. General rules (and, of course, specific ones as well) will be interpreted by each side in the light most favorable to its own interests.

On occasion, it may be in the U.S. interest to *not* seek specificity, either because we want flexibility for our conduct, or because we wish to avoid any implication that by prohibiting certain specified actions, we are implicitly accepting the propriety of closely related—equally troubling—ones. Some things, in short, are better left to future case-by-case determinations. But such instances are the exception, not the rule.

In particular, in a comprehensive agreement of any kind, setting the borderline conditions, saying what systems and actions are limited, will be both important and controversial. An especially important issue in an agreement that tries to be very comprehensive is how to deal with dual purpose systems. Prior SALT agreements have focused heavily on two types of weapons—SLBMs and ICBMs—that are unusual in that they are, for all practical purposes, limited to a strategic nuclear mission. This is the exception; most nuclear systems also have some actual or potential conventional role. Even "heavy bombers" proved hard to define in the SALT context, partly for this reason. The Soviet Union uses Bear and Bison airplanes for both bomber and non-bomber missions. We had to agree on a system for determining which would count against the SALT ceilings. The example of Backfire in the SALT II negotiations is a classic boundary case: Should this plane be counted (or frozen) as a strategic nuclear bomber? There is no question that it is an airplane which, under certain conditions, is capable of reaching the United States; if that makes it a bomber, then it ought to be in. But if that's not the definition of what the sides want to limit (and it wasn't the general U.S. definition, though it was, in a sense, the Soviet one), then there is a strong case for excluding it.

The endless debate over the essentially marginal Backfire issue in SALT barely hints at the problems that would be involved for a freeze in defining, for example, exactly which Soviet and U.S. theater aircraft are to be treated as having a nuclear role. And these arguments are never abstract; the issue is instead always one of how a particular definition affects the two sides' actual forces and plans, not what is the "right" definition in some platonic sense. (Even the Backfire issue doesn't disappear in the freeze case, for there is the problem of how you deal with the half of the total Backfire force that is part of the Soviet Navy, assuming the Backfires in the Long Range Air Force are limited automatically.)

A host of similar definitional issues will have to be faced: One general concept advanced in some freeze proposals is to limit development tests but permit crew training. That's a meaningful concept, but it is not self-defining. The sides would have to agree on what features would distinguish tests that are to be permitted for crew training and reliability from those that are prohibited as part of an improvement effort—and those features would have to be capable of observation by the other side and reasonably resistant to faking. If there is to be a numerical quota on tests (perhaps as a way to avoid having to sort out motives), the sides have to agree on what is a "test" and what is a "failure" that doesn't count against the quota. (For those, embarrassed arguments that "we learned a lot before the rocket blew up" have some validity.) They would also need to agree on what (if any) space shots count against the quota. Similarly, if "replacements" and "maintenance on existing systems" are permitted, but "improvements" prohibited, what is understood to be the difference?

In a sense all these issues have to be resolved during the negotiations in order to *permit* a side to comply even if it wants to—and they are certainly necessary to enable conduct to be challenged convincingly.

Some criticisms of the complexity of arms control agreements are, in effect, criticisms of a high standard of verification. But clarity in negotiation is not just a matter of preventing clandestine advantages—it contributes to arms control's ability to serve one of its important purposes, namely increasing confidence between the parties. We must *assume* that the Soviets will cheat (i.e., act illegally) if they believe they could do so clandestinely and usefully (i.e., that they would gain an advantage thereby). But we *know* that they (and probably we) will press to the limit of permitted conduct. When the borders of permitted conduct are obscure, an ambiguous agreement can be a source of constant conflict and dispute. (This has for example, been true for the 1962 agreement—cast in the most general terms—whereby the Soviets undertook not to have nuclear forces in Cuba.)

An effort to anticipate every possible case, and resolve *all* ambiguity is obviously doomed to failure. Some issues can safely be remitted to later resolution in the Standing Consultative Committee (SCC). But that instrument works far better when it can deal with specific cases against the framework of an explicit and concrete set of rules. (An important, and largely confidential, role of the SCC is that it can be and has been used not only to resolve disputes, but to clarify and specify detailed rules of future conduct in areas where problems have arisen.)

Freeze proposals generally envisage limits on things with multifold interactions with non-nuclear activity—from civil nuclear power and space programs to conventional weapons. Therefore, if they are to be verifiable they necessarily involve detailed and tedious negotiation *on their substance*, quite apart from any special monitoring-aiding measures that may be agreed on. When a new agreement can piggy-back on already agreed details, the process can go much faster. Therefore, if speed of negotiation is a virtue, a freeze proposal should make maximum use of the already agreed terms of SALT I and II, and of whatever progress is made in Geneva in START and INF, simply to avoid duplication of effort and reopening settled issues.

Agreement on Cooperative Measures

Adequate precision of the terms of the limitation is necessary even if a freeze (or any other agreement) is to be monitored exclusively by National Technical Means (NTM). However, for many more far-reaching limitations, agreement on measures to assist monitoring will be *necessary* and in almost every case it will be *useful*.

It is important to realize that agreed or "cooperative" verification procedures can never be more than a backup to national technical means. Cooperative measures that require the equivalent of joint U.S.-Soviet manning of the Soviet Strategic Rocket Forces or SAC are something neither side is likely to be keen on. Cooperative measures that are worthy of the name and sufficiently plausible to be worth consideration are those that (a) provide some kind of ostensible "correct" data point against which to measure conduct as observed by NTM, (b) make it easier for national technical means to work, as, for example, not encrypting telemetry makes it easier for national technical means to work, or (c) provide data we could not collect at all (or as well) with NTM.

Data Exchange. The first class of cooperative measures simply provides unconfirmed information. The kinds of exchange of information that could be required include declaring rates of production or giving numbers of systems in limited categories. The limits of such data exchange have to be acknowledged, for the data given are not self-validating. For example, the Russians at a certain point in SALT II duly told us that they had exactly 1,398 ICBM launchers. After they told us that, we did not really know anything more than we knew before, because 1,398 was the number we thought they had (counting their way). Given the openness of our system, we can never tell when they give us a piece of data whether it is the *correct* number, or whether they know we *think* it's the correct number, or whether it is merely the number *they wish us to think* is correct. (In SALT I, when they gave a number for Soviet SSBNs under construction that differed from our own, we were less than overjoyed at this manifestation of openness.) But such Soviet-provided data are still useful even though they don't increase our current information. This is because having such a Soviet-provided data base means that if we later find a 1,399th

Soviet ICBM the Russians can't argue (as they did with the brigade in Cuba), "Well, it was already there; you should have found it ten years ago when the treaty was negotiated!" In a freeze—whose focus is, by definition, on prohibiting change from a pre-existing base—such a system of explicit statement of the initial condition would be especially useful.

Generally speaking, the Soviets have proved increasingly willing to agree to such data exchange, quite possibly because they recognize the very real limitations on U.S. ability to tolerate their old position that both sides should work with U.S. estimates of Soviet forces, which they could then reject as inaccurate if it served their purpose.

Helping NTM. The second important class of cooperative measure is the one that makes NTM work better (or at all). In this class come both limitations—e.g., the SALT II ban on interference with NTM and the prohibition of deliberate concealment from NTM (like denial of access to telemetry when the denial impedes verification)—and affirmative required actions that alert and focus NTM collection systems, e.g., advance notice of tests, declaration of distinctive features of limited and non-limited equipment, or identification of production facilities. Special attention should be focused on these NTM-assisting measures. For in a critical sense, we always rely ultimately on NTM, i.e., on our own intelligence, and increased assurance of access by NTM may make risks acceptable by reducing uncertainties.

In theory, the Soviets have already agreed to the basic principle here: non-interference and non-concealment. In practice, the food for dispute is endless, as recent Soviet ballistic missile test encryption shows. This is an area where more far reaching agreement may need the backup of more precise agreement on specific rules, not just general concepts.

Independent Data. Finally, we come to those cooperative measures that provide raw data, not subject to Soviet control—and not obtainable (at least not so easily or accurately) from NTM. There are a great series of bright ideas in this field—all very hard to negotiate. The analysis of any proposal for such procedures should include hard-headed analysis of what precisely the data so obtained would be used for, and how they would increase our confidence, because the negotiating cost will be high, so it should be worth the effort.

On-site inspection (OSI) usually is a focus of speculation—or demands—in this context. I would argue, however, that OSI is vastly over-rated for everything except the CTB. The on-site inspection focus began there and OSI would still be useful in that context. But violations of a ban of the testing of nuclear weapons have almost unique characteristics. If there's been a seismic event at some definite place and you're trying to decide whether what made the seismograph jump was an earthquake or a nuclear explosion, you know just where you want to look, you can go look quite a while after the event, and it's real hard to clean up before the inspector arrives to make a nuclear explosion look like an earthquake. (No doubt there are people who think it's possible, but it's very difficult to do it.) But if you want to find out whether the accuracy of a Soviet missile has improved, and you don't expect to get the research protocol and a license to ruffle through the files, what are you going to inspect when you arrive on-site? One thing is sure: If you do get a look at the Soviet test report, the report will say (believe me, the report will say) that the accuracy was what it is supposed to be if that report is what Russians know the inspector is going to look at.

There are, fortunately, a number of more productive data-provision ideas than OSI. These come under the general heading of "black boxes" that collect data passively, i.e., that serve as officially tolerated in-country data collectors. Even this wouldn't be easy to get agreement on, but a first step has been made in the agreement for NSS in the CTB, so this is an area where the Soviets are far more likely to be interested and cooperative than they are on things that involve Americans physically inspecting in their country.

Verification as a Soviet Bargaining Chip

A final problem of negotiating verification-enhancing provisions is that they are not only complex in themselves, but for all practical purposes verification is a strictly American concern. The Soviets occasionally talk about verification as if they were interested, but this almost always simply as a debating point. The Soviets understand perfectly well that they do not need special verification arrangements. They may not "trust" us any more than we "trust" them. But they have to recognize the impossible political difficulties of any deliberate U.S. cheating on a significant scale and in any event, they have a big national technical means system of their own, they have a lot of agents, and they have the American open society as a way of finding out what's going on. For all practical purposes the Russians rightly understand every verification provision that gets into a treaty to be a concession that they are making to us. That makes such provisions extraordinarily difficult to negotiate.

Negotiating a verifiable agreement, even assuming agreement on basic concepts, is not simply a matter of getting a group of technical people, Russians and Americans, in a room and saying, for example, "Monitoring a ban on fissionable material production is tough, but our leaders have agreed to the ban in principle. Now as technicians, we can agree that *if* one knew all these things, then we would each be able to monitor fissionable materials production. So now we've got the technical answer. Now our bosses can agree on it." That is not the way the process works. Instead, every stage is a significant negotiating effort—which the Soviets expect to be a two-way process, with Soviet concessions on verification (both monitoring and precision) compensated by U.S. agreement on points of concern to the U.S.S.R. This—like a good deal else about U.S.-Soviet relations—isn't right and it isn't fair. But it is a fact to be recognized.

All this does not mean that verification of comprehensive, innovative agreements is impossible. But it does mean that proposals for a freeze, whatever they include, cannot realistically be built on the assumption that it would be possible to get quick agreements *even assuming general Soviet agreements on concepts*. If we were interested primarily in a so-called negotiator's pause—a largely symbolic tonic for real negotiation—or if one judged that a particular program is particularly dangerous and you'd like to stop it for a while during talk about permanent solutions—it may be possible to have a "soft" agreement to stop. But if you're interested in long-term agreements, then verification negotiation is going to be extended.

* * *

Judging the Freeze: The Inevitable Trade-Offs

Leon Sloss

Introduction

I have been asked to assess several freeze proposals in terms of their coverage, verification, and timing (which really is related to negotiability). These are important considerations for a freeze, or for any arms control proposal. However, there are other—and I would argue more important—criteria by which any arms control proposal (including freeze initiatives) must be judged; the same criteria ought to be applied to any arms program as well. It would be useful if proponents of various arms proposals and arms control proposals could use the same criteria in making assessments, for in theory (and one would hope in practice) arms programs and arms control ought to be directed at the same national security objectives. This obviously is too much to hope for in an imperfect world, but, nevertheless, the subject of criteria for assessment is discussed briefly below in order to add some breadth and perspective to this analysis.

Coverage, verification and timing are important aspects of any freeze proposal. There are clearly trade-offs among them. It will be argued here that timing is the essential characteristic of a freeze. This sets the freeze-type of arms control proposal apart from other types. In the final analysis, any freeze proposal, trading among timing, coverage, and verification, will of necessity encounter strong pressures to compromise the latter in order to obtain an early agreement.

Criteria

Any arms control proposal or any arms program should be designed so as to foster a political-military environment that will enhance U.S. security. Few would disagree with that broad statement, including the implicit assumption that arms influence political relationships in peace as well as the military results of war. There will be less agreement, I am sure, in this forum and in the broader strategic and arms control community about specific criteria by which various arms and arms control programs should be judged, and the relative weight to be given each. In particular, there are differences about the role nuclear weapons can and should play in U.S. security. These range from the view that nuclear weapons can only be used to deter the use of nuclear weapons to the view that they can be used in fighting wars. However, it should be possible to establish a set of criteria that could be applied to the assessment of the political-military situation or regime resulting from a defined set of weapons deployment and arms control measures.

Such a framework should include the following criteria:

1) *Deterrence* - Does the regime reduce the prospects of war? There is, of course, a particular concern with nuclear war in this nuclear era. But the risks of

Leon Sloss *is president of Sloss Associates, Arlington, Virginia.*

nuclear war are closely related to the risks of any war when nuclear powers are involved. In terms of this criteria, it would be illusory to adopt a scheme or program that controlled, reduced, or increased nuclear arms in the belief that such a scheme would reduce the risk of nuclear war, if the result was to increase the risk of non-nuclear war, for such a war between nuclear states readily could escalate. For example, "no-first-use" proposals that are not offset by corresponding increases in non-nuclear capabilities are open to such criticism. The notable proposal by Messrs. Bundy, McNamara, Smith, and Kennan recognizes this fact. Certainly, insofar as the U.S. and the Soviet Union and their close allies are concerned, the risks of any war directly involve the risk of nuclear escalation, so deterrence must contend with both types of risk.

2) *Assurance* - Does the arms program/arms control regime establish a sense of security, relatively free of coercion, for the U.S. and its allies? The regime will have both a peacetime and political role and a wartime and military role, and this is specifically applicable to nuclear weapons. For years American nuclear weapons have had a central role in cementing U.S.-allied security relationships. Not only are nuclear guarantees or assurances an essential underlying feature of U.S. treaty relations with NATO and Japan, they are also an important part of U.S. efforts to curb nuclear proliferation. However, it has become clear that nuclear weapons can convey positive assurance or can undermine assurance. Recent changes in the nuclear weapons balance, and the way in which the U.S. has dealt with them, have had some negative effects on both domestic and allied confidence in U.S. policies.[1]

3) *Coercion* - Does the regime support U.S. foreign policy objectives? Arms program/arms control regimes also play a coercive role in support of U.S. foreign policy. Often this role is implicit, but sometimes military power is displayed (i.e., showing the flag) or, still more rarely, actually used. There are serious questions about the utility of military power in these more overt forms, particularly when nuclear escalation is a serious possibility. However, there can be little doubt that U.S. military power has had political influence in the past, and will likely be called upon in this role in the future—even in the nuclear era. For example, there can be little doubt that the existence of U.S. military power was an influential factor in the Middle East in 1973 both in keeping the Soviet Union out of the conflict and in bringing hostilities to a prompt conclusion.

4) *Reducing the consequences of war* - Does the regime reduce the consequences of war, if hostilities do in fact occur? The consequences of war can be political and social as well as military and territorial. The consequences of the Vietnam War for American society are a good example. In the nuclear era, however, it is not surprising that public attention has been focused on the physical effects of nuclear weapons. Both arms programs (e.g., counterforce weapons and defenses) and arms control measures (e.g., deep reductions and the freeze) have been proposed to mitigate the physical consequences of nuclear war. Given the massive arsenals of nuclear weapons that exist today, neither approach offers

very satisfactory solutions. The prevention of nuclear war remains by far the most attractive means of limiting its consequences. Nevertheless, any state must take care that policies designed to prevent nuclear war are balanced by an equal determination to resist coercion. Preventing war can never be the sole security objective of a nation, or it can readily fall victim to blackmail.

5) *Reducing the burden of arms* - Does the regime minimize the economic and social burden of arms, in a manner *consistent with the security objectives and obligations of U.S. policy?* Arms control proposals have as one objective reducing the cost of arms programs. However, one must be careful in assessing the economics of freezes or other nuclear arms control proposals. Any such analysis must take into account possible offsetting defense expenditures that may be required to maintain current security responsibilities. In the past, reliance on nuclear arms has been a way of achieving security "on the cheap." This has been particularly true in Europe. Such a policy no longer appears viable in light of vast changes in the military balance. However, the alternatives are by no means clear. Major reductions in nuclear arms (of a magnitude which would have a marked effect on the federal budget and deficit, for example) will require a reassessment of U.S international security objectives and priorities unless reductions in nuclear arms can be offset by comparable reductions in the other side's nuclear arms or increases in our own non-nuclear capabilities. It should be recalled that nuclear forces represent only 10 percent of the total U.S. defense budget. This is not to suggest that freezing or reducing nuclear arms might not help to reduce prospective budget deficits and/or freeze resources for other defense or non-defense uses. However, care is required in order to be sure that cost savings are both real and do not impair overall security.

6) *Lay a basis for future reductions* - Does the regime establish a better basis for negotiating future reductions? Advocates of arms programs often argue their proposal will create leverage which will enhance Soviet incentives to negotiate. Advocates of various arms control proposals (including freezes) maintain their proposals will create an "appropriate atmosphere" for future negotiations. Whether carrots or sticks are the incentives most appropriate for successful negotiations and what mix will best advance negotiations are complex and controversial issues to which we shall return below. However, there is little doubt that the effect of a given arms program/arms control regime on the prospects for future negotiations is a criterion that must be considered so long as the U.S. government retains a commitment to arms control negotiations.

Assessment

1) *The nature of freezes* - A freeze is an approach to arms control with a fundamental assumption—that time is of the essence. Advocates of freeze proposals presume that the future is going to be far less satisfactory than the present and that we are thus better off to halt the nuclear competition here and now rather than negotiate some future balance with a different mix and lower level of

forces. This is not to say that freeze advocates are at all satisfied with the *status quo*, but that they see a freeze as the essential first step to changing the current situation. This contrasts with advocates of reductions, who believe that if we are going to expend time and effort on arms control we should get something more than a freeze and also not preclude changes in force postures that might enhance strategic and particularly crisis stability. Some advocates of reductions also believe it is necessary to restore "a balance" in order to create incentives for the other side to negotiate.

For advocates of freeze proposals it is axiomatic that a freeze should take place promptly, because the future is sure to be worse. The precise timing of an agreement does remain an issue in the freeze movement, and there is admittedly a growing tendency to compromise on timing a bit in deference to "current political realities." Nevertheless, a freeze in 1988, say, would not meet the primary objective of freeze advocates at all, for most of the "bad developments" envisioned by freeze supporters would have occurred—e.g., MX, D-5, and the proliferation of cruise missiles, not to mention what the Russians may have done in the meantime (which many freeze advocates have a tendency not to mention at all). Even a freeze in 1985 would permit many new programs to escape out the freezer door before it is closed.

Coverage is clearly important in freeze proposals, for the broader the coverage, the more comprehensive the restrictions on dangerous future developments. Yet there is a tension between coverage and time urgency, the more complex and time-consuming negotiations become. Coverage of certain systems (e.g., cruise missiles) or processes (e.g., weapons production) creates severe verification problems, which could take years to negotiate. Failure to include these elements in a freeze will create certain "loopholes." Their inclusion, however, will likely require prolonged negotiations, or compromises in verification, or both.

2) *Coverage* - There are several aspects to coverage:
- Whether a freeze should apply only to warheads, only to delivery systems, or to both. If it applies to delivery systems, what systems would be covered? If systems are dual-capable, how would *nuclear* systems be defined? Should a freeze include other strategic force elements, such as C^3I?
- Would the freeze apply to deployment only, or to production, development, and testing as well?
- Will the freeze apply to strategic forces only, to long-range forces (including INF), or to all nuclear forces?

Broad coverage is desirable if a freeze is to be effective and credible. If the goal is primarily to create a better atmosphere for future negotiations, the simpler the freeze the better; but atmospherics may be transitory. It is necessary to assess carefully whether once a freeze is achieved, the objective incentives for further negotiation will in fact be greater or less.

If the goal is to reduce the risks and consequences of nuclear war, the more comprehensive the freeze the better, but a comprehensive freeze may be difficult to verify and prolong negotiations, thereby vitiating the main purpose of a freeze—to curb future developments before they occur.

3) *Verification* - Others will have more to say than I will on this topic, but it is important to recognize that verification is not absolute. This is not to say that it is not important, for it is. However, verification should be judged in relation to the consequences of a violation rather than by some abstract standard. Both freeze advocates and proponents of reduction seek ever more detailed limits that make verification more difficult. Many freeze advocates seek to limit production, which can be very difficult to verify. Many reduction advocates want to limit warheads or throw-weight, which are also difficult to verify. There are trade-offs between coverage and verification. The proper balance is not easy to identify, but one can envision cases where some reduction in verification assurance can be warranted in order to expand coverage—e.g., non-deployed missiles are important to cover in a freeze or a reduction, but cannot be verified in these cases—i.e., through counting rules such as those established in SALT II. However, compromise on verification can only go so far. Unless verification is credible, confidence in an agreement will rapidly erode. The American public and the Congress do not trust the Russians and do not want to be "taken by an agreement."

4) *Negotiability* - Negotiability is really very difficult to assess. It involves judgments about Soviet objectives and how best to deal with them. There are several schools of thought about how the U.S. should negotiate any arms control agreement.

- The *"necessary evil"* school - which sees negotiations primarily as a response to public pressures.
- The *"hard bargaining"* school - which believes in proceeding at a deliberate pace and waiting for the other side to take the initiative. This has been the approach, to date, in INF and START.
- The *"flexible"* school - which believes in adjusting U.S. proposals frequently as negotiations progress in order to respond to the other side's objections and provide impetus to negotiations. This often was the approach in the SALT I and II negotiations.
- The *"unilateral initiative"* school - which believes the U.S. should take initiatives to reduce arms in order to advance negotiations.

While the two extreme schools can be rather easily dismissed as lacking realism, there are respectable arguments for each of the "centrist" positions. If we give in to what the Soviets want, negotiations will move more easily, but at what point does such negotiation become concession? Will such a position be more likely to lead to further negotiations the U.S. can find more acceptable or make such negotiations more difficult? On the other hand, if the U.S. will not compromise with the Soviets in any areas, that is not negotiation either. If Soviet interest is serious, reasonable proposals, effectively advanced and cogently argued, will produce a true negotiation with at least the prospect of an acceptable outcome. If Soviet intent is propaganda and political warfare, concessions will just feed their appetite, and acceptable results will be difficult to achieve. For these reasons, how we negotiate should depend on how we assess our adversary's objectives. If negotiations are to be successful, the proposals set forth on both sides must meet the legitimate security concerns of both parties and be negotiated patiently, but vigorously. The U.S. should advance proposals it can sustain throughout the negotiating process. All of this will take some time, even in the best of circumstances.

5) *Conclusions*

- The greatest appeal of a freeze is in its simplicity and the promise of early results.
- However, an early freeze will generate great pressures to sacrifice in the areas of comprehensiveness and/or verifiability to advance the objective of negotiability in order to obtain a timely agreement.
- To the extent that a freeze proposal is less comprehensive or less subject to verification than a competing reduction proposal, a freeze will suffer in any comparison. (The current U.S. START proposals have serious flaws on both counts.) On the other hand, to the extent that negotiations are prolonged to achieve more coverage or tighter verification, the freeze loses its primary appeal, which is early agreement.

Thus, it seems inevitable that, when applied in practice to U.S.–Soviet strategic arms talks, the freeze proposals will have to compromise on coverage and verification, if they are to meet the essential objective of timeliness. Yet to compromise on coverage and verification is to reduce both the utility and credibility of a freeze. This is a major dilemma that confronts the freeze movement.

---

1. See Michael Howard, "Reassurance and Deterrence: Western Defense in the 1980s," *Foreign Affairs*, Winter 1982/83, p. 309.

* * *

Do Freezes Satisfy Ethical Criteria?

Ethical Dimensions of the Nuclear Danger

Sister Mary Hennessey

As the first panelist in this area of concern, I would like to offer a general introduction to the ethical considerations. Let me first remark that I think that we are indebted to Paul Doty for having included the moral dimensions of the freeze in this conference. I think that religion has had a very unhappy history in trying to deal with the values and place of science, and I am afraid that science has returned the compliment. This has created a chasm between the scientific and religious communities that endures even now when we are working on the same side, as it were. I find this reflected in the tendency of professional scientists to belong to groups of their own when they address the threat of nuclear war and the same tendency among those whose concern over nuclear arms is religiously motivated. Let us hope that we can leave the stereotypes of the past behind in order to be open and enriched by whatever anyone can contribute to the effort of avoiding nuclear destruction.

History indicates, as Barbara Tuchman has remarked, that in most instances nations stumble into war, lacking the time, freedom, information, and perspective required to make ethical examination of their act. Whatever else may be said regarding the over thirty years of cold war, detente, and deterrence, it has been during this period that scientific analysis and evaluation of nuclear weaponry and moral judgment regarding it have entered the mainstream of our Western world. The popularity of the nuclear freeze movement is evidence of this new level of awareness and judgment.

We now have substantial numbers of citizens from diverse sections of society who have examined this nation's nuclear arms policy and have begun to ask questions that touch its ethical marrow. They want to know what right the United States has to continue the escalation of nuclear arms, how the cost of the arms race can be justified, whether the United States has the right to even contemplate nuclear war.

Explicitly or implicitly, the ethical considerations that have been raised are contained in the principles of the "just war theory." This theory provides a compre-

Sister Mary Hennessey is Director of Ecumenical and Interreligious Affairs, Diocese of Worcester, Massachusetts.

hensive framework and reflects moral values that are consonant with our cultural heritage. It may be well, therefore, to review this theory briefly:

For a just resort to war (*ius ad bellum*), 1) competent authority must make the decision; 2) in the name of a just cause; 3) with the right intention of achieving solely just redress; 4) after all other reasonable means have been exhausted; 5) with legitimate hope of success; 6) at a cost not disproportionately greater than what waging the war might achieve. For a war to be judged just in the way that it is carried out (*ius in bello*), 7) the violence done must not be indiscriminate, i.e., it cannot be directed against those not responsible for or participating in the war, and 8) the destructiveness wrought by the war must never exceed the good sought in waging the war.

The most recent and well-publicized application of this theory is found in the second draft of the National Conference of Catholic Bishops' Pastoral Letter, "The Challenge of Peace: God's Promise and Our Response."[1] The Bishops have condemned nuclear war as immoral. Their condemnation is based on the judgment that both the conditions of discrimination and proportionality required for waging a just war could not be realized in a nuclear war.

Those who reject the absolute condemnation of nuclear war (and there are many Catholics among them) rely upon the principle of a "just cause," i.e., the right to legitimate defense. For them the threat that Russia poses is so overwhelming that defense through nuclear war is legitimate even to the point of first strike. Some among them would justify the potential destructiveness of such a war by accepting Michael Walzer's dictum: "decent men and women, hard pressed in war, must do terrible things and then they themselves have to look for some way to reaffirm the values they have overthrown."[2] Even assuming that there will be a "then," the tragic aftereffects that still haunt the veterans of the Vietnam jungles should make us less sanguine about the viability of the theory. Others believe that the proportions of the war may be limited to a tolerable level.[3] They are likely to justify the continuing expenditures on nuclear research and development in order to achieve that level of sophistication which will allow precision targeting of the immediate enemy. Curiously, they seem to be untroubled by the possibility of retaliation and the manifold forms that it could take.

Currently, then, those who have considered the morality of nuclear war have come to quite opposite conclusions. Some see nuclear war as totally immoral and never justified. Others see nuclear war as morally justifiable, even necessary, under some circumstances. Both positions contain unresolved weaknesses. Those who judge nuclear war as absolutely evil have to acknowledge the part that deterrence has played in forestalling nuclear war and the risk of untried alternatives. But if nuclear war is in all cases unjustifiable then one can never seriously intend to engage in it, and deterrence is robbed of its power.

Yet there is also a risk involved in the judgment of those who support continuing to rely upon deterrence and accept the possibility that a nuclear war might occur. The risk is the gamble that nuclear war, once begun, could be contained. This is a risk which, as Jonathan Schell, among others, strongly warns, no one has the right to take for the world.[4] That is, they fail to recognize that no nation, or nations, has the competent authority to justify exposing all present and future humanity to the possibility of annihilation. A second weakness of the deterrence policy as now pursued is that the level of expenditure that it is reaching, the level of governmental subterfuge and manipulation that it is generating and the level of tension and despair it is causing in youth all threaten to cause the collapse of the very society it is dedicated to preserving. Finally, the escalation of capabilities and the magnitude of destructiveness of newly designed weapons, together with the growing comfortableness of military and political leaders with strategies that take for granted "thinking the unthinkable," advance the likelihood that nuclear war will begin and limits the enduring effectiveness of deterrence. Official language seems to recognize this, and has slipped rather too easily into speaking of initiating limited nuclear war. Ethically they have made a quantum leap when they shift from speaking of having nuclear arms only in order to be able to threaten to retaliate if someone should attack us, to considering how to initiate the first strike.

At this juncture, however, and happily so, the impetus and initiative seem to be with those who do not accept nuclear war under these conditions. They have made widely available to the public the three central weaknesses in the government's current deterrence model: its growing comfortableness with the likelihood of nuclear war, the draining effect of the current policy on every aspect of our lives, and the enormous devastation contained in nuclear weaponry. The minimal basis for security and hope required for living genuinely human lives is seen as being triply eroded.

It is in the face of these judgments that the proposal of a nuclear freeze has caught the imagination of a large and extremely diverse cross-section of our nation and the Western world. I believe that this is a literal statement of what has happened: It has caught the imagination of countless people, and this should not be lightly dismissed. It represents a vital breakthrough for many from what Robert Jay Lifton saw as first prevailing: psychic numbing, that "emotional and intellectual anesthesia," which "interferes with our capacity to cope with the weapons themselves . . . [and] extends into all our perceptions of living and dying."[5] It also goes beyond that despair described by Erik Erikson, which "expresses the feeling that the time is now short, too short for the attempt to start another life and to try out alternate roads to integrity."[6]

That the reasonable desire to halt the arms race is often passionately expressed should come as no surprise. In a debate in which the issue involves the future of all humankind, feeling and passion cannot be dismissed as inappropriate. Rather, they can provide the energy and urgency required to deflect the world from the single-minded pursuit of arms as the sole source of security. Detached rationality has let some objectify nuclear war to such an abstract level that it has become almost a plaything in the sandbox of their computerized theories. Thus technical inventions that qualitatively increase the destructiveness of nuclear weapons are celebrated as producing new "generations" of weapons, as if they were somehow new signs of life rather than further treacheries to the possibility of life. There was a parallel effort made to mask the reality of the most sophisticated and lethal of weapons by calling it a "Peacekeeper."[7] These rationalizations fly in the face of reality and provide further proof of the dangers inherent in allowing nuclear war even a modicum of respectability. A major benefit of the nuclear freeze effort is its adamant refusal to hide from any of the realities of the present policy or to be paralyzed by them.

But if we are to answer the demand inherent in the popularity of the nuclear freeze, I would posit that it can be seen only as a first step in a far more complex and far reaching process. To be ethically responsible, it cannot be seen as a permanent level of nuclear arms toleration. As the World Council of Churches notes,[8] it is not to be used as a tactic to avoid making decisions or to delay decisions. Rather it is to provide the time needed to begin prudent patterns of disarmament, to develop alternate ways of resolving international conflict and to pursue those economic, political, and social conditions required for making war a less desirable option.

Past efforts at arms reduction negotiations seem to have been undermined because nuclear arms levels were not held stable while treaties were hammered out. A nuclear freeze would provide this needed stable framework. Understanding the freeze as a first step in the mutual dismantling of weaponry, to proceed in a mutually agreed upon way, could also defuse some of the anxiety regarding the conflicting data as to whether the U.S. or the U.S.S.R. at this moment enjoys some superiority.

As noted earlier, a good proportion of the public has been educated to understand the cost, on so many fronts, of the nuclear arms race, the growing possibility of nuclear war, and the destructive consequences of such a war. They have learned to question whether deterrence can continue to be effective under the changing circumstances of our world. There is a growing openness to undertake some form of disarmament, though to what level is not yet clear. Now there is need to face much more realistically the cost that we, as an affluent nation, with a position of global superiority and leadership, must pay if we truly seek a climate conducive to peace. If war is the ultimate form of conflict resolution, then not only other forms of conflict resolution must be studied, but also the causes of the conflict. To suggest that all conflict for the U.S. rests on the bipolar division of U.S. and U.S.S.R., to ignore the growing complexities of the divisions of North from South is to oversimplify dangerously our obligations and responsibilities. It is important to see the nuclear freeze within a larger context. To immobilize or even remove a sword that dangles over the head does not lead to health if feet are still treading on burning coals.

John Earnest has put it well: "If there is a viable solution—and we have no choice but to proceed on that assumption—it will probably require unprecedented and painful revision in our political and economic institutions, our standard of living and in our world view and philosophical orientation."[9] For those who do not believe that such a major transformation is possible for human society, Earnest cites the transformations called for in founding the United States, in the massive re-orientation of China, in the changing relations between Germany and France.

More issues remain. They include a closer examination of the relationship of deterrence and disarmament to the freeze, the legitimacy of weapons at ready alert during the freeze, what should be complementary to what alternative strategy, and, most especially, the issues of non-nuclear arms, upon which the public is far less educated.

In general summary, though, the nuclear freeze proposal merits the support of those who question the morality of nuclear war, and those who question the morality of our current nuclear arms policy. To answer all ethical concerns, however, it must be able to marshal the world to stop focusing on nuclear arms as the final form of security, the ultimate sign of power. It should push us to ask how long we can tolerate controlling nuclear war through ethically questionable methods, and how long nuclear war can be controlled if we are unjust in our methods.

I close with two reflections.

The first, from the speech of Pope Paul VI to the United Nations: "It is true that the task in question is extremely arduous, but it is not beyond the tenacity and wisdom of people who are aware of their own responsibilities before humanity and history—above all, before God. This means the need for higher religious awareness. Even those who do not take God into account can and must recognize the fundamental exigencies of the moral law that God has written in the depths of human hearts and that must govern people's mutual relationships on the basis of truth, justice and love."[10]

The second, a small section from Plato's *Republic:*

". . . 'Really, Socrates, it seems ridiculous to me to ask that question . . . are we to believe that, when the very principle by which we live is deranged and corrupted, life will be worth living so long as a man can do as he will and will do anything rather than to free himself from vice and wrong doing and to win justice and virtue?'

" 'Yes' (Socrates) replied, 'that is a ridiculous question.' "[11]

---

1. National Conference of Catholic Bishops, "The Challenge of Peace: God's Promise and Our Response," New Draft, Origins v. 12 #20, Oct. 28, 1982.

2. Michael Walzer, *Just and Unjust Wars* (New York: Basic Books, 1977).

3. E.g., Colin S. Gray and Keith Payne, "Victory Is Possible," *Foreign Policy*, vol. 39, Summer 1980.

4. Jonathan Schell, *The Fate of the Earth* (New York: Avon, 1982).

5. Robert Jay Lifton, "Acceptance Speech for the 1969 National Book Award in the Sciences," in *History and Human Survival* (New York: Vintage Books, 1971). See also Lifton & Richard Falk, *Indefensible Weapons* (New York: Basic Books, 1982).

6. Erik Erikson, *Childhood and Society* (New York: W. W. Norton, 1973).

7. Cf., Stephen Hilgarten et al., *Nukespeak* (San Francisco: Sierra Club Books, 1982).

8. World Council of Churches, Church and Society, *Faith, Science and the Future* (Geneva: WCC, 1978).

9. John Earnest, "A Call to the Conscience of the University Community," *The Center Magazine*, Vol. 20, No. 1 (January/February 1982).

10. Paul VI, "Message to the United Nations' General Assembly at a Special Session on Disarmament," May 24, 1978, in *Peace and Disarmament*, documents of the World Council of Churches and the Roman Catholic Church, Geneva, 1982.

11. Plato, *The Republic of Plato* (Oxford: Oxford University Press, 1941).

* * *

The Freeze Movement as an Ethical Achievement

Jack Mendelsohn

The freeze has democratized the nuclear debate, reaching far beyond the customary discussions of experts, strategists, politicians, and diplomats. It is taken to heart by an impressively wide and diverse public. Winston Churchill once called democracy the worst system of government there is—except for every other system. I have a more positive opinion of democracy. But even if it is only the least worst of systems, I submit that to democratize the discussion of an issue as fateful as the threat of nuclear war has to be considered an ethical achievement.

The unhappy truth is that most citizens through the 70s abdicated their nuclear responsibilities. Enforced secrecy and cultivated nukespeak produced massive psychic numbing. Exaggeration and emotionalism ruled each succeeding presidential campaign. Who could penetrate the confusion? Who wanted to risk the mental chaos if you did? Ratification of SALT II died not with a bang but with a whimper—the whimper of a gulled, bushwhacked, and spent citizenry.

Yet in barely two years, extraordinary grass-roots political upheaval has taken place. Apathy is dissolved. Policy is no longer left to specialists. All kinds of people, tens of millions of them, want to be involved in reducing the grimmest threat to humanity's existence in four million years. They want a part in facing the gravest challenge to democracy since the Athenians gave birth to the idea of self-government.

Perhaps it would have occurred without the freeze as catalyst. Who can say? Maybe it was the hand of God. All we really know is that the freeze was thoughtfully formulated. A plan for promoting it was painstakingly devised. A campaign little larger than a mustard seed was sown. I was close to the handful, then the dozens, then the hundreds who joined the process. I know at first-hand the soul-searching agony of the early, hesitant steps, and the cumbersome frailties of those who risked them. I know too how demonic and misguided are allegations of subversive manipulation, and of amateurish over-simplification.

The results, as we know, have been spectacular, perhaps because of old wisdom about an idea whose time has come. But I wouldn't be happy with that if I didn't also believe that there are reasons for the inspirational power of the freeze that meet ethical criteria of a high order.

First, recognition that the nuclear monster is threatening to slip its leash, ending civilization as we know it, laying waste the entire product of humanity's past history, and snatching from future generations the privilege of living a life on this earth. A first responsibility is to secure the beast's chains. That's what the freeze is about. A

Reverend Jack Mendelsohn is Pastor of the First Parish Church in Bedford, Massachusetts.

first step. Secure the chains. Civilization is not the property of our generation; we are only its custodians. We did not create it; we inherited it. It was bestowed upon us. Our responsibility is to cherish, preserve, and deepen it, and to pass it on—elevated if possible, but at least intact—to those who are supposed to follow us.

To respond to this moral imperative as the freeze movement consistently does—prudently, soberly, responsibly, imaginatively—is quality ethical behavior.

Any such movement is open to criticism, and should be. I am aware of no freeze leaders who expect less, or who see themselves involved in anything but the barest beginnings of what must be done. Because the freeze is dramatically embraced by so many, it inspires a remarkable flow of searching critical literature and artistic expression, from highly qualified professional communities, most of whom were not earlier engaged. Overwhelmingly these expressions support a halt to the deadly spiral of the nuclear arms race, and demand an accounting of the policies that brought us where we are today.

This brings us to a second reason for the freeze's dynamic ethical worth. It identifies and celebrates fundamental, graspable, irrefutable principles of human experience. Nothing can be propelled forward and backward at the same time. Before an arms race can become an arms reduction, it must first stop being an arms race. If you want to back up your forward-moving car, you must bring it to a halt, or strip the gears. One of the basic tenets of Alcoholics Anonymous, an organization in intimate touch with a substantial portion of Americans who, therefore, are not likely to miss the freeze point, is that, before you begin to deal with the causes of your alcoholism, you must stop drinking, period.

There is a second universal principle that complements the first. Enough is enough. How many gallons will it take to paint your house? Why, then, go out and buy ten times as much, or forty times as much? How many nuclear warheads would it take to wipe out America and the Soviet Union as viable societies? If each already has far more than enough survivable ones to do the gruesome, unthinkable job, isn't that enough? Why more?

The freeze takes hold because there is visceral ethical appreciation of these principles. The various statistical comparisons between Soviet nuclear arsenals and our own, absorbing and confusing as they are, pale when one's mind centers on an existing volume of weaponry capable of putting an end to both superpowers several times over.

A third ethical credential of the freeze is its recognition of a long, hard road. Miracles, devoutly to be wished for, are unlikely to appear. Establishment bastions, like the *Wall Street Journal*, will rail against unilateralism, ignoring the freeze's stoutly bilateral character. Others will pick at verification details, as if they are a peculiar dilemma of the freeze. Our government, which alternates between accusations of Moscow-controlled subversion and brushing off an annoying insect, will not suddenly change its spots or its tune. It was the Carter Administration after all, not Reagan's, that first advanced the grisly notion of moving from mutually assured destruction to a winnable nuclear war.

The freeze movement must be credited with opting not for paroxysms of self-righteousness, but for persistent struggle—organizing, educating, anticipating, involving, lobbying, doing precinct work, raising money, bearing adversity, minimizing egocentric excursions, turning the other check, enduring. A credit to ethical standards.

Let me speak personally. I am a freeze-as-a-first-step supporter. I am convinced of its soundness. I also believe that superpower use of deterrence has become a moral crime against the future of the human race. I am willing, however, to get at that somewhere down the road. First, a freeze. I believe that the Reagan Administration, in whatever heart of hearts it possesses, really wants a nuclear arms race. I am not interested in scoring that point. I'll settle to begin with for a freeze, under whatever name. I believe that positioning informed, aroused public opinion on the broadest possible base is what we have going for us, no matter who's in power in Washington, or Moscow. I believe that among neither of the superpower populations is there an inherent compulsion to use nuclear weapons against the other or anyone else—against men, women, and children never seen or known, and whose innocence or guilt can in no way be measured.

I believe that the present course of our government, and that of the Soviet Union, is a presumption of monstrous proportions, an offense to humanity and to God. I know I must do all I can to stem this course, and reverse it; and to persuade others to do the same. I cannot directly influence the people of the Soviet Union, or their rulers, but I believe that our interest in survival coincides, and that we can reach out to one another to avoid a human indignity of infamous dimensions.

This is what the freeze means to me, and to the multitudes who, like me, are galvanized and empowered by it. Why can't the nuclear menace be stopped in its tracks so that we can begin sensibly and rationally to diminish it? Why can't the approach be made lean enough to leap over "bargaining chips," "relative advantage," and "windows of vulnerability"—all the excuses for increases in nuclear weaponry behind which arms control discussions screen themselves?

Why not a major first step, with the promise of further steps to follow? What would it accomplish? Nothing less than an easing of tensions through the world. Nothing less than freeing up a spirit of cooperative action so essential for solving the deepening socioeconomic problems which all nations have in common.

In summary, what I see the freeze saying to us is: don't be discouraged by past darkness. There are practical and achievable ways to overcome a sense of helplessness, to multiply efforts for a saner, better world, and to acquire and spread a deeper understanding, not only of ourselves but of those whom so many of us regard as our enemies, but without whose increased sense of security, and without whose collaboration, there will be not just non-peace but non-existence.

To those who ask "Is this possible?" I offer a reply George Kennan devised for such occasions: "Why not?"

*   *   *

"Acceptable" Deterrence and The Freeze

Bruce Martin Russett

My assignment, to discuss ethical dimensions of the freeze movement, is an impossibly broad one. In the first place, it is not entirely clear what would be meant by "the" freeze, as there are different interpretations as to exactly what weapons, and especially just what modernization or replacement programs, might be covered. In the second place and more seriously, the ethical criteria that might be applied to an evaluation are virtually infinite, varying with the very different moral premises to be found throughout our pluralistic society and even more diverse world. Quite obviously, some freezes meet some ethical criteria, and others do not. On the one hand, no freeze, by itself, could possibly satisfy the full requirements of a pacifist. On the other hand, a unilateral or unverifiable freeze would hardly meet the requirements of one who asserts the ethical imperatives of self-defense in a disordered world. In the space here available to me I can only give serious consideration to a single case, taking as an example the United States Catholic Bishops' apparent endorsement of one kind of freeze ("immediate, bilateral, verifiable, agreements to curb the testing, production, and deployment of new nuclear weapons systems") in their draft Pastoral Letter on War and Peace.[1]

Several aspects of this endorsement deserve immediate comment. First, it is obvious that the Bishops' stance toward the freeze is too favorable to satisfy one who conceives the United States and/or NATO as a whole to be at a present military disadvantage, and who therefore insists on a Western increase in military force before accepting a freeze. At the same time, the emphasis, here and elsewhere in the draft, is on the bilateral and verifiable nature of the proposal. The Bishops do praise "independent initiatives," but define these as "carefully chosen limited steps which the United States could take for a defined period of time," and explicitly decline to advocate unilateral disarmament. Similarly, they repeatedly require verifiability in arms control and disarmament. Versions of the freeze that were not, by some reasonable criteria, verifiable presumably would not receive their approval.[2]

Finally, the Bishops' draft, rather gingerly to be sure, recognizes a need for conventional weapons. Elsewhere in the Letter they "strongly support negotiations aimed at reducing and limiting conventional forces," but also, with commendable political realism, acknowledge the argument that "in the absence of nuclear deterrent threats, more troops and conventional (non-nuclear) weapons would be needed to protect our allies. . . ." At several points in the document it is clear that the Bishops have much sympathy for pacifists and pacifism; in strong terms they endorse the pacifist option as legitimate for individuals. But at the same time they emphatically acknowledge a fundamental right of self-defense on the part of governments. These are real conflicts of interest in the world, and real values of justice and freedom to be

---

Bruce Russett is Professor of Political Science at Yale University, New Haven, Connecticut.

defended. "A government threatened by armed, unjust aggression *must* defend its people." The exercise of this right is elaborately hedged in by the limitations of the just war tradition which make the resort to lethal violence only justified as a last resort. Nevertheless, in these and other passages it is clear that the Bishops did not write a pacifist document. Nor, as I shall discuss, do they completely repudiate all aspects even of nuclear deterrence, at least for the present and immediate future. In that context, and with their advocacy of a freeze only as "bilateral" and "verifiable" and their openness to improvement of conventional military defense as an alternative to reliance on nuclear weapons, they could hardly satisfy a pacifist's criteria.

In some observers' minds there has been a question as to whether the Bishops' position, both specifically on the freeze and on nuclear deterrence more generally, satisfactorily meets the Bishops' own criteria for ethical consistency. There was some ground for that question in the working of the second draft, which left some deliberate or inadvertent ambiguity. I believe, however, that the third draft clearly and effectively removes that ambiguity.

The Bishops' Committee rather early decided that it wanted to write a strong anti-nuclear statement, but judged that neither the majority of the Committee nor a majority of the entire Bishops' Conference was prepared to embrace pacifism with the full authority of the church. They worked—and this is very explicit in the third draft—from an elucidation of the just war tradition rather than from the precepts of non-violence. Yet as understood by the Committee, the traditional just war criteria, elaborated with great care over the centuries, are extremely restrictive in the nuclear era and nearly converge with nuclear pacifism. In particular, the requirements of discrimination (the immunity of civilians from direct attack), proportionality (the damage to be inflicted must be proportionate to the good expected in any exercise of violence), and of a reasonable probability of success are extremely hard to satisfy when contemplating the *use* of nuclear weapons. It might be comforting to distinguish between the use of such weapons and merely their possession, or the threat or intent to use them only for purposes of deterrence, but analytically that distinction does not really hold up. Deterrence may possibly fail, in which case the issue of potential use cannot be avoided (quite apart from specific Catholic moral difficulties with intending though not actually committing an evil act). Hence the Bishops felt their moral and theological traditions hemming in their set of possible options in drafting this part of the Letter.

The solution is composed of three elements. One is a strong condemnation of any strike, even in retaliation, against population centers or against military targets where civilian damage would be disproportionate. The second element is a position against "first use" of nuclear weapons: "We abhor the concept of initiating nuclear war, on however restricted a scale. Because of the probable effects, the deliberate initiation of nuclear war, in our judgment, would be an unjustifiable moral risk." As a result, they support "NATO's moving rapidly toward the adoption of a 'No First Use' policy." In this latter statement there is an acknowledgment that implementation of a "No First Use" posture cannot come immediately, that adequate conventional forces to deter a Soviet conventional attack in all circumstances may not yet be in place. The

American Bishops are aware that many Europeans—including some European Bishops—are not ready to forgo the threat of nuclear retaliation for conventional attack, and that in any case "development of an adequate alternative defense posture" will take time. Nevertheless that clearly is what they advocate.

The third element is a very carefully crafted section on whether the use of nuclear weapons, even in extremely restricted form, in retaliation, could ever be acceptable. If *no* such acceptable use could be imagined, then the Bishops would have had, as well, to reject a posture of deterrence based on any intent to use nuclear weapons, since in their moral theology the intent to commit an act is as reprehensible as actually committing the act.[3] The Bishops therefore characterize nuclear deterrence "based on balance" (employing words of Pope John Paul II which were impossible for them to evade) as something that "may still be judged morally acceptable," "not as an end in itself but as a step on the way toward a progressive disarmament." This thrust is reinforced by an emphasis on only "strictly conditioned" acceptance, and forceful calls for mutual disarmament. The whole draft, but especially the section on deterrence, is strongly anti-nuclear in tone, and seeks rhetorically—though not in explicit complete rejection of any use—to build a barrier against notions of limited nuclear war.

In keeping the door open, however slightly, to use, the Bishops left themselves vulnerable to two kinds of misunderstandings—misunderstandings that posed very serious, though very different dangers. The first was the danger that their acceptance of nuclear deterrence would be seen only as a means to achieving a good end (disarmament) and avoiding a bad one (nuclear war). Under that interpretation the Bishops would have run afoul of critics from within their own moral tradition, calling forth charges that they had violated their own rules of moral discourse. The first draft of the Letter, which employed a formula of "tolerating" the deterrent as a means to good ends, provoked just such a response, and some ambiguities on this matter which remained in the second draft continued to draw strong fire. "Traditional" or "conservative" moral theologians vehemently reject any suggestion of "doing the lesser evil" or achieving a good end by morally evil means. In their formulation, one may never do evil; at most one can seek to achieve a good end by morally neutral means. Anything else smacks of an unacceptable "consequentialism." While it is true that there are "liberal" Catholic theologians who advocate one form or another of consequentialist ethics, the Bishops Conference as a whole simply could not do so. The requirements of its own ecclesiastical polity forced the Committee to avoid any whiff of consequentialism in the final draft. Accepting an evil deterrent merely to avoid war, or even to achieve disarmament, could not survive the rigors of public debate within the Catholic community. Some other formulation had to be used.

Their answer took the form of regarding at least some form of deterrence—and hence some possible use of nuclear weapons—as at least morally neutral and hence "acceptable" though hardly good in itself. This immediately raised the danger of playing into the hands of those who, in the construction of counterforce strategies of "limited" nuclear war, adopt "warfighting" and "prevailing" postures with the very great risk that nuclear war will erupt and prove, in reality, not to be limitable in any way recognizable by the survivors. This danger was real, especially in light of the administration's declaration—for example in a letter from National Security Adviser

Clark to Cardinal Bernardin, quoted in the draft, which stated, "For moral, political and military reasons, the United States does not target the Soviet civilian population as such." In so doing the administration seemed to be implying that adoption of a counterforce strategy and avoiding targeting population centers *per se* (the traditional just war criterion of discrimination, advocated by the Bishops as *one necessary* condition) very nearly is a *sufficient* condition for such a deterrent. In the Bishops' opinion it most certainly is not, and they were not about to give some sort of "Good Housekeeping Seal of Approval" to limited nuclear war. Rather, they expressed the severest doubts about "the notion that nuclear war is subject to precise rational and moral limits," and about the likelihood that "a purely counterforce strategy may seem to threaten the viability of other nations' retaliatory forces, making deterrence unstable and war more likely."

To buttress this position the Bishops invoked two other traditional just war criteria, those of proportionality and reasonable hope of success. After acknowledging the administration's statement about not deliberately striking civilians they nevertheless say:

> The statement does not address or resolve another very troublesome problem, which is that an attack on military targets or militarily significant industrial targets could involve "indirect" (i.e., unintended) but massive civilian casualties. We are advised, for example, that the United States nuclear targeting plan (SIOP) has identified 60 "military" targets within the city of Moscow alone, and that 40,000 "military" targets for nuclear weapons have been identified in the whole of the Soviet Union. . . . While any judgment of proportionality is always open to differing evaluations, there are actions which can be decisively judged to be disproportionate. A narrow adherence exclusively to the principle of non-combatant immunity as a criterion for policy is an inadequate moral posture for it ignores some evil and unacceptable consequences.

They further note that "a purely counterforce strategy may seem to threaten the viability of other nations' retaliatory forces, making deterrence unstable and war more likely," and warn that "Modern warfare is not readily contained by good intentions or technological designs." And elsewhere in their discussion of limited nuclear war they invoke the third criterion: "One of the criteria of the just war tradition is for a reasonable hope of success in bringing about justice and peace. We must ask whether such a reasonable hope can exist once nuclear weapons have been exchanged. The burden of proof remains on those who assert that meaningful limitation is possible."

Their "profound skepticism about the moral acceptability of any use of nuclear weapons" leads them to a declaration and an implicit threat:

> It is precisely this mix of political, psychological and technological uncertainty which has moved us in this letter to reinforce with moral prohibitions and prescriptions the prevailing political barrier against resort to nuclear weapons. Our support for enhanced command and control facilities, for major reductions in strategic and tactical nuclear forces, and for a "No First Use" policy (as set forth in this letter) is meant to be seen as a complement to our desire to draw a moral line against nuclear war.

Any claim, by any government, that it is pursuing a morally acceptable policy of deterrence must be scrutinized with the greatest care. We are prepared and eager to participate in our country in the on-going public debate on moral grounds.

In other words, while they are not prepared to condemn nuclear deterrence in entirety, they are aware of how easily any "strictly conditioned" acceptance can be distorted. They are aware that they have not themselves fully resolved all the dilemmas of constructing an adequate moral analysis of nuclear weaponry. They also know that public discussion of the technical and moral aspects of an acceptable deterrent strategy will long be a part of American political culture. Having already raised many of those issues in a strikingly public way, they intend to continue to take part in the debate and to ensure that their "strictly conditioned" acceptance is not perverted.

Just as the freeze proponents understand that a freeze would be only a first step, to be followed by substantial reductions in the superpowers' nuclear arsenals, the Bishops know that even a refinement and limitation of deterrence policy is hardly a satisfactory long-run solution to the risk of world catastrophe. They refer to "the historical evidence that deterrence has not, in fact, set in motion substantial processes of disarmament," and repeat the passage in Pope John Paul II's full statement on the moral acceptability of deterrence:

> In current conditions "deterrence" based on balance, certainly not as an end in itself but as a step on the way toward a progressive disarmament, may still be judged morally acceptable. Nonetheless in order to ensure peace, it is indispensable not to be satisfied with this minimum which is always susceptible to the real danger of explosion.

Their long-term vision therefore calls for "accelerated work for arms control, reduction and disarmament," "continued insistence on efforts to minimize the risk of non-nuclear war," "efforts to develop nonviolent means of conflict resolution," and the promotion of social justice in the world. Some of the latter measures seem more like distant ideals than immediate possible realities. But the role of Bishops, after all, is not only to be politically "responsible" and "realistic," but also to set forth goals worth striving for and to express a vision of hope for a better future.

The process by which this Pastoral Letter was created is perhaps fully as important as the content of the Letter. It began as an initiative by "peace" Bishops in 1981, who persuaded the entire Conference to set in motion the formal mechanism of preparing a Pastoral Letter. That process involved creation of a politically "balanced" committee that was to hear personal testimony from approximately 50 witnesses and to read voraciously in a technical and politicized literature. The Letter went through three drafts which were scrutinized in full public view. It generated an enormous volume of response within the American Catholic community, within the much larger American polity, and worldwide. Two full-scale debates on the Letter were held in view of the world's media. The division of opinion was exposed, lay participation in the debate was immense, and it was explicitly acknowledged that "on some complex social questions, the Church expects a certain diversity of views even while holding to the same general moral principles." In other words, the Bishops recognize that the moral debate on these crucial issues is, even within the church, quite out of their hands. They have begun a process of examination with great potential for their church as well as for the American political system.

---

1. Unless otherwise indicated, all references here are to the third draft of the Pastoral Letter of the National Conference of Catholic Bishops, *The Challenge of Peace: God's Promise and Our Response* (Washington: U.S. Catholic Conference, April 1983). I have been involved as the principal consultant to the Bishops' Ad Hoc Committee on War and Peace in preparing all the drafts of the document. A consultant is just that—one who can suggest, caution, and reason—but only the Bishops on the Committee possessed a vote. Probably no one, Bishop or staff, was entirely satisfied with every word in the document. My own position nevertheless is one of very great agreement with the central premises, reasoning, and conclusions of the draft; it has my wholehearted support in virtually every respect as a progressive, politically responsible statement.

2. Some observers may regard the Bishops' position on the freeze as ambiguous. The second (October 1982) draft of the Letter called for "agreements to halt the testing, production and deployment of new strategic systems." In the third draft "halt" was changed to "curb" and "strategic systems" was changed to "nuclear weapons systems." The first change, from halt to curb, is undoubtedly to introduce a weaker verb, reflecting some concern about the practicality of aspects of a freeze. But the change from strategic to nuclear is clearly to broaden the coverage, and to eliminate any impression of sympathy toward tactical nuclear weapons or notions of fighting limited nuclear war. As indicated below, elsewhere in the draft the Bishops make clear the generality of their skepticism about nuclear weapons and nuclear war. Overall, these two shifts in this passage should *not* be interpreted as a weakening of the endorsement, by the majority of the Committee, for urgent steps toward ending testing, production, and deployment. Of course, the details of this endorsement may be modified by the full body of Bishops when they vote on the document on May 3.

3. It might have been possible for them to adopt a position declaring that the threat to use nuclear weapons might be acceptable so long as one had no intention of carrying out that threat. But they wisely, in my opinion, resisted the temptation to use such an escape hatch. One reason is that they still would have had, in their moral-theological tradition, difficulty with the idea of making a threat whose execution would have been immoral. More important, it is very hard to see how the threat to use nuclear weapons could be credible in the absence of a real intent, and even more so in the absence of physical capabilities and strategic doctrine for use that would in the event of attack be extremely difficult to keep under reliable restraint. Thus some possibility of retaliatory *use* could not be entirely disavowed.

* * *

Ethical Aspects of Nuclear Freeze Proposals

Charles H. Fairbanks, Jr.

This paper represents the views of the author, and should not be construed as representing the policy of the United States Government.

In order to answer the question posed to members of this panel, "Do Freezes Satisfy Ethical Criteria?," the first order of business, clearly, is to establish what our ethical criteria are. I would argue that the ethical criteria for judging a nuclear freeze agreement are no different from the ethical criteria for judging any arms control agreement. All arms control agreements must be examined in terms of the morality of their means, the morality of their ends, and their comparative effects upon the parties to the agreement, each of which occupies a particular moral standing of his own. I propose to apply these three ethical criteria to the nuclear freeze movement.

The means by which proponents of a nuclear freeze propose to achieve arms control is by halting the additional deployment, production, and testing of nuclear weapons and nuclear launch systems. The problem arises in how we might achieve such a halt. In doing so, we may adopt courses that tend to blind people to moral reality, to the crucial ethical problems which lie at the heart of the nuclear age. Thus, instead of producing a heightened sense of moral awareness—of moral "wakefulness," if you will—the nuclear freeze movement can act as a sort of moral soporific, a means of moral evasion. Let me explain what I mean by this.

The theory of nuclear deterrence constitutes a genuine paradox: that the moral result of avoiding nuclear war was only attained through a reliance on weapons that are immoral in the destruction they threaten. In other words, immoral means have secured—and continue to secure—a moral end. And all the members of our society, insofar as we are committed to the survival of our society—and insofar, too, as we have no intellectual alternative to the policy of deterrence—are morally implicated in these evil means.

A genuine debate on the morality of a freeze would raise these issues, in much the same way that the noted theologian Paul Ramsey did in the course of an earlier debate on the ethics of nuclear war. The nuclear freeze movement, however, does not stimulate such a debate. Its moralism is ultimately self-indulgent, in that it encourages its members to feel good about themselves simply by being against nuclear weapons. It offers the cheapest way out of some very serious moral dilemmas—by saying that the problem is not in us but in "them"—meaning the government, the "militarists," the Pentagon, anyone, that is, but ourselves. It constitutes, in other words, an evasion of moral reality.

Charles H. Fairbanks, Jr. *is Deputy Assistant Secretary for Human Rights and Humanitarian Affairs of the Department of State, Washington, D.C.*

Nor is this the only ethical evasion that the nuclear freeze movement can lead to. Perhaps even more damaging, from an ethical viewpoint, is the tendency to evade or gloss over the real evils of our time in order to promote a freeze agreement. The reasoning, I believe, goes something like this: avoiding nuclear war is the most urgent task of our time; a nuclear freeze is the best means of avoiding a nuclear war; in order to secure a nuclear freeze agreement, we need to promote better Soviet–American understanding; the Soviets' invasion of Afghanistan, and their resort, either directly or through proxies, to chemical and biological weapons in Afghanistan, Laos, and Cambodia, stand in the way of better Soviet–American relations; therefore, we must play down Soviet human rights violations in Afghanistan, Laos, and Cambodia. We must, that is, be kind to the human rights violators, and cruel to the human rights victims. All this in the name of higher morality.

Turning now to the second criterion of any arms control agreement—its comparative impact on the parties to the agreement—the most obvious point to be made about the arguments for a nuclear freeze is that such considerations appear to be utterly alien to them. For example, apart from a passing reference to the need for "verifiable" agreements, considerations of the ethical standing of the Soviet Union and the U.S., and of the comparative effects of a nuclear freeze on the U.S. and the Soviet Union, are notably absent from the congressional resolutions and from the Catholic Bishops' draft pastoral letter. Yet unless one assumes that the Soviet and American political systems are ethically equivalent, it surely behooves us to ask which side will benefit more from a nuclear freeze.

To bring out the ethical dimension of this question more clearly, let me briefly review for you the 1935 Naval Treaty between Great Britain and Nazi Germany. According to the terms of this treaty, Nazi Germany could build up to 35 percent of parity with Great Britain in surface warships, but up to 100 percent of parity in submarines. That this treaty actually benefitted Nazi Germany far more than it did Great Britain should have been obvious at the time, and became tragically obvious in retrospect. The submarine, after all, is a weapon that can *only* be efficient if used inhumanely—that is, to kill civilians aboard merchant ships. For obvious reasons, Nazi Germany was more likely than Great Britain to use weapons inhumanely. An arms treaty that benefitted Nazi Germany more than Great Britain—that increased Nazi Germany's power relative to Britain's power—was, I would argue, *ethically* objectionable.

If we examine the comparative effects of a nuclear freeze on the Soviet Union and the U.S., the first point to consider, surely, is that of a total American G.N.P. of $2 trillion, the U.S. spends some 5 percent on defense. By contrast, the Soviet Union, with a G.N.P. of $1.374 trillion (1979) spends 11–13 percent on defense. In other words, the U.S.S.R. maintains military parity or better with the U.S. by devoting a much greater effort to the development of war material. (This fact alone provides a very important clue to the differences between the two countries' priorities and interests.) Given its economic and technological superiority, however, the U.S. could, in the event of a deep world political crisis, build up its strategic arsenal far more quickly than the Soviets. In preventing such a strategic buildup, a nuclear freeze would have a far more disabling impact on the U.S. than on the U.S.S.R.

The comparative impact of a freeze on the Soviet Union and the U.S. becomes clearer still if one considers the history of the postwar arms race. Between 1950 and 1964, the U.S. occupied a position of strategic superiority. From 1964–1980, the Soviet Union began an unprecedented buildup to parity and beyond.

The Soviets attained parity or better essentially through a historical accident: the effect of the Vietnam war on American defense spending and morale, on the one hand, and the policies of a new Soviet leadership, on the other hand. The freeze movement literally wants to *freeze this historical moment of relative Soviet superiority*. At a time when the Reagan Administration is beginning to reverse the imbalance in strategic nuclear forces and, equally important, intermediate nuclear forces, the proponents of a freeze want to tie its hands.

Of course, if the Soviet leadership occupied a morally higher plane than the U.S. leadership, such a result might well be ethically desirable. But in the wake of the massive Soviet human rights violations in Afghanistan, Laos, and Cambodia (not to mention Soviet violations of the human rights of its own citizens) can any ethically serious person make such an argument? Indeed, when one remembers that even between 1958 and 1961, when the Soviet Union was in a position of strategic inferiority, Khrushchev openly threatened to use nuclear weapons during the Berlin crisis, then the prospects for the survival of liberty in an era of Soviet strategic superiority are none too bright.

Yet here, once again, the nuclear freeze movement is guilty of a moral evasion. The moral reality of our time is that the world is an exceedingly dangerous place. It is dangerous because human nature is sinful, and because totalitarian political systems give freer rein than others to human sinfulness. The nuclear freeze movement concentrates not on the dangers of what imperfect human beings do and intend, but on hardware, on the existence of missiles. By failing to address the tragic dimension of human existence, by focusing all its moral energies on "technical fixes," the freeze movement loses its claim to moral seriousness. In its view that moral problems are caused not by human imperfection but by hardware, the nuclear freeze movement resembles nothing so much as the temperance movement of the 19th and early 20th centuries. This movement also sought to address problems whose origins are in the human heart—the multitude of personal vices ascribed to "demon rum"—by removing bottles of liquid from the shelves.

Would a Nuclear Freeze Diminish the Chances of Nuclear War?

Let us turn now to the question of whether nuclear freezes would be ethically attractive in terms of achieving their own ends. It has long been recognized in all moral discourse that a good man cannot be a man who destroys everything that is good by his action, nor can an action which has these consequences be evaluated as good. In the first book of Plato's *Republic* Socrates is able to refute the definition of justice as returning deposits by asking whether one would return a weapon to a madman who had deposited it with you earlier. This appeals to the common sense awareness that a morally disastrous outcome means that the action itself cannot be considered adequately moral. This logic applies to the anti-nuclear campaign with even greater force, because the end it seeks is a very practical one: the avoidance of nuclear war. If nuclear freezes do not make nuclear war less likely, or less terrible, the ethical arguments for them appear very weak. In considering whether current nuclear freeze proposals would achieve their own ends, it is useful to consider the canonical aims of arms control, as defined many years ago: decreasing the chance of war, and limiting the terrible consequences if it should occur. The latter question is simpler so we can address it first.

The nuclear freeze movement, and the present anti-nuclear movement in general, obviously rests on a sense that nuclear war is a real possibility. If it is a real possibility, it would be morally irresponsible to block measures that would limit nuclear war if it did occur—with the important reservation that any measures taken to limit the damage of nuclear war should not have the simultaneous effect of making the transition to some form of nuclear war more likely. One of the most obvious effects of nuclear freeze proposals is to stall the movement which has been taking place towards creating a capability to avoid civilian targets in nuclear warfare, minimize collateral damage, and direct nuclear war if possible toward military rather than civilian targets. The freeze proposals have this tendency because they would ban the testing of new technologies which are necessary to develop such capabilities—although the rather limited and unsophisticated range of technology which is to be controlled in current freeze proposals will have a partial and random effect on such innovations. It would be misleading to think that in discussing whether technologies permitting more limited forms of nuclear war should be stalled, we are discussing primarily the limitation of the effects of war if it should break out. This is a frequent mistake in debates over the limited nuclear war issue. Most of the thinkers who have devised strategic doctrines involving more limited forms of nuclear war have understood that the chance of limiting a nuclear war once it begins is very small. But they have felt that the consequences of an all-out nuclear war are so unspeakable that it would be irresponsible not to seize whatever small chances there might be to limit nuclear war once it was beginning. This aim is still a morally compelling one, but a secondary aim and one that is very delicate in the light of the need not to make nuclear war an ordinary instrument of policy. But the primary interest of the thinkers who have tried to develop doctrines and technologies that would limit nuclear war has actually been not in the limitation but in the prevention of war. The extreme consequences of the decision to attack cities with nuclear weapons create enormous uncertainty about the conditions under which such an attack would actually be carried out. And since deterrence relies on an expectation that nuclear weapons would be used under certain circumstances, the extreme consequences that underlie the logic of deterrence also tend to undermine it. It can easily become highly uncertain which conventional war actions will be met with a nuclear response. The primary interest, at least since the mid-60s, in limiting nuclear war has been to fortify the credibility of deterrence, and thus to make nuclear war less likely. The current nuclear freeze proposals will obviously interfere with efforts in this direction.

The decisive question about whether a nuclear freeze would achieve its ends is evidently whether it will decrease the chances of nuclear war. It is usually assumed that a freeze would do so, without examination of how it would do so. In fact, if one thinks about the issue, it begins to seem that a nuclear freeze would increase the chances of nuclear war. The freeze intends to halt the development of strategic nuclear forces at this point in history. This point in history is a point at which land-based ICBMs have ceased to be invulnerable to a disarming counterforce attack. In other words land-based ICBMs, as now deployed, have ceased to be a good deterrent, and have become a magnet that attacks preemptive attack. That is, these weapons are now creating an increased chance of war. But at this point in history the United States has not yet put into place new technologies that would overcome this problem, such as the MX/CSB system. Thus the major effect of a nuclear freeze would be to *prolong the age of simple land-based ICBMs past the point at which they continue to serve deterrence.* There is no escaping the fact that there is presently one factor in the "arms race" which creates the greatest danger of nuclear war: the vulnerability of land-based ICBMs. The current nuclear freeze proposals do nothing to help with this problem. Instead they make it worse. By prohibiting the testing and deployment of new systems, they block the technical improvements which might diminish or eliminate this problem. (Not only survivable land-based systems such as the MX, but even taking our missiles to sea would be excluded by current nuclear freeze proposals.) There can be no question that the current nuclear freeze proposals would increase the chance of nuclear war. Nothing could be more immoral than this outcome.

It is worth analyzing a little further why proposals for a nuclear freeze negate their own aim. Such proposals represent a retrogression in thinking about arms control. They are based on an unsophisticated and simplistic view according to which the problem is "the arms race," undifferentiated. Since Samuel P. Huntington discussed the difference between qualitative and quantitative arms races in 1958, arms control thinking began to attain much more precise understanding of the complex processes summarized under the label "arms race" and where in these processes the problem lies. Since the work of Albert Wohlstetter, Andrew Marshall, and Graham Allison over a decade ago, it has been realized that the traditional understanding of the arms race as an action/reaction process between the two sides is highly misleading. It has come to be realized by many thinkers about arms control that not all weapons increase the danger of war. Historically certain weapons developments such as missile silos and ballistic missiles for submarines have played an essential role in keeping war at a distance. The nuclear freeze proposals completely lack any awareness of these factors. They are completely indiscriminate on their face. The intention is to freeze *all* nuclear weapons. And this simply does not address the problem.

The intellectual background of the nuclear freeze movement is in fact the simplistic notion that nuclear warheads and launch vehicles are the essense of deterrence. As Elliott Abrams pointed out in his speech "Nuclear Weapons: What Is the Moral Response?" prosaic and civilian substances, like cement for missile silos, have played a decisive role in the development of deterrence. A nuclear freeze proposal that does not cover areas such as hardening technology, ASW, and command and control would be a kind of gesture. It would cover items that are symbols, simply because they are bigger, but not those that really make the difference for war or for peace. On the other hand, if nuclear freeze proposals were made more sophisticated and tried to control more technological aspects affecting deterrence, they might end up in an attempt to control the whole development of technology, civilian as well as military. Is it practical to control cement?

This problem is heightened by the well-known mechanism by which armed forces and nations react to arms control agreements. They characteristically divert energy and funds from the systems limited into aspects which are not limited. The Washington Naval Treaty of 1921 limited battleships, at the cost of diverting effort into cruisers and aircraft carriers. The current nuclear freeze proposals have no means of dealing with this problem and seem to be unaware of its existence.

Let us consider for a moment how arms control proposals have been able to achieve their aims. To genuinely decrease the chances of war, arms control proposals need to make use of—not ignore—the current state of technological development and the current international situation. Two examples of arms limitation agreements, in the broadest sense, illustrate this.

In 1908–1909 the follow-up meeting to the Second Hague Peace Conference met to codify and refine limitations on maritime warfare, and specifically limits on the vulnerability of peaceful commerce to wartime action. Two important provisions of the resulting Declaration of London were a great narrowing of the contraband list and the failure to apply the doctrine of continuous voyage to conditional contraband. Under the first provision items essential for war such as rubber, aircraft, oil, coal, metallic ores, and foodstuffs could not be seized at all (that is, they were "free goods") or could be seized only if bound for an enemy port ("conditional contraband"). In the case of conditional contraband such goods were liable to capture only if destined for an enemy port and to the enemy government; the doctrine of continuous voyage, by which goods destined for an adjacent neutral port for forwarding to the enemy could be seized, did not apply. At the beginning of World War I, these provisions of the Declaration of London were rapidly abandoned, first by the Allies, and then by the Central Powers. The reasons are clear. These limitations did not realistically correspond to the state of technology nor to the international situation. In the late 19th century technological development had made the possession of an industrial base for war all important. This meant that items such as ores, rubber, and foodstuffs were truly as important for making war as weapons themselves. At the same time the development of railroads had made it easy to transfer goods from neutral ports to belligerent countries, making the failure to apply the doctrine of continuous voyage to conditional contraband unreasonable. Both of these provisions of the Declaration of London were profoundly opposed to the interests of the strongest naval power, Great Britain, and therefore bound to be broken in any war that Great Britain was a party to. In fact the Declaration of London was not even ratified by Great Britain.

Other arms control agreements have been successes because they used constructively the existing state of technology and the international situation. For hundreds of years, privateering was a recognized mode of naval warfare. It was certainly an undesirable thing, because it tended to obliterate the distinction between warfare and piracy and involved peaceful commerce in the business of war. Privateering was finally outlawed by the Congress of Paris in 1856. The statesmen who met at Paris seized this opportunity to exploit the changes that were taking place in technology. Because of the invention of steam propulsion and iron hulls for ships, warships and commercial vessels were becoming increasingly differentiated. This development made privateering a less attractive form of naval warfare. Those who worked to limit warfare at the Congress of Paris built on technological and political realities rather than fighting them. Future arms control initiatives in the West should attempt to do the same rather than ignoring realities and basing themselves on simplistic perceptions of the problems as current nuclear freeze proposals do.

* * *

Soviet Interests and Initiatives

Moscow's Arms Control Agenda

Stephen J. Flanagan

The statements contained herein reflect the author's opinions alone, and do not necessarily represent the views of the Select Committee on Intelligence or any other U.S. government entity.

While commentary emanating from Moscow has fostered the perception that the Kremlin supports the goals of the nuclear freeze movement in the United States, the Soviet leadership has studiously avoided official endorsement of specific freeze proposals. The Soviets have expressed more explicit approval of the aims of the various West European groups opposed to the deployment of U.S. intermediate-range nuclear forces (INF) in their countries. During the past few months, the Kremlin has been uncharacteristically public in delineating its own arms control agenda, and it differs considerably from the comprehensive freeze proposals. Soviet leaders have expressed interest in interim freezes during formal negotiations leading to reductions in the number of deployed nuclear weapons delivery vehicles and qualitative restraints on certain weapons systems which they find destabilizing. However, senior Soviet officials have made it clear that modernization of their nuclear forces will remain an essential requirement of their national security planning and would be allowed under the several arms control accords they have proposed.

Since both Moscow and Washington have lately been treating arms control as a component of public diplomacy, as was the fashion in the 1950s, rather than a matter for quiet diplomatic bargaining, which was characteristic of negotiations during the past 15 years, it is a fairly straightforward task to sketch the kinds of nuclear weapons freezes or other arms limitation arrangements that are favored by the Kremlin. It is a much more speculative endeavor to assess the kinds of arms control regimes Moscow is likely to accept under various circumstances and the political and strategic opportunity costs of pursuing certain negotiations with the Soviets. Nonetheless, this essay addresses each of these issues briefly. Much of the analysis is drawn from a review of the Soviet media and statements by the Kremlin leadership.

Moscow's policy preferences are a manifestation of its long-standing approach to arms control and of certain military and economic realities. Soviet arms control diplomacy has consistently reflected a determination to control the risks of war and to constrain improvements in U.S. military capabilities that could result in a shift in

Stephen J. Flanagan *is a Professional Staff Member of the Select Committee on Intelligence, United States Senate, Washington, D.C.*

the balance of forces. A bilateral freeze on Soviet and American nuclear weapons would not eliminate third country threats to Soviet security. It is evident from Moscow's recent proposals for an INF agreement as well as from its statements that the START negotiations must take into account "the general strategic situation in the world," that the Soviets believe the military threats posed by China in the coming years require that any bilateral arms control arrangements must allow for improvements in Soviet offensive, and probably defensive, nuclear capabilities designed to deal with this problem.

Another factor likely to inhibit Moscow's acceptance of a comprehensive nuclear freeze is the conversion of the large segments of the country's scientific, industrial, and technical communities involved in nuclear weapons programs to other military and non-military endeavors that such an accord would require. Such a conversion could not be achieved without severe economic dislocation and alienation of important political forces.

Given this political and military context, negotiations on a comprehensive nuclear freeze run the risk of diverting effort from more pressing and achievable arms limitations.

Soviet Statements on the Freeze and Their "Freeze" Concepts

The Soviets have advocated a number of informal, interim freezes or moratoria on nuclear weapons deployments, ostensibly to help establish a climate conducive to success in formal arms control negotiations.

For example, in February 1981, President Brezhnev proposed a moratorium on the "establishment" of new facilities in Europe for NATO and Soviet medium-range nuclear missiles that would extend from the time negotiations on the limitation or reduction of such facilities commenced until the time a permanent treaty was concluded. Of course, on March 16, 1982, soon after the INF negotiations began, Brezhnev announced that he had imposed a unilateral moratorium on the deployment of "medium-range nuclear armaments" in the European U.S.S.R. specifically noting a "freeze" on deployment of SS-20 IRBMs.[1] Since that time, the Soviets have continued to caution, in increasingly threatening tones, that this freeze on SS-20 deployments is conditioned on reversal of NATO's plans to deploy 108 Pershing II MRBMs and 464 ground-launched cruise missiles (GLCMs) in Europe as well as conclusion of an accord limiting all medium-range nuclear weapons systems.

Similarly, in a speech to the Komsomol Congress on May 18, 1982, Brezhnev expressed Moscow's interest in an interim, quantitative freeze on Soviet and American strategic armaments, coupled with restrictions on force modernization, as soon as negotiations on strategic arms reduction reconvened. This freeze was also couched as a measure that would facilitate "headway toward radical limitation and reduction" of strategic arms by precluding actions that would upset the stability of the strategic situation.[2]

The timing of both these Soviet "freeze" proposals suggests they were designed primarily to intensify Allied and domestic pressure on the Reagan Administration to commence the INF and START negotiations and to forestall deployment of the INF systems and the MX ICBM. Nonetheless, it is revealing that these informal freezes would not preclude force modernization.

The Soviets adopted an analogous stance on nuclear testing at the 1982 U.N. Special Session on Disarmament. The U.S.S.R. proposed, among other things, a moratorium on all nuclear tests, including peaceful nuclear explosions, once trilateral negotiations on a comprehensive test ban treaty resumed.

Perhaps the most explicit official Soviet pronouncement on the various Western freeze proposals was made by the late President Brezhnev, and his comments underscore the Kremlin's reluctance to give all but the most general endorsement of the freeze concept. In his June 15, 1982 message to the U.N. Special Session on Disarmament, Brezhnev remarked that the Western freeze proposals "on the whole . . . go in the right direction."[3] The Soviet leader also stated that the idea of a mutual freeze of nuclear arsenals as a first step towards their reduction ". . . is close to the Soviet point of view."

Foreign Minister Gromyko provided further insight into the type of freeze the U.S.S.R. might find acceptable during his October 1, 1982 speech to the U.N. General Assembly when he characterized the Brezhnev strategic moratorium as his country's "concrete response" to calls for a freeze on the existing level of nuclear arms.[4] This stance seemed to be reaffirmed by Chairman Andropov in his November 22 speech to the CPSU Central Committee and in his report, "60 Years of the U.S.S.R.," on December 2, 1982.[5]

Soviet media commentary has also reflected this strategy of general endorsement of the freeze concept coupled with favorable discussion of more traditional arms control arrangements. For example, in an early November 1982 English-language radio program, the Soviet commentator noted that while the U.S.S.R. "supports a nuclear freeze," every favorable Soviet statement about the concept is used by opponents of arms control in the U.S. to prove that the freeze is in the Kremlin's interest. Yet, the Soviet observer went on to elaborate Moscow's arms control goals by extolling the virtues of SALT II.[6]

Thus the Soviets appear to favor a quantitative freeze on Soviet and American strategic arms, coupled with stiff, but undefined restrictions on force modernizations that might upset "the stability of the strategic situation" while the START negotiations are underway. Such an amorphous, declaratory freeze would grant Moscow considerable flexibility in deciding which U.S. force improvements would be destabilizing.

Soviet Arms Control Proposals

Given the Kremlin's enunciated views on the freeze and its preference for interim deployment moratoria while formal agreements are hammered out in the various negotiating fora, the types of nuclear arms limitation arrangements the Soviet leadership appears to favor remain to be considered.

In early 1983, Soviet officials publicly expressed their interest in concluding a strategic arms agreement which would reduce the total number of strategic nuclear delivery vehicles to 1800 units, a 25 percent cut in existing Soviet forces. It is worth recalling that this 1800 figure is the same limitation on strategic delivery systems advanced in the Carter Administration's March 1977 "Deep Cuts" proposal, albeit without that earlier concept's coordinate subceiling of 150 on heavy ICBMs. This delivery vehicle ceiling would be accompanied by as yet unspecified reductions in the total number of "nuclear charges" (bombs and warheads) in the Soviet and American operational inventories to equal levels. A *Pravda* editorial of January 2, 1983 stated that this proposal presupposes no increase in U.S. nuclear forces capable of reaching targets in the U.S.S.R.[7] This noncircumvention concept reflects the Soviets' continuing desire to develop an explicit linkage between negotiations on strategic arms and intermediate-range nuclear force deployments.

The Soviet START proposal reportedly contains certain qualitative limitations, including prohibitions on new types of weapons. In particular, the proposal calls for a ban on all types of cruise missiles with a range in excess of 600 kilometers. The Soviet concept also includes limitations on modernization according to certain unspecified parameters.

Pravda reported that the Soviet proposal also advances a number of confidence-building measures such as: bans on flights of heavy bombers and cruising of aircraft carriers in certain zones along the periphery of the U.S. and the U.S.S.R.; advance notification of "mass takeoff" of forward-based heavy bombers and aircraft; and establishment of zones for the operation of ballistic missile-carrying submarines in which anti-submarine warfare (ASW) activities would be proscribed. The first two measures underscore further Moscow's interest in linking U.S. forward-based systems to START. The ASW-free zones concept is an old one, but enhancing the survivability of their SSBNs through arms control measures is certain to be an increasingly important Soviet objective as a larger percentage of Soviet strategic weapons are deployed at sea.

The most complete exposition of Soviet INF proposals came in General Secretary Andropov's December 21 report, "Sixty Years of the U.S.S.R." Andropov noted the initial Soviet proposal called for NATO and the U.S.S.R. to reduce the level of their medium-range nuclear weaponry deployed in Europe by more than two-thirds. This concept implies a ceiling of roughly 300 on "medium-range systems" since, according to the Soviet count, there is rough parity (975 for the U.S.S.R. and 986 for NATO) in this category of weapons delivery systems.[8] Announcing a slight variation of their opening stance, Andropov expressed Moscow's willingness to reduce the number of medium-range missiles deployed in the European U.S.S.R. to a number equal to the aggregate missile forces of France and the United Kingdom so long as the U.S. halted deployment of the 572 Pershing II and ground-launched cruise missiles. In tandem with such a pact, the Soviets would like to reach an accord reducing to equal levels the number of medium-range nuclear-capable aircraft deployed by NATO and the U.S.S.R. in Europe.

While Andropov's offer marks a retreat from earlier Soviet insistence that missiles and aircraft be addressed in the same accord, its overall significance is, as yet, unclear. The scope of reductions under the new scheme might not be much different than under the concept of a ceiling of 300 on medium-range systems. However, the new plan would constrain Soviet freedom to mix the composition of medium-range forces by precluding deployment of more than 162 missile systems. However, missile deployment in the eastern U.S.S.R. would clearly be unconstrained. Furthermore, Andropov did not indicate whether the Soviets are willing to dismantle the launchers, missiles, and support facilities in the European U.S.S.R. for the SS-20s and other medium-range systems. Without dismantling, SS-20s could be stored at facilities east of the Urals and reintroduced into the western U.S.S.R. during periods of heightened tension.

Andropov did not specify the scope of the aircraft limitations, and previous Soviet statements suggest that most U.S. forward-based aircraft, as well as some deployed in the continental U.S., would be subject to accounting. Nevertheless, this proposal does appear worth probing. If this is not Moscow's last best offer, as some Soviet commentary has hinted, there would appear to be room for compromise. Indeed the July 1982 Nitze-Kvitsinsky "understanding" on INF limitations suggests that there may be some flexibility in the Kremlin's position on several of these key issues.[9]

Would the Soviets Be Interested in a Freeze?

Given the Soviet positions outlined thus far, it is conceivable that the Soviets might be willing to enter into an informal moratorium or a negotiated freeze on further deployments of strategic nuclear weapons systems and would welcome a freeze on deployment of new intermediate-range delivery vehicles. However, it is most *unlikely* that Moscow would embrace a freeze on testing and production of all nuclear weapons systems.

In looking at likely trends in the strategic balance, the Kremlin has undoubtedly realized, as Stephen Meyer illustrates elsewhere in this volume, that a freeze on strategic force *deployments* at the current level is much more favorable to Soviet interests than the unconstrained situation in the late 1980s is apt to be if all U.S. force modernization initiatives are realized. However, in order to accept a freeze on modernization and production of nuclear weapons, Soviet leaders would have to be relatively content with the existing capabilities of their forces. Such a sense of satisfaction is not reflected in their ongoing weapons improvement programs.

A comprehensive freeze would preclude several aspects of Soviet strategic force modernization that the military finds desirable in the context of the current U.S. threat. Even with the limited existing U.S. counterforce capability, the fact that 80 percent of their strategic missile warheads are fitted on fixed ICBMs makes Soviet planners uneasy. The Strategic Rocket Forces have already identified a requirement for a solid-fueled, mobile ICBM to alleviate their vulnerability problem, a problem whose solution would become even more urgent if the MX ICBM is deployed. The Soviets are also working on a number of programs designed to enhance the effectiveness and survivability of their sea-based missile force. The Soviet Navy is still in the early phases of deploying MIRVed SLBMs. Soviet SLBMs, including some of the newest missiles, have not demonstrated a high level of reliability. The deployment of new, long-range SLBMs that enable Soviet SSBNs to operate closer to home ports, thereby reducing their vulnerability to hostile ASW capabilities, would likewise remain an important goal unless some arms control arrangement imposed restrictions on ASW. This enhancement of intercontinental forces is complemented by similar improvements in intermediate, medium, and short-range nuclear delivery systems.

In contrast, the Soviet air forces have a new intercontinental bomber, the Blackjack, under development. The Blackjack program is hardly the most valued component of their strategic force modernization program, and the Soviets could accept strict limitations on its deployment so long as the U.S. B-1B were also constrained. Similarly, Soviet officials, reflecting concern with the U.S. technological edge, have stated publicly that they have a long-range cruise missile program under development which they would be willing to forfeit in the context of a START agreement that banned all such systems.

Realization of a comprehensive freeze would require not only a dramatic reduction in international tensions, but a fundamental shift of political power within the Soviet system. It is evident that the military and other powerful forces in the Soviet polity would object strenuously to any consideration of a freeze on the testing and production of nuclear weapons. At this point in the leadership transition, it is unclear whether the Soviet military's influence over resource allocation is increasing or declining. However, a December 9, 1982 article in *Krasnaya Zvezda* by General A. Gurov reflects the military's likely objections to a freeze on the production and modernization of nuclear weapons. Echoing similar recent statements by members of the General Staff, Gurov argues that the pace of modern weapons competition requires that every major weapons system must be completely replaced every 10-12 years and that this can only be accomplished by the maintenance of a dynamic economy and an "advanced scientific and technical potential."[10] This disposition, coupled with the problems of conversion that Stephen Meyer discusses, make realization of a comprehensive freeze unlikely.

Alternative Approaches

Negotiations for a comprehensive freeze would raise public expectations in the West that could probably not be fulfilled, leading to a disillusionment of the valuable support for arms control that now exists. Despite its superficial simplicity, negotiation of a comprehensive freeze would undoubtedly involve a very lengthy process of hammering out an agreement laden with understandings about maintenance and reliability testing of frozen nuclear weapons systems and allowances for nuclear-capable conventional weapons that would make the SALT II treaty look simple.

The history of SALT—particularly SALT II—demonstrates that broad, complex arms control arrangements are difficult to negotiate. Implementation of such accords has been encumbered by compliance disputes that often turn on differences in interpretation of intricate limitations, which undermines public confidence in the process. Given the Soviet wariness of a comprehensive freeze and these lessons of the SALT experience, Western diplomatic efforts could be more productive if devoted to building an arms control regime comprised of an interrelated series of very narrow agreements that impose strict controls on the most destabilizing weapons testing and deployment activities.

1. "Text of Brezhnev Speech to the Congress of Soviet Trade Unions," *Tass*, March 16, 1982. In *Foreign Broadcast Information Service (FBIS) Daily Report-Soviet Union*, March 16, 1982, p. R8.

2. "Text of Brezhnev Speech to Komsomol Congress," *Tass*, May 18, 1982. *FBIS-Soviet Union*, May 18, 1982. p. R5.

3. "Brezhnev Message to U.N. Disarmament Session," *Tass*, June 15, 1982. *FBIS-Soviet Union*, June 16, 1982, p. AA2.

4. "Gromyko Statement at 37th U.N. General Assembly," *Tass*, October 1, 1982. *FBIS-Soviet Union*, October 4, 1982, p. CC8.

5. "Andropov Plenum Speech," *Tass*, November 22, 1982. *FBIS-Soviet Union*, November 23, 1982, p. R9 and "Andropov Report—Sixty Years of the U.S.S.R.," *Tass*, December 21, 1982. *FBIS-Soviet Union*, December 21, 1982, pp. P9-10.

6. "Commentary on U.S. Arms Freeze Movement," Radio Moscow, November 5, 1982. *FBIS-Soviet Union*, November 8, 1982, p. AA1.

7. "The USSR and the USA—Two Approaches to START," *Pravda*, January 2, 1983. *FBIS-Soviet Union*, January 3, 1983, pp. AA1-5.

8. The Soviet tally of NATO forces includes: U.S. and German Pershing I missiles; British Polaris missiles and Vulcan bombers; French IRBMs, SLBMs and Mirage-4 bombers; and U.S. carrier-based aircraft (F-4, A-6, A-7), other aircraft in Europe (F-111), as well as U.S. FB-111s based in the continental United States. Moscow's count of its own forces is: 496 land-based missiles (SS-20, 4, 5); 18 SLBMs (SS-N-5); and 461 medium-range bombers (Backfires, Badgers and Blinders). See Leslie H. Gelb, "Moscow Indicates Easing of Stance on Cuts in Missiles," *New York Times*, December 12, 1982, pp. 1 and 22.

9. See John Newhouse, "Arms and Allies," *New Yorker*, February 28, 1983, pp. 70 and 73.

10. General A. Gurov, "Combat Readiness of the Soviet Armed Forces," *Krasnaya Zvezda*, December 9, 1982. *FBIS-Soviet Union*, December 21, 1982, p. V2.

* * *

Soviet Military Programs and the Freeze

Stephen M. Meyer

Introduction

At the time of the signing of the SALT II treaty in 1979, President Jimmy Carter is reported to have raised the possibility of a total freeze on nuclear weapons with Soviet President Brezhnev. Brezhnev's immediate response was: nyet! In contrast, the Brezhnev leadership in 1982 made a number of public statements evincing a willingness to discuss a nuclear freeze. Are recent Soviet expressions of interest in a nuclear freeze mere propaganda—part of the Soviet peace offensive as many in the West believe? Or, have changes in "objective conditions" over the last several years provided incentives for the Soviet political and military leadership to consider a freeze seriously?

This brief paper attempts to explore two areas where relevant changes may have occurred: Soviet military programs and the Soviet economy. Specifically, three hypotheses are examined:

1. A freeze in 1983 would be significantly less disruptive to Soviet military programs and military-industrial plans than a freeze in 1979.
2. There were significant changes in Soviet perceptions of relative and absolute U.S.–Soviet operational capabilities between 1979 and 1983.
3. A freeze on nuclear weapons (including their production and testing) offer opportunities to improve the Soviet economy, and Soviet leaders would feel free to take advantage of those opportunities.

1978–1982

Table 1 is a listing of major Soviet nuclear weapons systems that were in production for deployment between 1970 and 1982.[1] When the data are aggregated, the result is a time-series plot of the number of Soviet nuclear weapons systems (undergoing deployment) in production as is shown in Figure 1. Between 1973 and 1979 the number of such programs in production increased three-fold. Indeed the reputed Carter freeze initiative occurred right at the peak in Soviet production effort.

Figure 2 breaks the data up into intercontinental attack systems and peripheral attack systems, and reveals an interesting pattern. On the one hand, intercontinental attack programs show a fairly stable production effort with a base of four programs in production in a given year. A noticeable bulge can be seen during the period 1973–1980. We see that production related to Soviet intercontinental attack missions was in the midst of a cyclical surge precisely when the Carter freeze was suggested. On the other hand, programs in production related to peripheral attack missions start from practically a "zero" base and grow substantially over the entire period. In other words, the Soviets were conducting a massive modernization of their entire INF pos-

Stephen M. Meyer is Associate Professor of Political Science at the Massachusetts Institute of Technology, Cambridge, Massachusetts.

ture from short-range battlefield missiles and tactical aircraft to long-range IRBMs and intermediate-range bombers), which peaked in 1980. Reasonable projections of production rates, deployment rates, and force posture requirements suggest that a significant decline in activity could not occur before 1983–1985.

One can hardly imagine a period during which a freeze on nuclear weapons testing, production, and deployment would have had more disruptive effects on the Soviet military industries and its industrial economy in general—not to mention military planning. In particular, the Soviet system of central planning and direct resource allocation severely constrains options for flexibility and real-time revision of 5-year industrial plans and associated (in-phase) ten-year military production plans. Once the plan is underway, a kind of industrial "grid-lock" occurs that imposes high costs on any major change. Consequently, since military production has such a cen-

TABLE I
Soviet Nuclear Weapons Programs in Production 1970-1982

Weapons Type	Core Years in Production
ICBMs	
SS-9	1970-1972
SS-11	1970
SS-13	1970-1972
SS-17	1975-1980
SS-18	1975-1980
SS-19	1975-1979
SLBMs	
SS-N-6	1970-1974
SS-N-8	1973-1977
SS-NX-17	1978-1979
SS-N-18	1978-
SS-NX-20	1982-
SSBNs	
Y-CLASS	1970-1975
D-CLASS	1973-1982
TYPHOON	1982-
INF-SSMs	
SS-20	1977-1982
SS-21	1978-
SS-22	1979-
SS-23	1980-
INF-SLCMs	
SS-N-12	1979-
SS-N-19	1980-
INF-AIRCRAFT	
MIG-27	1971-
Tu-26	1974-
Su-17	1974-
Su-24	1974-
INF-ASMs	
AS-6	1977-

FIGURE 1: Total Number of Soviet Nuclear Weapons Programs in Production for Deployment

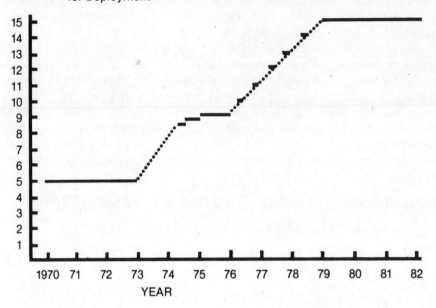

FIGURE 2: Soviet Nuclear Weapons Programs in Production—Peripheral Attack vs. Intercontinental Attack

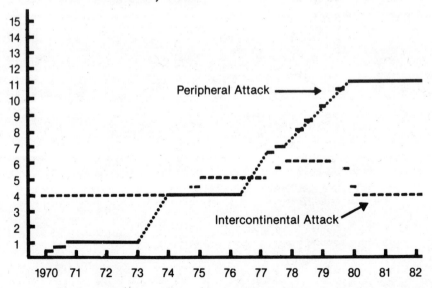

tral position in the Soviet economy there are very strong economic-industrial disincentives against major alterations of the military-industrial plan once it is in place. Thus, even ignoring military considerations, the Soviet rejection of the Carter freeze offer is fully understandable.

It was during this period that the long coveted and long pursued capability to destroy hardened military targets in the U.S. (e.g., ICBM silos) first began to come within reach. This represented a fundamentally new operational capability for Soviet intercontinental attack forces. The theoretical ability to implement the basic principles of Soviet military strategy in the struggle against U.S. strategic nuclear forces was being made possible by the production of the Soviets' first reliable, high alert, accurate MIRVed ICBMs: the SS-18 and SS-19.

In the peripheral theaters the ability to destroy all soft and hardened targets (e.g., nuclear storage igloos) had been within the range of Soviet operational capabilities for well over a decade. SS-4 and SS-5 regional missiles were sufficient to cover all prospective soft targets (e.g., airbases), while the combination of LRA intermediate bombers and peripherally targeted ICBMs (about 120 targeted on Western Europe) provided the means for hard target strikes. In this respect, the introduction of neither the SS-20 IRBM nor the BACKFIRE bomber can be said to have provided Soviet military planners with any categorically new operational capabilities. Yet, the Soviet theater posture was significantly enhanced by the acquisition of these weapons. Here, critical improvements revolved around reducing operational uncertainties: much improved systems reliability, greater force readiness, reduced maintenance and logistical requirements, enhanced C^3 responses, greater targeting flexibility and versatility, and improved survivability.[2] No doubt, these weapons and the improvements in the Soviet force posture they brought at that time were deemed critical by Soviet military planners.

The modernization of Soviet short-range TNF (SRTNF) during this period was the first such full scale effort in over a decade and a half. Here as well, no new operational capabilities emerged, but improvements related to reducing operational uncertainties were made. Unlike the case of the longer-range TNF systems, however, improvements in SRTNF operational capabilities were of considerably less priority to Soviet military planners.

Meanwhile, the U.S. was going about the task of eliminating or otherwise scaling back many of its planned nuclear weapons programs. The B-1 bomber and enhanced radiation battlefield weapon programs are two examples. To some extent, Soviet perceptions that President Carter might unilaterally restrain U.S. nuclear weaons programs may have led them to believe that a "window of opportunity" for one-sided nuclear modernization had been briefly opened. Indeed, the U.S. was not about to add any new operational capabilities, nor significantly enhance existing operational capabilities.

In sum, the period 1978-1982 was one in which Soviet leaders had every reason to expect that important new operational capabilities and important improvements to the existing force posture were going to be acquired by the Soviet Union, while no significant change in U.S. operational capabilities was likely to occur.

1983-1988

What about 1983 and the years beyond? As Soviet ICBM production for deployment winds down, four new ICBMs are in R&D. Since full scale testing has only begun on one design, none are likely to be slated for production at this time. Moreover, while the ICBM is the preferred Soviet weapon for intercontinental attack for a variety of reasons, under SALT II the Soviets did agree to test and deploy only one new ICBM. The allowance for one new ICBM permits the Soviet military to pursue the one intercontinental attack weapon that they deem important, but that has eluded them for two decades: a reliable and mobile solid-fueled ICBM. Nevertheless, Soviet willingness to accept a major limitation on their normally robust ICBM development programs indicates a basic satisfaction with their present ICBM posture—largely a product of recent deployments.

None of the Soviet ICBMs on the drawing boards can be expected to offer fundamentally new operational capabilities. The most important changes already were accomplished with the deployment of the current generation of Soviet ICBMs. In contrast, the MX does hold out the possibility (if procured in sufficient quantity) of giving the U.S. the operational capability to destroy an array of hard targets in the U.S.S.R. The U.S. would regain an operational capability it has lacked for well over a decade and a half. Moreover, if the MX is deployed in a mobile/deceptive basing mode, the result will be a serious decline in Soviet operational capabilities—irrespective of any new Soviet ICBMs that might be deployed. In other words, Soviet operational capabilities would be better in a world where neither the U.S. nor the Soviet Union deployed a new ICBM than in a world where both did. Consequently, I believe that the Soviet military, much aware that deployment of the MX would seriously undermine newly attained Soviet operational capabilities to attack U.S. ICBMs and that MX will be far superior to any Soviet analogue, would accede to freeze on all ICBMs—"sacrificing" deployment of their own mobile solid-fueled ICBM—if it meant halting testing, production, and deployment of the MX.

The TYPHOON/SS-NX-20 program, now underway, is solidifying the capabilities attained with the DELTA/SS-N-18 program: reliable SLBM coverage of the U.S. homeland from "controlled and protected" deployment areas adjacent to the Soviet Union. In appearance if not substance, this is the counterpart to the U.S. TRIDENT I program. The TRIDENT II program, however, may be seen as being far in advance of Soviet R&D capabilities and more importantly as the most pressing threat to Soviet ICBMs and other hardened military structures in the presence of freeze on ICBMs stopping the MX program. Moreover, for technical, internal, and institutional reasons a Soviet TRIDENT II counterpart is not likely to have high priority among the Soviet political and military leadership—especially in comparison to a new mobile solid-fueled ICBM. For these reasons, the Soviet military might look favorably upon an SLBM freeze that set equivalence between the TRIDENT I and the SS-NX-20, while blocking testing, production, and deployment of the TRIDENT II and its putative Soviet counterpart.

Missions and roles for long-range bombers in intercontinental attack planning have not figured prominently in Soviet military writings for two decades. The arthritic pace with which the new BLACKJACK (Ram-P) long-range bomber has moved through R&D—the first such bomber in two decades—underscores its low priority in Soviet military planning. With the only logical candidate for targeting in intercontinental bomber missions—the mobile MX ICBM—frozen out of deployment, there is every reason to believe that the Soviet leadership would gladly sacrifice BLACK-JACK to stop B-1, the Stealth bomber, and corresponding ALCM deployments.[3] Indeed, they would most likely accept a freeze on new bombers—in the absence of an ICBM freeze—just to stop B-1 and Stealth.

In terms of peripheral attack programs, the present SS-20 IRBM deployment is more than sufficient, quantitatively and qualitatively, to fulfill all primary and secondary IRBM missions. The SS-20 follow-on in R&D is an incremental improvement over the SS-20 design that would not add much to existing Soviet operational capabilities. However, the deployment of the U.S. PERSHING II and GLCM would seriously erode Soviet operational capabilities in the theater. As was the case regarding new ICBMs, the Soviets would be better off if neither side was able to modernize its long-range TNF than if both did. Therefore, the Soviet military would quickly accept a freeze on new long-range TNF production and deployment if it meant a halt to production and deployment of PERSHING II and GLCM. To be sure, a freeze on long-range TNF falls substantially short of General Secretary Andropov's recent offer to reduce the SS-20 deployment facing Europe in exchange for halting the PERSHING II/GLCM deployment.

Ongoing changes in Soviet military strategy and operational art suggest that Soviet military planning for theater warfare is not as dependent as it once was on operational-tactical and tactical ballistic missiles.[4] The secondary role which these weapons now seem to play in Soviet theater planning, as well as improvements in their SRBM force currently being secured, suggests that the Soviet military would agree to curtail the further modernization of the SRBM force if it would mean a freeze on NATO's SRBM posture.

Tactical airpower (TACAIR) is a pivotal element in Soviet theater warfare planning. For all intents and purposes, without massive conventional TACAIR there is no Soviet conventional theater warfare capability. Correspondingly, the prospect of a possible freeze on dual-capable TACAIR might first seem to pose a major dilemma for the Soviet military. However, here again changes in Soviet military planning suggest that most, if not all, of Soviet TACAIR is intended for initial non-nuclear missions in the theater. In conjunction with a freeze on TNF, the imposition of design requirements (for verification purposes) that marked TACAIR as unambiguously nonnuclear would not be of any real consequence to ongoing or planned Soviet military production programs or Soviet operational capabilities.

TABLE 2
Growth Rates for Machinery Output

	1966-1970	1971-1975	1976-1980	1981
Civilian Machinery	8.6%	9.0%	5.8%	1.8%
Military Machinery	3.5%	4.5%	3.4%	6.0%
RATIO (C/M)	2.3	2.0	1.7	0.3

TABLE 3
Planned Growth in Consumer Durables Produced
by the Military Sector

Industry	Planned Growth 1976-1980	Planned Growth 1981-1985
Aviation	50%	45%
Communications Eqpt.	90%	60%
Radio Eqpt.	200%	80%
Electronics	200%	85%

What should be clear is that the period 1983-1988 reflects a reversed image of the period 1978-1983. In the earlier period it was the Soviets who were deeply engrossed in relevant military production activity and the creation of new and enhanced operational capabilities while the U.S. did little outside of R&D (i.e., no production). In the later period it would most likely be the U.S. that moved heavily into military production, creating new operational capabilities for itself and simultaneously undermining newly acquired Soviet operational capabilities.

Economic Opportunities?

Obviously, a thorough analysis of the implications of a nuclear freeze for the Soviet economy is well beyond the scope of this brief paper. Nevertheless, some insights may be gained by examining several aspects of Soviet military-industrial activities over the last decade.

First, a comparison between the production of civilian machinery and military machinery in terms of average annual growth rates of output reveal a steadily increasing bias towards military production. (See Table 2.) Both current investment in military sector capital construction and 1981-1985 planning targets for growth in production of consumer durables by the military sector suggest continued bias in allocating new investment towards military needs. (See Table 3.) Thus, under current plans any real modernization and expansion of the civilian sector of the economy will be pushed further into the future, exacerbating current imbalances and bottlenecks in the Soviet economy.

Second, in contrast to popular perceptions of continuous and incremental growth in all areas of Soviet military investment (of which procurement is 90 percent), the fact is that there are a number of noticeable "spending" cycles within mission areas, as well as trade-off patterns among them. (See Figure 3) True, expenditures (i.e., resource allocation in the Soviet context) for overall military procurement appear to have grown at a fairly steady rate, but the corresponding distribution of those resources among mission areas has not. As can be seen, mission "funding" over the past decade reveals a number of expansions and contractions, where the expansion of procurement programs in one mission area was "paid for" by the contraction of funding for mission areas. In other words, there appears to be a pattern of choice reflected in the shifting "procurement budget" distributions—not a pattern of mindless acquisition.

Thus, despite growing problems in the civilian sector, the Soviet leadership has chosen to allocate increasing shares of machinery output to military needs, while taking any "savings" produced by the cyclical contractions in one mission area and redistributing it among other mission areas.

What opportunities for correcting the investment imbalances in the Soviet economy might a nuclear freeze present to Soviet leaders? CIA analyses suggest that had Soviet military procurement been held constant during the 1970s and the additional output in defense production diverted instead to produce durables for investment purposes, then the resulting increase in capital stock (e.g., plant and machinery in transportation, chemicals, etc.) may have added about 2 percent to the Soviet GNP in 1980.[6] Using this as a guide, a freeze on nuclear weapons procurement in 1970 might have added about 3 percent to the Soviet GNP by the end of the decade, assuming that all resources formerly dedicated to nuclear weapons production were reallocated for the production of producer durables in the civilian sector. Thus, under the most favorable assumptions a nuclear freeze might be expected to provide the opportunity to add at most 0.3 percent per annum to the Soviet GNP, and of course, any such gain would take a number of years to materialize.

What about near-term increases in the production of consumer durables by the military sector to relieve shortages and break up bottlenecks? Unfortunately, the military industries that would be most affected by a nuclear freeze are the ones that could contribute least to increasing the production of consumer durables. (See Table 4)[7] For the most part, we are talking about the missile industry. The aviation industry would simply have to stop making its strike and bomber aircraft dual-capable, which would have no noticeable impact on aircraft development, testing, or production. Naval yards producing SSBNs would most likely switch to producing SSNs in order to increase protection of Soviet SSBNs from U.S. ASW forces. Then too, the missile industries would have to continue to crank out spare parts to maintain the frozen Soviet missile force, as well as space launchers.

TABLE 4
Consumer Products Produced by the Military Sector

Industry	Consumer Product
Missiles/aviation	civilian aircraft
Naval surface vessels	pumps, machine tools, mining eqpt.
Submarines	pumps, machine tools, mining eqpt., large pipe
Tanks	construction and transportation eqpt., trains, etc.
Armored vehicles	construction, agriculture, and transportation vehicles
Artillery	construction, agriculture, and machine tools

Sources: Joint Economic Committee, *Allocation of Resources in the Soviet Union and China* (Washington DC: GPO, 1974-1982).

Of course, what has been described is past and planned Soviet economic behavior. The Soviet leadership could choose to break with the past trends if it so desired. However, for the reasons outlined here, the resource cuts and changes in production priorities would have to be borne by the military industries that support Soviet general purpose forces (GPF)—not those "freed" by the freeze. And herein lies a problem. With a nuclear freeze newly in place, it is likely that the Soviet military will strongly argue the case for increased and stable investment in the heavy industries supporting the general purpose forces elements of the Ground Forces, the Air Forces, the V-PVO, and the Navy. Thus, not only will it be difficult to redirect resources from these GPF industries for civilian needs, but it is quite probable that a substantial portion of the resources freed by a nuclear freeze would be redistributed among the GPF military industries.

In short, there is little reason for the Soviet political leadership to believe, *a priori*, that a nuclear freeze can provide near-term opportunity to improve the investment or the production imbalances in the Soviet economy.

Concluding Observations

For at least the last decade U.S. and Soviet nuclear weapons programs have been "out of sync" with one another. Thus, one of the complicating factors in trying to negotiate any major nuclear arms control measure—let alone a total freeze on nuclear weapons testing, production, and deployment—has been the desire by both

Allocations Within the Soviet Military Procurement "Budget"

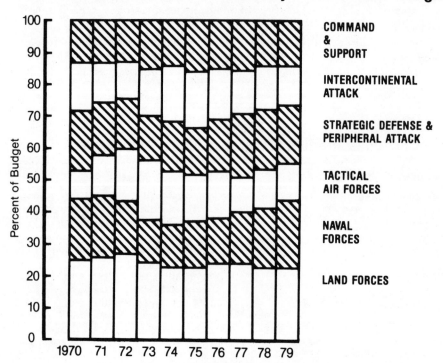

sides to "make the last move" in procurement and deployment before an agreement was solidified. Thus, it should come as no surprise to learn that the Soviet military leadership at this time probably is more interested in constraining U.S. nuclear programs than in expanding their own. Indeed, they must recognize that a nuclear freeze now would give them the "last move" and, correspondingly, lock in what is likely to be their maximal position vis-à-vis the U.S. in terms of nuclear force capabilities.

However, I must hasten to emphasize that this does not mean that a nuclear freeze would necessarily be detrimental to U.S. national security. What is nominally the Soviet Union's maximal position vis-à-vis the U.S. may represent no more than fundamental nuclear parity. Similarly, allowing the Soviets the "last move" in nuclear modernization does not necessarily imply U.S. nuclear or military inferiority.

Finally, while a nuclear freeze might offer some prospect of industrial adjustment in the far term, in the near term it cannot be expected to solve the fundamental problems confronting the Soviet economy that must occupy the minds of the present Soviet leadership.

---

1. Data taken from *The Military Balance* (various years) (London: IISS).

2. For a detailed discussion see Stephen M. Meyer, *Soviet Theater Nuclear Forces: Capabilities and Implications*, Adelphi Papers (London: IISS, 1983).

3. Soviet military writers argue that the utility of long-range bombers is tied to their capability to carry out real-time search and destroy missions against mobile targets. As of yet there is nothing in this target category. A mobile MX would, in fact, be the first as early notions of making MINUTEMAN were never implemented.

4. See Meyer, *op cit.*

5. Ibid.

6. Joint Economic Committee, *Allocation of Resources in the Soviet Union and China—1981*, Part 7. 97th Congress, 1st Session (July 8 and October 15), p. 271.

7. Soviet machine tools tend to be specialized and dedicated to particular tasks. Even Soviet numerically controlled tools are remarkably inflexible. Thus, retooling an industry is a much more complex, costly, and time-consuming process than is commonly believed.

*   *   *

Why Andropov Would Reject a Bilateral Freeze

Dimitri Simes

As for Soviet interest in the American freeze, I think they have clearly endorsed it. They clearly think it is a great idea. It is not a priority item for them for a very simple reason. I asked a Soviet scholar why they don't talk more about the freeze in the Soviet Union and he said, "We are a practical people and we know that the Americans would never accept something like that. If there would be a change in administration. . ." And he looked at me and repeated, "We are a practical people."

Another rather revealing statement was made by the Chief of the Central Communist International Information Department. He was asked on Soviet TV on an interesting talk show where he frequently appears what he thought about the idea of a freeze, and he said that there were several different freeze proposals, that they were interesting, but that there were some problems with them, they were quite complex. But then he added, "On the other hand, we are very much in favor of freeze movements in the United States and we find this movement entirely constructive."

Now if you think that something is not negotiable on one hand but helps you to constrain programs of your adversary, you obviously will be mildly enthusiastic about this venture. I agree with Stephen Meyer that the Soviets probably are more concerned about American systems than at any time since 1971 when they were very concerned about a combination of American ABM and MIRV. Yet we know that decisions regarding weapons systems are made not only on the basis of substantive analysis but also for political reasons. When we want to assess Soviet attitudes to freeze, we have to discuss the political climate in the Soviet Union at this point.

Here is a speech in *Pravda* by Comrade Yuri Andropov delivered to the Joint Session of the Central Committee and the Supreme Soviet on the occasion of the Soviet 60th anniversary. He said a number of interesting things, and I will comment on some of them. But what I found much more interesting and revealing was not what he said but where he got applause and what kind of applause he got. They had three different forms of applause. First, just applause; second, prolonged applause; and third, stormy applause. Let me give some indication where they applauded and what received particularly enthusiastic applause. "Attempts to kill Socialism in the Soviet Union never worked even when the Soviet Union was a young state and was alone. Now nobody can seriously believe that attempts like that would work." Stormy, prolonged applause. Then Andropov talks about Soviet commitment not to use nuclear weapons first. No applause. They are willing to negotiate agreement not to use first all kinds of weapons including conventional weapons. No applause. "However, as far as the American side is concerned, we regrettably see a totally different attitude.

Dimitri Simes *is Professor of Political Science at the School of Advanced International Studies at Johns Hopkins University, Baltimore, Maryland.*

They appeal for radical reductions but in practice they want to reduce only the Soviet strategic potential. It is absurd to think that we would discuss something like that." Stormy applause. Then he says that the Soviet Union is willing to cut its strategic forces by 25 percent. No applause. They are willing to discuss limits on all systems, not just in ICBMs. No applause. He is saying that during the negotiations they suggested a freeze on all strategic systems. No applause. "Problems in unilateral growth of armaments would not force the Soviet Union to make unilateral concessions. We would respond to the American challenge by deploying our analogous systems. We would respond to MX by an analogous ICBM. We would respond to cruise missiles with our own cruise missile which is being tested right now." Prolonged applause. "Those in Washington who believe that new systems of armaments would become bargaining chips believe in dreams." Stormy, prolonged applause.

I'm trying to give you an obvious picture. You are dealing with a national security consensus in Moscow. You are dealing with a political succession where a new leader is remarkably dependent on the military and on security services. I do not know any other Soviet leader who is equally dependent on this particular part of the Soviet establishment. We are similarly talking about a man who, contrary to conventional wisdom in this country, won precisely because he was *not* perceived to be a closet liberal. There's a very good article in the most recent issue of *Problems of Communism* analyzing public statements made by Konstantin Chernenko who is a man who for ten years was talking about the need for political pluralization, greater interparty democracy, and an emphasis on consumer goods production. I am not suggesting that Mr. Andropov would not tend to be liberal. And I'm not suggesting that if Mr. Chernenko would somehow prevail in the power struggle he would not tend to be a hard-liner. There is no way to predict how a person would behave once in power on the basis of his previous statements when he was a subordinate. What I am trying to say is that the current public record indicates that it was Mr. Chernenko, not Mr. Andropov, who was a public spokesman for reform, for pluralism, and for tolerance.

I think it is also fair to say that Mr. Andropov knows fairly well that the Soviet economy is in deep, deep trouble. I believe that he approaches Soviet economic reform seriously and responsibly. Some people say that he would be nothing because he did not move during the first sixty days. Anyone who would move during the first sixty days, particularly as a former security chief, without having any experience in dealing with the Soviet economy, would be irresponsible, would be criticized, and probably would break his political neck. Mr. Andropov set up a commission studying different economic reform proposals. I do believe that he is going to move. But he is also an ultimate politician. As one Soviet official described him recently having worked for him in the past, "Mr. Andropov is a remarkable man. He has no hobbies. Unlike Leonid the Leech, he is not interested in women and hunting. He is not interested in tennis. He is interested in substantive policy, but he is really an ultimate politician." As an ultimate politician, Mr. Andropov knows full well that if he wants to press on with economic reform, he has to build a political coalition.

How do you build this political coalition under current Soviet conditions? Economic managers and scientists are not sufficient to overcome resistance from the Party apparatus of central economic planners and the huge central economic/industrial bureaucracy in Moscow of numerous ministries, ninety of them. Mr. Andropov will need support from the military. He had a chance to refuse this support because the military said on many occasions, including the Minister of Defense and a Chief of the General Staff, that they need a more balanced economy because without a more balanced economy, as they called it, you cannot have an effective militarization.

Which brings me to a final point: if Mr. Andropov wants to improve his economy, he cannot seriously negotiate any freeze on deployment for reasons which were outlined, but if we are talking about really freezing the arms race, not simply allowing the Soviets to have a pause, then I think we don't have particular reasons for hope.

A final, very brief comment on the Soviet connection with the freeze movement. I think that the Soviets clearly are involved with the freeze movement and there is no question in my mind that they are trying to penetrate it is much as they can. As you know, there were several instances in Western Europe when different people connected with the anti-nuclear movement were clearly receiving money from the KGB. Mr. Baron and Mr. Bukokovsky are quite correct in suggesting that the Soviets are trying to penetrate the American freeze movement and that they are also trying to manipulate it wherever possible. I think that the Soviets are also trying to penetrate the White House, the CIA, the State Department, and on occasion I think they very effectively penetrated in the past the Committee on Present Danger. I think it is up to us to decide which particular movements and which particular initiatives are helpful to the Soviet government. That is a matter of opinion.

*   *   *

Consequences of a Freeze

The Political Importance of the Freeze

Richard J. Barnet

The importance of the freeze is almost entirely political. Even if the freeze were adopted the destructive power that would remain in the world would, of course, be enormous. The measure stands or falls on what kind of a political process it initiates. In making that judgment you need to look at three audiences—the Soviet Union, our allies, and the United States population. There are other audiences, but these are the most important.

The freeze is fundamentally an exercise in political communication. The measure makes two basic points that I think are incredibly important. One is that there is no technological solution to security at any level of expenditure. If there were to be a recognition by the United States and the Soviet Union of that fact, it would be an extremely important development.

I think the second statement the freeze is making is that any differences in the military balance—or the balance of imbalances—is less significant than the destabilizing effect of another spiral of the arms race, particularly the one in prospect. The new round of the arms race is important to prevent, not only because of the nature of the technology which has been discussed—the increased concern on the part of the military planners on both sides because of the increasing counterforce threat—but also because of the historical moment. The new round of the arms race follows a failed detente. The perception now is of an arms race out of control following a time when it appeared to many people that it was in control, and this is especially disturbing.

I would agree with Randy Forsberg that despite what are clearly internal resistances within the Soviet system to doing anything as radical as production cutoffs, the development of a consensus on a set of proposals for a freeze would put considerable pressure on the Soviet Union. I think this is a political reality that would influence them. The political climate has influenced them in the past. The freeze idea has great potential influence on them precisely because it is a popularly backed movement. For the first time in a long time, perhaps since the Partial Test Ban, an arms control proposal appears to have a wide popular backing in the United States. I do not believe that the Soviets are so naive to think that that popular backing can be manipulated by them to cause the United States to make proposals or agreements that will not be in its own interest. Rather I think it suggests to them that perhaps we have come to a time when they can count on a certain stability in American arms

Richard J. Barnet *is Associate Director of the Institute of Policy Studies in Washington, D.C.*

control policy precisely because it has flowed out of the narrow confines of expert discussion, which is apolitical, into the political arena. If that happens, this overcomes one concern which they have clearly had: the tenuousness and uncertainty of official understandings, such as those relating to the extension of credits in the early 1970s which were undermined by Congress with the Jackson Amendment, or the failure to ratify SALT II. Administrations come and go and proposals that they believe are signed do not get ratified. So the notion of an arms control consensus that goes beyond the experts is something that should, I would think, enlist considerable Soviet interest.

The effects of a freeze on America's relations with its allies would be positive. Relations with allies improve as we go in the direction of peace or perceived peace and they get worse as we go in the direction towards war. My experience in Europe, and I've been spending quite a lot of time there in the last two years, is that many, many people who have been strong supporters of the United States have increased their concern about the United States precisely because they do not see our policy as either consistent or sufficiently concerned with their security interests. I think it's worth going back to the origin of the Euromissile discussion, the original speech of Helmut Schmidt to the International Institute for Strategic Studies in 1977. Schmidt's message was not so much that the Euromissile balance was a pressing problem, but rather that European interests were being ignored because the superpowers were engaged in a very clumsy way over a very long period in making a deal which did not address the interests of Europe. In the 1970s we had a most peculiar situation in which the political situation greatly improved and the arms race in Europe, certainly on the Soviet side, took a big leap forward. What Schmidt was saying was that these things have to be dealt together. The effect was rather clumsy, and it ended up badly for him and for other European politicians. But we are now in a situation where, if the only prospect that the United States can offer the European allies is an increasing arms race in which the "bargaining chip" strategy of putting in the missiles to achieve a significant reduction of Soviet missile threat to Europe is not convincing either to the European leaders or to the public, then Europeans will increasingly go their own way on defense matters. I think they should, but as a consequence of a sensible U.S.-European consensus, not out of frustration with U.S. policy.

A French/German nuclear entente is one possibility. Nuclear pacifism, which I think is significantly underrated as an historic political force, is another strategy. In any event, the perception of the world that we have and our allies have in Europe and Japan will further diverge. It is in our interests to be able to demonstrate that if we are interested in leading an alliance, then we have sufficient sense of the common concerns to take bold actions to control this danger that hangs over everybody.

Finally, it seems to me that over the last three years many people in our own country have had a growing sense that the security system, the war prevention system on which we spend so much energy and so much money is spinning out of control, that we don't really know how to run it, that our leaders don't seem to know how to run it. The Reagan Administration has made statements about what is going to happen that seem fundamentally incredible to many people, certainly incredible to me. The basic view that the President put forward in the campaign and that has been repeated on various occasions since his election is that we are in an economic race with the Soviet Union and that if we are prepared to make the major investment in the arms race, the Soviets—being a troubled economy, more troubled presumably than we—will not keep up and that there will be some happy outcome. It is very hard to believe this on the basis of past Soviet behavior, and this makes more and more people skeptical about the way in which our leaders have developed plans for protecting us.

This fear of war which is growing is directly addressed by the freeze. The reason the freeze is so popular is that it seems at least to be a reasonable, moderate recognition that the course we are now taking is going to increase the shadow of war.

We have very much underestimated in this country the effect on our people of this lack of a believable national security strategy. It is not just the waste of economic resources; I absolutely agree that the arms race has a major effect on the nation's ability to marshal its economic resources. But the psychological effect on our people, particularly our young people, is an equally serious national security problem that gets almost no attention.

The real security problems of this country require the release of energy to rebuild the country. I think the peace movement has a very modest Utopia in mind: rebuilding the cities and the industry and the employment possibilities of our country, none of which at this point looks very promising. The deepest fear that motivates the freeze activists is that we are going to lose that, indeed lose everything, in a kind of dice-rolling strategy to restore a degree of security in the world that we can never have again. The statement "enough is enough," that neither of the superpowers can ever get a political advantage with nuclear superiority, that nuclear wars cannot be fought and certainly cannot be won, is a powerful and positive message that is essential to restoring some kind of political, economic, and psychological health to our country.

*   *   *

Western Europe and the Freeze

William E. Griffith

As to the change in West European attitudes toward the nuclear freeze, it is counter-productive to talk about this subject. There are attitudes in various countries. Those of you who know much about France will know that on this and other subjects France is a very special case indeed. There has been one general change which has occurred in almost all of Western Europe: the change in the left-wing intelligentsia. Until ten or fifteen years ago, the leftist intelligentsia was not critical of many aspects of Soviet policy. This is no longer the case. Indeed, in some places, particularly in France (this change began, not surprisingly, on the Left Bank of Paris), the left intelligentsia is much more critical of the Soviet Union than it is in this country. This is a very major change in European politics. It explains in large part, for example, why Mitterrand is much more critical of the Soviet Union than was Giscard d'Estaing, who was not noticeably supported by the Parisian left intelligentsia.

There has been another general change, which is also less strong in France than elsewhere: a much more critical West European attitude towards the United States. Its causes include many of the things discussed here today, ranging from perception of a greater danger of war, a more hostile attitude toward Reagan than toward Carter, greater economic competition, etc. It has produced in the West German extreme left an ideology of "a plague on both your houses"—that the important thing is that Europe be independent of both superpowers. This attitude would probably be much more criticized in this country if more people read German, but it is very strongly criticized in the Soviet Union, for it runs against the Soviet view that there are two camps and that one should be more favorable to the camp of socialism than to that of imperialism.

For many reasons, including the fact that France has an independent nuclear deterrent and therefore feels much less dependent on the United States, French attitudes not only toward the Soviet Union are more hostile. In any case, the support for a nuclear freeze in France is so small that one doesn't need to discuss it. The current attitude of the French government, and I think this is generally shared in France, is that French nuclear forces should be increased while those of both superpowers should be decreased.

The attitude in West Germany is very different. The principal cause of this difference relates to the general national consensus in West Germany to retain the gains of Ostpolitik, particularly the human contacts with East Germany, and therefore to maintain détente with East Germany and with the Soviet Union because of East Germany. For essentially national reasons, therefore—holding open the door for German reunification—the West Germans' attitude toward the Soviet Union is bound to be different from that of the U.S.

William E. Griffith *is Professor of Political Science at the Massachusetts Institute of Technology, Cambridge, Massachusetts.*

There is, as you know, a revival of the unilateral disarmament movement in Britain, but I think that it, like Britain, is less important. We know more about it because we read their language. Mrs. Thatcher retook the Falklands. She will probably be able to ensure that INF be deployed in the United Kingdom.

What of the concern in Western Europe about the increase in Soviet weapons deployment and, as various speakers have agreed, the approaching increase in the effectiveness of American weapons? The former: a) is understood, b) has in general created fear and concern (perhaps more in many cases than in this country, because West Europeans are weaker and more dependent on us), but c) has generated differing attitudes as to how to meet it. It has, on the one hand, made the major governments of Western Europe—Britain, France, West Germany, and Italy—favor INF deployment (indeed, it was Helmut Schmidt who began the process). On the other hand, this fear has certainly fed the rise of the West German peace movement, especially when contrasted with some of the Reagan Administration's pronouncements. On balance, though, although support of the freeze movement is growing in Western Europe, I think that what is growing more is something more radical than the freeze movement: a combination, in varying proportions, of the rejection of deterrence, of essential equivalence, indeed of all nuclear weapons, and within this context, outside of France the idea of Europe between the two superpowers.

Many, probably most, French remain Gaullist. But they do not reject nuclear weapons or equivalence. On the contrary, France is increasing its defense expenditures. Since the polls still show that in the U.K. and West Germany the conservatives are leading, the left has declined (in Britain it has split and in West Germany it is not exactly characterized by monolithic unity), this probably means more suspicion of the Soviet Union and greater support of INF deployment.

I think it is fair to say that if one isolates the so-called Eurostrategic balance—there are many military arguments why one should not do this but it is a political fact of life that it is done—the modernization which produced the SS-20 has given the Soviet Union a very considerable degree of imbalance in its favor compared to any U.S. missiles of that category deployed in Western Europe. Secondly, this has produced in Western Europe, as has the loss of American strategic superiority, what Congressman Gore called the "political radiation," which has increased West European fear of the Soviet Union, decreased confidence in American—and NATO—deterrence. This is why Chancellor Schmidt in 1977 said that something should be done about this. Steve Meyer is about to publish his Adelphi paper, which, I think, will finally demonstrate in great detail that this problem can be taken care of militarily by other means, such as sea-based missiles.

But that is not the point. The purpose of INF deployment, like SS-20 deployment, in Europe is primarily indeed political, not military. It is to change political attitudes in Western Europe and the Soviet Union. That is why the West European governments now involved—Britain, France, West Germany, and Italy—favor it. As the INF contest has gone on, it has of course had the additional effect of making it a test on the one hand of U.S. and NATO determination, and on the other whether or not the Soviet Union can contribute significantly to postponing or preventing the deployment. And in the process, the Soviet Union has been, with some success, pushing its campaign to split the United States from Western Europe.

Now a few words on the peace movement in Western Europe as compared to the peace movement in the United States. They share certain common characteristics. First, a greatly increased fear of nuclear war—I happen to think largely without justification, but that is not the point. That they have this fear is an important fact. They display, I would agree, as these movements have throughout history, a revival of Utopianism—that is to say, a belief that one can very rapidly bring about something like heaven on earth. America has been especially, and chronically, addicted to this kind of revivalism. Indeed, I would compare the present freeze movement more to the religious revivals than I would to either the temperance or abolition movements. It is not an accident, I would suggest, that it is one of the two semi-religious revivals now going on in this country. (The other, the Moral Majority, at least has the virtue of not wanting to bring about heaven on earth, but only in heaven.)

The West European peace movement is not only more radical, but it has in it several other characteristics. Therefore, comparisons, despite the common factors, are dangerous. It has in it a certain amount of anti-Americanism. It occurs almost entirely in Protestant countries. (You may say, "Why, then, the Catholic role in the peace movement in the United States?" Well, a, they may have been affected by Protestantism, and b, American Catholicism was Irish before Jansenist in origin, and Jansenism is as close to Protestantism as the Catholic Church ever came.) The peace movement in Catholic Italy is small and largely Communist, and in Catholic France even smaller and also largely Communist. That France has an independent nuclear deterrent also, I think, discourages the anti-American aspect there.

It is important in this country to try to understand that the West German peace movement cannot accurately be called primarily nationalist or pro-Soviet. Indeed, its primary political ideology, as I said before, is a more independent Europe between the two superpowers. But it is not surprising that a minority in it is concerned with what one can call nationalist or patriotic motives. After all, Poland was divided for one hundred and twenty-five years and did not lose its desire for "reunification." Finally, the attitudes toward the Soviet Union, I think, are significantly different in the various countries where the peace movement is active.

Finally, what are the relationships between the peace movement here, the peace movement in Western Europe, the freeze here, the largely anti-INF movement in Western Europe, and the whole INF situation? I would make only two points—they are interrelated. The first is that I suppose some of you might believe, although I hope you would not, that if the United States had not proposed to deploy INF, Andropov would have unilaterally offered to decrease SS-20 deployment. I hope you would not believe that because I think it is untrue. Secondly, while I believe that the freeze movement in this country helped to get American negotiations going with the Soviets in START, I equally believe that it is now one of the elements that discourages the Soviets from agreeing to a compromise. I therefore think that it is more likely that the

Soviets will agree to a compromise—and I think they probably will, for reasons Steve Meyer gave—after some deployment has begun.

One final point which has hardly been mentioned here: it is characteristic of most Americans objectively to act as though they and the Soviet Union decide these things. This is of course what the Soviets would like to do. I would argue that we should not. One can hardly believe that either the French or the Chinese would agree to a nuclear freeze. Moreover, a nuclear freeze between the United States and the Soviet Union without the involvement of China and Japan and against the will of France would: a) cause great difficulties in our alliance in Europe; b) would clearly menace the Chinese and the Japanese more; and c) would mean that the only two growing and moderniz- ing nuclear forces in the world (I'm assuming that the British would probably go along with this if only because they always have) would be the French and the Chinese. If you like the French and the Chinese enough and believe they are more responsible than we or the Soviets, as undoubtedly both of them believe, then you are not concerned about that. If you don't, I guess you are.

* * *

The Economic Impact of a Bilateral Nuclear Weapons Freeze

David Gold

No one would support or oppose a bilateral freeze on nuclear weapons solely or even largely on the basis of its likely economic impact. But there are economic impacts and, in terms of their size, differential effects, and possible long-term implications, they are not trivial. In this paper, I will outline four areas where such impacts are potentially important: the federal budget and the aggregate economy; the industrial base; business, labor, and communities; and long-term technological change and economic growth.

The Federal Budget and the Aggregate Economy

A bilateral nuclear weapons freeze would be accompanied by a reduction in expenditures for nuclear weapons. The possible reductions are substantial. The Reagan Administration's strategic weapons modernization program is expected to cost $260 billion, in current dollars, by FY87, including Department of Energy warhead costs.[1] On a year-by-year basis, nuclear weapons expenditures are climbing. Analyzing the FY82 Carter Administration budget authority request as amended earlier in 1981 by the Reagan Administration, Randall Forsberg estimated that nuclear weapons costs were 22 percent of the defense function, or $49.5 billion.[2] If the same percentage were applied to the Reagan Administration's budget authority request for FY84, nuclear weapons costs would be $60.2 billion.

A freeze would affect some portion of the money being projected for nuclear weapons costs. The amount of any "freeze dividend" depends on what programs are frozen and when the freeze starts. A Congressional Research Service study estimated that an immediate freeze would reduce defense outlays by $14.5 billion in FY83, which is about 7 percent of projected defense spending.[3] Since many of the systems that would be covered by a freeze are not scheduled to enter production until later in the decade, the reduction in outlays would be substantially larger later in the 1980s and into the 1990s.

The impact of cuts in nuclear weapons spending on the federal budget and the economy depends upon two major uncertainties. The first is the state of the economy at the time major cuts take effect, and the second is whether the cuts are compensated, or offset, by other changes in the federal budget. A cut in nuclear weapons spending by itself would reduce the budget deficit and contribute to a possible easing of monetary policy and lowering of interest rates, both welcome developments in the midst of a severe recession or an emerging recovery. A cut in nuclear weapons spending would also reduce aggregate demand by some multiple of the budget cut, which would reduce private spending and increase unemployment, hardly welcome

David Gold *is Director of Military Affairs at the Council on Economic Priorities, New York, N.Y.*

developments.[4] The existence of opposing impacts, positive from the financial side and negative from the spending side, is a reflection of a current dilemma: while there is a large amount of slack in the economy as a whole due to the length and depth of the recent recession, there is no perceived slack in the federal budget. Since large deficits are being projected well into the future, this particular dilemma is likely to continue.[5]

If the economy were to be in recovery the loss of purchasing power would be less serious. A recovering economy can more easily replace demand than an economy that is fighting to move out of recession. In addition, one benefit of a reduction in nuclear weapons spending could be a diminution of inflationary pressures, but that, too, would depend upon the state of the economy and, particularly, of the defense industrial base.

An alternative outcome is for the freeze dividend to be diverted to some other budget item, either within the defense function or in the remainder of the federal budget. An increase in the budget allocation for non-nuclear forces may be needed to buy political support for the freeze from the military and key members of Congress. There is pressure for substantial government investment in our economic infrastructure. And a number of social programs, for example Social Security and Medicare, would be powerful claimants on any money released by the freeze. If the freeze dividend is fully offset by other expenditure increases, there would be little or no effect on the budget deficit and little or no withdrawal of aggregate demand.

A compensated reduction in nuclear weapons spending may still, on balance, have beneficial effects for the economy as a whole. If the funds are transferred to infrastructural investment, the employment lost by the reduction would probably be more than offset by employment gains from the increase.[6] The gains from reconstruction of bridges and highways, increased funding for transportation systems, and the like would benefit other sectors of the economy as the costs of moving goods and people would decline. Such gains are likely to be greater than any economic benefits that are spun off from continued nuclear weapons spending.[7]

If funds were shifted from nuclear to non-nuclear weapons, there is evidence that the basic economic indicators would improve.[8] Even if the decline in nuclear weapons expenditures were accompanied by lower taxes, rather than increased non-nuclear expenditures, macroeconomic performance is likely to improve. In one such research experiment, lower levels of defense spending, accompanied by equal reductions in taxes, resulted in increases in employment, investment, and GNP, and less inflation.[9]

The Industrial Base

A reduction in spending for nuclear weapons would have impacts upon the industrial base of the U.S. economy. While defense spending accounts for about 6 percent of total spending in the United States, it represents a considerably larger share of manufacturing output. In the late 1970s, defense procurement took about 11 percent of the durable manufactured goods sold in the U.S. In the 1960s this ratio was over 15 percent, and it is rising again in the 1980s.[10]

The withdrawal of nuclear weapons money would have its greatest impact on the sector of industry known as the defense industrial base. Whether the impacts are beneficial to the economy depends, again, on the state of the economy and how the withdrawn funds are put to use.

The increase in procurement expenditures under the Carter Administration, which was quite a bit smaller than current increases, led to substantial strains within the defense industrial base. Production bottlenecks, long lead times, and rapid and large cost increase became widespread by 1980.[11] Since then, the problem has eased substantially, largely because the deep recession in the civilian economy freed labor, materials, and industrial capacity for use in defense production.[12]

The expected revival of the economy, while long delayed, would coincide with a major leap in defense production, as such large items as the B-1 bomber, MX missile, F-18 fighter-bomber, and two Nimitz class carriers move into production. There is some fear that defense industries have not expanded capacity sufficiently to handle this procurement bow wave.[13] Moreover, internal Pentagon changes designed to halt weapons cost escalation have so far not succeeded.[14] There is a very real prospect that, by the middle of the decade, bottleneck and cost growth problems will be even more severe than in the past.

A reduction in the demands upon the industrial base that would accompany a nuclear weapons freeze is likely to reduce inflationary pressures. This is true, although to a smaller extent, even if there is a compensating increase in expenditures for non-nuclear weaponry. Using the results of alternative budget scenarios developed by Data Resources Inc., Gary Guenther estimated that the budget with the heaviest emphasis on strategic forces would create the greatest strains on the industrial base, although there is substantial unevenness to the patterns. If strategic weapons spending were to be reduced, and replaced by spending on readiness or naval forces, two alternatives tested by DRI, there would be less pressure on the industrial base.[15]

The pressure would be even less if the money saved by reducing nuclear weapons programs were instead spent on civilian programs, given the substantial excess capacity in civilian industry. But as Guenther points out, this optimistic assessment "is based on the highly theoretical and not necessarily 'real world' assumption that these resources are readily transferable to these alternative uses."[16]

Companies, Government Installations, Workers, and Communities

A reduction in nuclear weapons spending, whether compensated or not, would result in a loss of contracts for companies, revenue for government installations, jobs for workers, and income for communities. Even if some of the losses were offset by increases from other government programs, there is no guarantee that the new revenues would go to the same companies, bases, workers, and communities that suffer the losses. A reduction in nuclear weapons spending will generate an adjustment problem, as its effects spread unevenly across the economy.

The problems faced by companies, bases, workers, and communities are not identical, and can vary substantially within each category. The large, prime contractors are frequently diversified, and have cushions against the loss of even a substantial contract. Moreover, they are well positioned to gain from increases in other government spending. Subcontractors are in general more vulnerable, but the impact would vary widely. There are probably tens of thousands of companies that are potentially affected by a reduction in nuclear weapons spending.

Military bases and other government installations, including nuclear weapons laboratories and processing and assembly plants, would also be affected. Some of these have other obvious uses; others do not. Similarly with personnel. As many as 300,000 private sector jobs could be directly affected, and another 150,000 to 200,000 jobs within the Pentagon.[17] Many of these people could be easily reassigned or reemployed, but others would have difficulty. Transferability of skills is a major problem. The decline in military procurement after Vietnam left large numbers of skilled and experienced people without employment.

Dollars and, to some extent, people are mobile but communities are not. The loss of a sizeable contract or the closing of a plant or military base can deprive a community of income. And in many cases, military business is the largest source of income for the community or even the region. Whatever the macroeconomic impacts of a freeze, there are many communities that are heavily defense-dependent, and they would suffer inordinately from the decline in weapons spending.

These problems of differential impact can be approached through greater coordination involving private and governmental agencies at local and national levels. There are examples where the adjustment away from heavy defense dependency has been accomplished with impressive results. But it is likely that a substantial national effort would be required in the case of the large and systematic withdrawal of resources that would accompany a nuclear weapons freeze. Perhaps one aspect of the freeze should be a revival of interest in conversion planning, which gained some supporters in the mid-1970s.[18]

Investment, Technology, and Economic Growth

Military spending in general, and spending on nuclear systems in particular, is heavily oriented toward high technology and research and development. Since 1960, about 60 percent of federal government spending for research and development, and about one-third of all U.S. R&D spending, has been for national defense.[19] The military share of all U.S. R&D expenditures dropped through the 1970s, and was 24 percent in 1980, but it is rising again in the 1980s. For FY82, nuclear weapons R&D was almost one-half the military total.[20] If those percentages hold, approximately one out of every six dollars spent for R&D in the United States in the 1980s will be for nuclear weapons.

Research and development spending has implications for long-term economic performance. While historians and econometricians may disagree as to how important R&D is, there is no disagreement that it is important. R&D leads to new products, improvements in production technology, and an increase in the skills and productivity of the work force. And these factors, in turn, make it easier to achieve higher rates of economic growth and higher standards of living. The very large share of the U.S. research and development effort that has gone to the military has led to a debate on the issue of how this has affected the performance of the U.S. economy in the period since World War II.

The primary economic argument in support of the positive impacts of military R&D is that such spending stimulates non-military efforts in basic research, product and process technology, and the generation of skills. Military R&D is seen as seed money. In the words of a senior Pentagon economist:

> Defense sets goals that are difficult to meet; and our new programs often tax the limits of technology. Only the Department of Defense's budget is rich enough to experiment with new approaches to complex problems. It is my belief that we cannot foretell exactly the future path that technology must take in the quest for new commercial applications and solutions to non-defense problems. In the same sense that we seed the clouds in the hope for rain, so too we seed our research laboratories in the hope for [sic] finding solutions to difficult problems.[21]

The problem with this familiar argument is that it is rarely, if ever, supported by systematic evidence. A few examples are given of industrial or consumer products that have their origin in military or space programs, such as radar, jet engines, nuclear power, Tang, and Teflon, but no assessment is given as to how typical are these products, how costly was the development effort, or how crucial was the role of military R&D.

There is no particular reason to expect that a substantial spin-off, or seeding, effect will remain in force for long periods of time. Most of the U.S. military production industry grew out of civilian industry, beginning in World War II. Many of the products and much of the process technology was similar; indeed, civilian industry was converted to military production, and then substantially reconverted after 1945. Innovations in each sector had a substantial degree of compatibility. Over time, military and civilian production diverged and the requirements and innovations of one had less and less relation to the other. The jet engine was transferable in a way that the supersonic aircraft has not been. The requirements of the military are determined by its own objectives, and there is no reason why these objectives should yield technology and products that are readily applicable to a civilian economy.

Studies of the relation between military spending and investment, manufacturing productivity, and economic growth suggest that military spending is negatively associated with these measures of economic performance. Higher ratios of military spending to total output have been found to be correlated with lower investment to output ratios, and lower rates of growth of productivity and total output, for the United States and other Western countries.[22] Case studies of the U.S. electronics industry suggest that while military demand was an important initial stimulant for the industry, military requirements are now contributing to the industry's relative decline in non-military markets. The technological needs of the military are seen as diverting resources, and altering incentives, to make U.S. industry less competitive in world markets.[23]

Whether the impact is primarily a quantitative trade-off, whereby military spending "crowds out" business investment, including R&D, or qualitative, in which military requirements and incentives tend to weaken civilian ones, a rise in military outlays can be seen as undermining the long-term growth potential of the U.S. economy. Conversely, a reduction in military outlays, and especially one such as implied by a nuclear weapons freeze with its emphasis on technology and basic research, has potentially beneficial implications for long-term growth.

Some recent economic research supplements this conclusion, at least for the long-term. Joel Slemrod of the University of Minnesota has estimated that an increase in the American public's fear of nuclear war measured, in part, by the size of weapons arsenals, can be expected to reduce the nation's savings rate, making long-term capital accumulation more difficult. An increase in the likelihood of a nuclear war and an increase in the destructive potential of such a conflict would reduce the incentive people have to save for the future and invest in physical goods. Slemrod measured changes in the probability of nuclear war by using the setting of the clock on the cover of the *Bulletin of Atomic Scientists*, and its destructive potential by the size of the Soviet arsenal. Using statistical methods, Slemrod found that, among other results, an increase in the perceived threat from its minimal level in the post-1945 period to its maximum level was associated with a decline in the savings rate of 1.7 percentage points.[24] The average postwar value of the savings rate was 10.2.

A bilateral nuclear weapons freeze would permit a reduction in U.S. military expenditures. Such a reduction would withdraw aggregate demand from the economy and cause substantial disruption among those workers, communities, and companies most affected. The impact of the withdrawal of aggregate demand would be more or less severe depending upon the state of the economy and the size of the federal budget deficit. However, these impacts can be offset through other spending and tax changes. Offsetting the disruptive impacts on those most directly affected is also possible, but we have little experience with nationwide conversion efforts and, so far, not enough of a political mandate to institute such efforts on a large scale.

Cuts in nuclear weapons outlays hold the promise of some important economic benefits. Such cuts would ease pressures on the federal budget, and give the government more options in allocating federal revenues, including the option of reducing the deficit. Pressure on the defense industrial base would also be relieved, reducing a prime source of inflation within the defense sector. And civilian research and development projects would improve both through the freeing up of money and resources and the removal of an element that has, in the past, distorted priorities.

---

1. William Hartung, "Economic Effects of a Bilateral Nuclear Weapons Freeze" in Dave McFadden and Jim Wake, eds., *Economics and the Freeze* (Mt. View, Calif.: Mid-Peninsula Conversion Project, 1983), ch. 3.

2. Randall Forsberg, "The Economic and Social Consequences of the Nuclear Arms Race," Occasional Paper 2, Institute for Defense and Disarmament Studies, March 1981, Table 1.

3. Gary L. Guenther, "The Implications of a Nuclear Arms Freeze for the U.S. Economy in the Short Run," Congressional Research Service, August 3, 1982, p. 5. The CRS study defined the terms of a freeze according to the joint resolution adopted by the House Foreign Affairs Committee (H.J. 521) on June 23, 1982.

4. Guenther, op. cit., p. 7, estimated that a cut in nuclear weapons spending of $14.5 billion could result in a decline in GNP of as much as $32.4 billion, both figures for FY83.

5. Congressional Budget Office, "Reducing the Deficit: Spending and Revenue Options," February 1983. The CBO projects federal deficits of 5.6 percent of GNP for 1984-88, assuming economic recovery. These are

historically high percentages and, according to CBO, deficits of this magnitude could frustrate the expected recovery. They suggest spending cuts of about $170 billion per year by FY88, with a substantial portion coming from defense.

6. David Gold, Gail Shields, and Christopher Paine, *Misguided Expenditures: An Analysis of the Proposed MX Missile System* (New York: Council on Economic Priorities, 1981), ch. 14, found that money spent on guided missile production generated fewer jobs, less investment in capital goods producing industries, and more inflationary pressure, than an equal amount of spending on new housing, solar equipment and energy conservation, inter-city and intra-city passenger vehicles, and new public utility construction.

7. *Ibid.*

8. Guenther, op. cit., pp. 10-19.

9. Roger Bezdek, "The 1980 Economic Impact—Regional and Occupational—of Compensated Shifts in Defense Spending," *Journal of Regional Science*, Vol. 15, No. 2, 1975, pp. 183-198.

10. Robert DeGrasse, Jr., *Producing Decay: The Economics of Military Spending*, (New York: Council on Economic Priorities), forthcoming.

11. Guenther, op. cit.,pp. 14-15; Defense Science Board, Task Force on Industrial Responsiveness, 1980 Summer Study.

12. *Aviation Week and Space Technology*, January 4, 1982, pp. 38-40, and January 11, 1982, pp. 64-73.

13. Among those expressing concern are Murray Weidenbaum, Chairman of the Council of Economic Advisors in 1981-82. See Weidenbaum, "Let's Examine National Defense Spending," *Challenge*, January/February 1983, pp. 50-53. Others raising the issue include *Aviation Week*, op. cit.; Bureau of Industrial Economics, U.S. Department of Commerce, "Sectoral Implications of Defense Expenditures," August 1982; Congressional Budget Office, "Defense Spending and the Economy," February 1983.

14. Gordon Adams, *Controlling Weapons Costs: Can the Pentagon Reforms Work?* (New York: Council on Economic Priorities, 1983). See also the testimony of Franklin Spinney before the Senate Armed Services Committee, February 25, 1983, as reported in *Time*, March 7, 1983.

15. Guenther, op. cit., pp. 16-19.

16. Guenther, op. cit., p. 14.

17. Hartung, op. cit.; Forsberg, op. cit., p. 3.

18. Lloyd J. Dumas, ed., *The Political Economy of Arms Reduction.* (Boulder, Co.: Westview Press, 1982), analyzes conversion.

19. DeGrasse, op. cit.

20. Forsberg, op. cit., p. 4.

21. David Blond, "On the Adequacy and Inherent Strengths of the United States Industrial and Technological Base: Guns versus Butter in Today's Economy," Office of the Secretary of Defense, Program Analysis and Evaluation, n.d. (probably 1981).

22. Ronald P. Smith, "Military Expenditure and Investment in OECD Countries, 1954-1973," *Journal of Comparative Economics*, Vol. 4 (1980), pp. 19-32; DeGrasse, op. cit.

23. William Baldwin, *The Impact of Department of Defense Procurement on Competition in Commercial Markets: Case Studies of the Electronics and Helicopter Industries* (Washington: Federal Trade Commission, Office of Policy Planning, December 1980); Robert Reich, "Japan in the Chips," *New York Review of Books*, November 19, 1981; Mary Kaldor, *The Baroque Arsenal* (New York: Hill and Wang, 1981); Michael Borrus, James Millstein and John Zysman, *International Competition in Advanced Industrial Sectors: Trade and Development in the Semiconductor Industry* (Washington: Joint Economic Committee, February 1983).

24. Joel Slemrod, "Post-War Capital Accumulation and the Threat of Nuclear War," Working Paper No. 887, National Bureau of Economic Research, May 1982.

★ ★ ★

A European Perspective on the Concept of a Nuclear Freeze

Johan Jørgen Holst

At the outset it seems necessary to differentiate between the general concept of a freeze on the one hand and particular constructions of that concept on the other. The concept commands broad popular sympathy and endorsement; particular constructions beg detailed issues with respect to implications and ramifications. The ambiguity of the American debate with respect to the inclusion or non-inclusion of INF, not to speak of battlefield nuclear weapons, makes it difficult to generalize about assessments as well as attitudes on the European side of the Atlantic.

The American freeze movement shares many concerns and characteristics with the European peace movement, but there are also important differences. There is a shared concern about an open-ended arms race, about a momentum which defies political control, about a need to turn the tide and a sense that enough is enough. In a very fundamental way the two movements reflect tensions and contradictions in the relationship between state and society in the West. However, while the freeze movement is advocating negotiated solutions, the peace movement in Europe frequently expresses disdain about negotiations and sees direct political action as a substitute for the diplomatic effort. In Europe the peace movement is much stronger and commands more attention in the Protestant countries of the north than in the Catholic lands of the south, which happen also to be the countries with strong indigenous communist parties. The peace movement in general is neither neutralist nor pacifist, although it contains such trends as well and it could move more clearly in that direction in the future.

The American freeze movement is viewed in Europe as being inspired very largely by exasperation with the apparent reluctance of the Reagan Administration to engage in serious arms control negotiations with the Soviet Union, and it is often credited with having moved the present administration to the negotiating table. In this sense it supplemented the efforts of West European governments. But there is also the residual concern that the freeze movement has opened and continues to nurture an internal U.S. debate which may have a diversionary impact on the negotiating performance of the Reagan Administration. The latter may be paying more attention to the internal debate with its critics than to its bargaining with the Russians in Geneva.

The European disaffection with arms control negotiations in large measure is due to the meager results which have emerged so far. The U.S. failure to ratify the SALT II treaty contributed to the malaise and was, it should be recalled, regretted by all governments in Western Europe. The latter turned less on a detailed assessment of the merits of the treaty, although its merits should certainly not be denigrated, than on

Johan Jørgen Holst *is Director of the Norwegian Institute of International Affairs, Oslo, Norway.*

the serious and negative political implications of the President of the leading power in NATO being unable to persuade the legislature in his own country to ratify a major treaty which he had negotiated with the Soviet Union and which had been endorsed by the European allies of the United States.

The major reason for European concerns about the directions of American security policy at present is the apparent absence of a coherent policy for structuring the long-term relationship with the Soviet Union. The notion of an open-ended conflict, sustained *inter alia* by a rather indiscriminate weapon-building program, and at times inspired by visions of or references to the eventual collapse of the Soviet system through the pressures of competition, is far from reassuring to European societies cognizant of sharing a continent with the Soviet Union. In these circumstances the general notion of a freeze on the production, testing, and deployment of nuclear weapons to many assumes the quality of a compelling imperative.

Several issues must be addressed, however, in connection with attempts to operationalize the concept of the freeze. First of all, there is the issue of coverage. Does it extend, e.g., to battlefield nuclear weapons? From the point of view of general concerns about stability, about how governments could be driven across the nuclear precipice, the present posture of NATO in Europe is very far from reassuring. The forward emplacement of a large number of nuclear munitions in fairly vulnerable sites, to be moved to equally vulnerable launch positions, and to be fired by systems which are outranged by the comparable systems on the other side of the hill, could create almost irresistible pressures for early release and use; decisions could be enmeshed in a "use them or lose them" syndrome. The destabilizing impact of the posture is compounded by a doctrine of first use unencumbered by agreed political guidelines for follow-on use. Here then is an urgent need for reductions, restructuring, and withdrawal. A freeze is not only insufficient, it could be counterproductive if it were to perpetuate a very undesirable situation. We have to be concerned lest ceilings become floors, and lest the concerns about future dangers overshadow the urgency of those of the present.

Another potential source of instability in the current posture is related to counter-air operations. They could come to be perceived as the most time-urgent missions in the early phases of a war. They would be directed principally, although not exclusively, against the major operating bases of the opponent. If there are strong expectations that tactical aircraft for such missions would use nuclear weapons, pressures for preemption with nuclear counter strikes would seem to grow (destroying the aircraft in their protected shelters or otherwise before takeoff). Hence, it should be considered whether stability could be improved by a stand-down of quick reaction alert aircraft and, possibly, moving towards "conventionalizing" tactical aircraft. It is possible to envisage a confidence-building measure which would prohibit collocating special munition sites for nuclear weapons with tactical airbases. Here more would be required than a freeze of existing deployments and missions.

Similar concerns are connected with INF, but for different reasons. There is time urgency about the INF negotiations because of the scheduling of NATO deployments. A freeze is an insufficient end-state for the INF negotiations, primarily in political terms, and it falls far short even of what Mr. Andropov seems to be offering at the present moment. It should be recalled that the European concern about the SS-20 had more to do with the political balance within the security order in Europe, particularly in the relations among the nuclear and the non-nuclear weapon states, in the context of Soviet–American strategic parity than with military requirements. What seems important is to draw down Soviet intermediate range forces and fix a ceiling for the future. The scale of the draw-down is a subject for negotiation, but not the principle. The problem is to develop criteria for establishing objectives with respect to Soviet concessions. The zero-zero solution while desirable is clearly not negotiable. In political terms we must consider the scale of Soviet reductions which could permit NATO to forgo deployment of Pershing II and GLCMs in Europe or, alternatively, to reduce and restructure the prospective deployment. I should think that a double criterion may be explored: The total number of Soviet M/IRBM warheads should preferably be lower than what existed prior to the deployment of SS-20, and the number of SS-20 launchers smaller than the number which was deployed in December 1979.

It is becoming increasingly clear that the INF negotiations and START must be relinked and treated as elements of the same process aiming for an integrated agreement. Separate negotiations and agreements would seem to generate decoupling effects, to weaken the links between the defense of Europe and the American guarantee. They also make it very hard to deal with the thorny issues in a negotiable manner.

An agreement on INF could be viewed as a partial and interim agreement for subsequent incorporation in a comprehensive agreement encompassing strategic forces as well as intermediate range forces. Even such an interim agreement would need to contain several freeze provisions in order to protect it against circumvention. Specifically, provisions may have to be sought barring the forward deployment of additional shorter range missiles, deployment of SLCMs to naval forces operating off the continent of Europe, as well as deployment of INF forces to areas immediately beyond the agreed zone of reduction and limitation.

In addition to giving specific precision to the concept of the freeze as a means of stabilizing an agreement on reductions and limitations, the two superpowers could endorse the concept as an interim measure, possibly through parallel declarations, observe the freeze, at least on deployment but possibly extending also to testing and some aspects of production, while negotiating a comprehensive agreement on reductions. It seems necessary, in other words, to find ways of welding together agreements on reductions as well as freeze, of cutting through false dichotomies and rather sterile and abstract debates about what should come first as well as about possible tensions between the two approaches to arms control.

It is enormously difficult to generalize about European attitudes to the idea of a nuclear freeze. Important differences may exist between elite opinions and popular opinions. There are certainly differences of opinion among governments and political parties. Opinion in the nuclear weapon states in Europe, England and France, would differ from the rest as more immediate interests and constraints are at stake. Part of the popular power and appeal of the idea of a nuclear freeze is its simplicity. But equally, part of the reason for equivocation within the elites is the ambiguity of the idea when related to specific issues.

Some key issues which are raised by the INF negotiations affect European perceptions and interests. There is no sense in denying the existence of British and French forces. However, neither Britain nor France participate in the INF or START negotiations. Russians and Americans cannot negotiate about the forces of third parties. They can agree, however, to take them into account when negotiating their obligations. How they do that is of considerable political importance. The major portion of the British and French forces is made up of submarine-launched missiles. Such systems are counted as strategic systems in the context of SALT/START. It will seem rather arbitrary to classify them differently because the submarines fly non-superpower flags. Their missions are, furthermore, clearly strategic in nature. They are not theater weapons.

Furthermore, applying different counting rules to European systems could contribute to a conception of a separate Eurostrategic balance which would tend to weaken the strategic unity of the Western alliance. It is questionable also whether a "balance" which is constructed on the basis of British, French, and Russian forces will provide the infrastructure for a legitimate political order in Europe. German and Italian apprehensions are likely to be nurtured by the inequity of an arrangement which appears to perpetuate the power relationships which were created by the outcome of the Second World War and which equates nuclear power status with the winning coalition. Issues of vulnerability and potentials for intimidation loom in the background. Furthermore, it is far from clear that stability and equity will be promoted by conceding to Moscow a right to match the power of every potential nuclear adversary separately. It is easier to mitigate such political connotations by constructing a comprehensive agreement which constrains both strategic and intermediate range nuclear forces within a single framework.

There is then a problem of the double standard. In addition, there is a problem of double bookkeeping. Thus it is difficult to understand why SSBNs which are assigned to SACEUR should be counted both as strategic systems (in SALT/START) and as intermediate range systems in the INF negotiations. That issue would not arise if the two sets of negotiations were joined. When NATO made the "dual track" decision on INF modernization in December 1979 it stated explicitly, and not accidentally, that the proposed negotiations should take place in the context of SALT. Europeans will resist the political implications of Europe's being considered an incidental extension of the Soviet-American central balance of strategic deterrence.

By this token many Europeans refuse to accept that the potential threat of Pershing IIs to the Soviet Union be considered fundamentally different from the threat of SS-20s to Western Europe (speed and accuracy are roughly equal) because the Soviet Union is a superpower. The right to security is not a function of the size of the state, and while the reality of the international system is such as to include gross inequalities, it would violate the principle and presumption of the equality of states to base a treaty on the notion of preferential rights for the superpowers.

A major issue involved for France and Britain, and for the Western alliance as a whole, is to avoid an agreement which concedes to Moscow a kind of *droit de regard* or even a *droit de controle* over British and French decisions concerning their nuclear forces in the future. They would urge the Americans to avoid agreements which would establish or even indicate such a supervisory role for the Russians. Similarly, Europeans would caution about the erosive consequences on the unity of NATO which would be the result of an agreement which appeared to establish a kind of duopolistic joint supervision by Moscow and Washington. We see then that the modalities of negotiations and agreements about arms may affect fundamental political relationships. Therefore, particular care must be taken to structure the modalities in a manner which is consistent with the protection of vital interests in the pattern of political influence on the European continent.

A basic proposition which is implicit in the preceding observations is that military power affects the structural quality of the political order in Europe. No impacts are simple or linear in nature, they depend on circumstances, conjunctions, and climate. The suggestion is not that impacts with respect to political behavior in Western Europe constitute the primary design considerations for the structuring and scaling of the military effort of the Soviet Union. But military forces have consequences in this realm, both in the normal peacetime conduct of diplomacy and, more potently, during crises. Attention must be paid, therefore, to the "soft" system effects of particular force deployments, force ratios, and arms control arrangements.

The question of verification plays a more prominent role in the American political discourse about arms control than in the European consideration. Generally speaking, claims about inspection requirements are viewed as constraints imposed by the political culture of the United States as much as by technical necessity. In any event, there will always be a need for political assessment of benefits and risks; foolproof control is never available. Some observers would be concerned also that agreements on verification inevitably involve Soviet concessions for which the United States will have to pay a price in other areas of the agreement in question. European governments are likely on the whole, with the exception of a comprehensive nuclear test ban and a possible agreement on a cut-off of fissionable materials, to accept American assessments concerning verification. In a situation in which views differ sharply in the American debate, European governments are still likely, with varying degrees of enthusiasm, to accept the judgment of the incumbent administration in Washington. The issue, of course, is much broader than a matter of monitoring capacities. Verifying a freeze agreement will require cooperative measures, data exchanges, and complaint procedures, the precise parameters of which need to be very carefully crafted.

The arguments which have been developed above indicate the need for a double linkage to be carefully considered: the first linkage to be effected is one between reductions and a freeze. It could be accomplished through specific provisions for freezes designed to prevent circumvention of agreements on reduction and limitation. Specific freeze provisions could be delineated, furthermore, with the aim of preventing destabilizing deployments according to agreed criteria. Finally, it is possible to envisage freeze agreements with build-down provisions requiring retirement of weapons to exceed the introduction of their replacements (within agreed parameters) by an agreed factor. Various schemes for combination and linkage should be explored.

The second linkage which should be made involves combining the INF negotiations and START, enabling the parties to trade off various choices within a common framework. A step-by-step approach may be envisaged. The first step might include a partial agreement which bans the deployment of Pershing II in return for commensurate reduction of the SS-20. The criterion for such preferential selection would be reciprocal concerns about high-accuracy, short flight-time missiles. Such a partial agreement would be coupled with an agreement to merge the INF negotiations and START with a view to negotiating a common and collective ceiling, taking into account the existence of *relevant allied* systems. The parties would be free to mix systems under the ceiling. Thus it would be up to either side to decide on how to distribute their assets among sea-based missiles, intercontinental range land-based missiles, bombers, or intermediate range systems. Such a formula would respond to the original political concerns about the SS-20 in Western Europe, i.e., that it constituted an unconstrained and additional threat to Western Europe, particularly the non-nuclear weapon states therein in the context of strategic parity. For NATO a new situation would thus have been created, enabling the alliance to agree to a freeze on preparations for deployment of new INF missiles pending the outcome of the negotiations and subsequent internal decisions concerning the mix of forces under the agreed ceilings. The collective ceilings could be defined primarily in terms of the number of warheads where the parties start from a position of approximate parity, and fixed low enough that they provide strong incentives for the parties to avoid concentrating many warheads in heavy missiles. The agreement need not contain detailed provisions concerning the force structure on either side. It would be designed rather to provide incentives for the parties to shun destabilizing deployments. The ceilings on warheads (and possibly sub-ceilings on launchers and missiles) could be progressively lowered through a permanent process of negotiation. In addition, of course, the agreement would need to contain precise provisions concerning the counting rules, boundary conditions in respect of dual role systems, complaints procedures, reliability testing, crew training, etc., etc. It is necessary to think in terms of novel approaches and logical combinations in order to break the present deadlock. In Europe it is necessary, most specifically, to get away from the tyranny of an approaching deadline for deployment, and substitute therefore a continuous process of negotiations about integrated solutions.

The concept of a nuclear freeze is not an analytical concept. It is an idea which has captured a mood. It amounts to an approach which must be orchestrated together with other means to produce viable arms control agreements. What is needed is the development of criteria for managing innovation and replacement in order to enhance stability and avoid destabilizing deployments. In this sense freeze must be preferential in nature. It should not become a protector of existing instabilities. The idea that enough is enough is sound, and the objective must be to create a downward trend. A dynamic freeze which incorporates mechanisms for a build-down of the arsenals as well as a structured arms control approach to modernization is needed. In some sense this takes us full circle, back to arms control, mutual restraint, and confidence building measures.

*   *   *

Political Perspectives

Fire and Ice

Senator Charles McC. Mathias, Jr.

It is a privilege to address this Conference on the Nuclear Weapons Freeze and Arms Control. I congratulate the Center for Science and International Affairs of the John F. Kennedy School of Government and the American Academy of Arts and Sciences for bringing together the right group at the right time to begin the crucial task of separating all that is good in the freeze proposal from what is awkward or unworkable.

In calling this conference, the Steering Committee put its finger on a potential problem that lends urgency to these deliberations. It pointed out that "The substantial and growing public support for the freeze may give way to disillusionment if ways are not found to translate general principles into viable proposals for arms control."

My greatest fear is that if the public becomes disillusioned, it may lose interest in arms control altogether. That is what brings me here tonight. And that is what has prompted me to suggest that we try to freeze a few ice cubes before we try to freeze a whole 100-ton chunk of ice.

Compared to most of you, I am no expert on nuclear disarmament. But, as a politician who has managed to survive in public life a fairly long time, I think I have some ability to sense the public mood. Right now, I think the American people—all the world's people—yearn for some immediate, tangible evidence of progress toward nuclear disarmament. And I think we can provide that evidence.

It is written in the Book of Proverbs that: "Hope deferred maketh the heart sick." So, if we are to avoid popular disillusionment, and perhaps worse, we must produce evidence of progress fairly soon.

Albert Einstein maintained that you should try to "make everything as simple as possible but not more so." And that seems to me to be pretty good advice when you consider a total freeze. The idea of a total freeze is very seductive; but I think it falls into Einstein's category of being too simple to be possible. Freezing huge chunks of ice just isn't as easy as it may seem to be.

What we need to do, if we are talking about freezing in a serious, mature way, is to talk about the various elements that could be frozen. We ought to be preparing ice cubes—of a usable, manageable, and practical size—that can be frozen quite easily individually. And then one by one they might gradually cool the nuclear arms race and bring it to a point where its direction could be reversed.

Charles Mathias *is a Senator (R-Maryland) in the United States Senate, Washington, D.C.*

There were moments in the last decade when it seemed that Americans might be able to develop a generally acceptable national security policy that combined the intelligent pursuit of arms control with prudent increases in our military force structure. SALT I and the Anti-Ballistic Missile Treaty, the Threshold Test Ban and Peaceful Nuclear Explosions treaties, all were accords that held the promise of greater things to come.

Some argued that ratification of SALT II, with amendments, would help to create a national consensus, which, in turn, would encourage our allies to believe that we were capable of sustaining a long-term national security policy spanning administrations. While none of these accords made a dramatic contribution to the control of nuclear arms, each was important as a confidence-building measure. And, most importantly, such small ice cubes were more easily digested by all concerned than one big block of icehouse ice.

Unfortunately, the anticipated consensus did not develop. Instead, this country's strategic policy direction has been pulled and hauled in a different direction every four years.

Today:

- We are embarked on still another set of U.S. strategic arms control initiatives, shelving, if not repudiating, the efforts of previous administrations;
- We continue to allow two painstakingly negotiated documents—the Peaceful Nuclear Explosions and Threshold Test Ban treaties—to languish unratified in the Senate;
- We have discontinued Comprehensive Test Ban negotiations;
- We are planning a large deployment of sea-launched cruise missiles and we are moving toward the militarization of outer space.

All of this projects an image of a nation unable to sustain an effective, coherent program for arms control and force structure that can retain strong public support. Our task is to change this perception. The way to approach this task is to work on those measures that will increase mutual confidence and promote nuclear stability. In this area, some ice trays are filled with water and are ready to pop into the freezer:

- As a first step, we must resume Comprehensive Test Ban (CTB) negotiations. In the 97th Congress, I introduced a resolution with Senator Kennedy and others that called on the President to resume trilateral negotiations toward conclusion of a verifiable CTB. We must press forward on this in the new Congress.
- A sensible next step would be to ratify the Threshold Test Ban and Peaceful Nuclear Explosions treaties. As you know, President Nixon signed the Threshold Test Ban Treaty (TTBT) in 1974 and sent it to the Senate in 1976. It has been gathering dust there ever since.

The Protocol to the TTBT provides for the exchange of geological and geographical data, which is essential for verifying the magnitude of a blast. The Protocol also designates specific areas as weapons test sites to assist verification. An agreement to exchange this and other more detailed data would plumb unprecedented levels of possible cooperation between the United States and the Soviet Union.

President Ford signed the Peaceful Nuclear Explosions (PNE) treaty in 1976. It, too, awaits Senate approval. Like the Threshold Test Ban, the PNE treaty contains verification provisions that make it a valuable confidence-building tool.

Articles IV and V of the PNE treaty establish the exchange of information and access to sites of explosions. The protocol to the treaty sets forth provisions for both detailed information and the rights and functions of observers at explosion sites.

The PNE treaty, combined with the TTBT, establishes a comprehensive system of regulations that would govern the underground nuclear explosions of the United States and the Soviet Union in a manner consistent with enhanced stability.

Other arms control initiatives of a practical size, while not yet ready for the freezer, must be addressed before they become unmanageable. The United States and the Soviet Union should agree on limitations on the deployment of sea-launched cruise missiles (SLCMs). Once major deployments of these missiles have occurred, any numerical limits we are attempting to secure through START will become meaningless. The easily concealable and transportable nature of the cruise missile will make United States and Soviet SLCM activity virtually impossible to verify. Once both sides possess equally effective SLCM systems, we will have sacrificed our ability to verify in the race to exploit this technology.

An analogous but even more dangerous situation exists in outer space. We are close to making outer space truly accessible; it is our next frontier. Clearly, certain outer space activity has contributed to arms control. But this positive aspect is threatened by a space technology that is rapidly providing the ability to destroy national technical means of verification. We must negotiate a treaty outlawing war and arms in space or prepare to defend our share of earth from space warfare.

There are six international treaties that govern the military uses of outer space, but apparently none is adequate for heading off the use of space for the next round of U.S.-Soviet brinksmanship. If we act now, the devastatingly expensive and lethal programs for the militarization of space could die a relatively clean, uncomplicated death. If we and the Soviets delay, we will be faced with an environment increasingly difficult to control and hostile to human beings a few hundred miles below.

A final ice cube worth exploring is the possibility of a ban on United States and Soviet new intercontinental ballistic missile (ICBM) flight tests. Earlier today you discussed Soviet initiatives and interests in a freeze. I think much could be made of this component of the comprehensive freeze proposal. Such a ban might lessen American fears of a Soviet first strike, which would almost certainly be directed at our land-based ICBM force. In addition to basing problems, our ICBM vulnerability depends on Soviet competence in delivering their ICBM warheads to their targets.

A complete ban on ICBM flight testing could, over time, erode Soviet faith in the reliability of their most important delivery vehicles. A country unsure of the reliability of its missiles would be much less likely to employ them in a preemptive strike or hair trigger reaction.

Would the U.S.S.R. buy the idea? That is hard to say. It is conceivable that they would have the same objections to this plan as they have to the START proposals. START, like an ICBM flight test ban, is aimed primarily at United States and Soviet land-based systems. But such a ban, unlike START, also would suspend our MX program. This might not be incentive enough for the Soviets to embrace a flight-test ban, but, since it would eliminate a major source of concern for the Soviet Union, it is certainly worth a try.

It is perhaps presumptuous of me to propose arms control measures in the presence of this company. But, in one respect, I may be uniquely qualified to speak. I visited Hiroshima and Nagasaki shortly after the bombs fell, before any of the cleanup had begun. Having walked through the atomic ruins of two cities, it is the fixed purpose of my life to assure that no city anywhere is ever again subjected to nuclear attack.

My longtime preoccupation with arms control stems from that experience with suffering and sorrow, death and destruction. My determination to seek solutions—ice cube by ice cube—is best conveyed by a memorable remark of David Ormsby Gore. He said:

"It would indeed be a tragedy if the history of the human race proved to be nothing more than the story of an ape playing with a box of matches on a petrol dump."

We may not be able to eliminate the petrol dump. We may not be able to confiscate the matches all at once. But we could start taking them away from the ape one by one.

* * *

Public Support for the Freeze:
The People Speak

Congressman Edward J. Markey

I appreciate having the opportunity to speak before this very impressive group. I understand that you will be publishing a report on this conference. I look forward to seeing that report. And, I hope you send a copy over to the Arms Control and Disarmament Agency.

I am honored to be speaking tonight with Mac Mathias, who has had a distinguished career on the Senate Foreign Relations Committee and who has long had an interest in arms control.

I am also particularly pleased to be the cosponsor in the House with Congressman Berkley Bedell of the same comprehensive test ban resolution that Senator Kennedy and Senator Mathias have sponsored in the Senate.

I am going to keep my remarks short and to the point. I have been pushing for the freeze now for almost a year. I have traveled all over the country talking about the freeze. I cannot count how many speeches I have given on it nor how many debates or arguments I have had on the freeze. I have listened to a lot of people out there express their hopes, their fears, and their frustrations about the nuclear arms race.

And I guess what I am trying to tell you is that I come here with a feeling of excitement that I think other people at this conference who have beaten the bushes organizing, educating, and speaking to the grass roots also feel—people like Randy Forsberg, Roger Molander, and Senator Kennedy who have helped make this issue a national issue.

I am excited because there is activism and energy and concern out there that we have never seen before in this country. People are just plain stirred up. And, here is my message to you in a nutshell.

The American people have presented you—the elite of the arms control community—with a golden opportunity. So, don't pass it up. Just think about it for a minute! On June 12, almost one million people rallied in New York City against nuclear war and for the freeze.

One million people!

Three years ago, arms controllers pushing SALT II were pretty lonely people. Can you imagine trying to organize that kind of rally during SALT II? So I think, above all else, we should be celebrating at this gathering—celebrating that finally there is now public enthusiasm for your work.

I noticed that the title of this conference is "The Nuclear Weapons Freeze and Arms Control" which seems to suggest that you are discussing two separate concerns here. I

Edward J. Markey *is a Congressman (D-Massachusetts) in the United States House of Representatives, Washington, D.C.*

do not see it that way. The fact is, the arms control initiative is out there in the grass roots. It was born out there, it grew out there, and it continues to grow out there. And so far, it has continued to confound the experts who said it wouldn't last this long.

In other words, the American people are ahead of you. So perhaps the more appropriate title for this conference is "How Can We Catch Up with the Freeze and Grab Hold." That is what this conference needs to do. You need to roll up your sleeves, buckle down, and figure out how we can have a freeze and reductions, not think up a hundred reasons why we can't.

The freeze is grounded in what should be the basic tenet of arms control—common sense. And as Ralph Waldo Emerson once said, "Nothing astonishes men so much as common sense." That is why the freeze has caught on in this country.

Lou Harris, I know, has already briefed you on the latest survey data on the freeze. I think the poll which I found was most revealing about how people feel about the arms race and how that feeling has been captured by the freeze resolution is a survey done by the *Washington Post* and ABC News last April.

A majority of the people polled did not believe the Soviets could be trusted.

A majority agreed that the Soviets would have numerical advantages over the U.S. in nuclear weapons if we froze now.

But three-fourths said it didn't matter because both sides have enough firepower to destroy the other no matter who attacks first.

And by a three-to-one margin, the people polled favored an immediate freeze on both sides.

Is that response a reaction to bumper sticker politics, as I have heard it called? Is that response simplistic? Is that response overcharged with emotionalism? I don't think so. I think it's more sophisticated and more level-headed than many would like to admit. As Paul Warnke has said, "What can possibly be wrong with stopping the arms race and proceeding with substantial reductions?" He hasn't heard a good answer yet. I haven't heard it. And neither have the American people.

Your job now is to figure out a way to stop the arms race so we can begin to reduce. I am a politician, not an arms controller. You are the ones who will have to work out the nuts and bolts of administering such a policy. But speaking as a politician, I can tell you that the grass roots movement has had a tremendous impact on my colleagues. E.F. Hutton has talked. And I can assure you the Congress is starting to listen.

The arms control community now has a big job ahead of it. But I urge you not to squander this opportunity. Don't let this public concern and activism slip through your hands.

*   *   *

Where Do We Go From Here?

Nuclear Arms Control: Nothing Until Everything?

McGeorge Bundy

I think that Paul Doty and his colleagues have done us all a great service in these last days. It's not easy to arrange the kind of careful and broad coverage of this very difficult subject that was arranged; both the quality and the temper of the discussion owe a lot, I think, to the arrangements made by the organizing committee. The freezers also deserve our thanks. Very often, when a movement gets going and has its own carefully defined and rather firm positions, it is not eager to expose itself to question and discussion. This meeting has been quite different in this respect, and I would like to say that I think it was a first-class performance, again both in content and temper.

Now, what kind of freeze do I want? The biggest one I can get. It seems to me the simple answer, and the only proviso I would put to that desire is that the result not be, in fact, destabilizing. One can imagine kinds of freezes which leave only the worst weapons. It seems to me possible that the Reagan reductions have this weakness, although the definitions given so far in public are insufficient to permit a clear judgment on the point. I think we would all have to agree, for example, that a treaty for zero warheads would be unstable. And that is one of the terrible facts about the world we live in. We have no way—and I think on this point our friends, the emeriti of the intelligence community, would agree—of verifying a zero warhead treaty. And so we can't have it. But, with that kind of obvious limitation, it appears to me that the right way of thinking about freezes is to think about getting the largest, broadest, strongest one you can. And, in a sense, it seems to me that the right process is to take all the proposals that have been seriously put forward here, and find out from the Soviet Union which starting points are best from its point of view. We can get a very helpful change in the international nuclear environment either with the broad freeze that Randy Forsberg represents or with the warhead freeze that Jan Lodal has presented. I think there is real promise in the approach taken by Congressman Gore and even if I didn't regard Senator Mathias as one of the wisest and most effective men of the center in American politics, I would be taken with his step-by-step approach. I wouldn't want to try to market this idea in the current White House because what Senator Mathias is doing is picking up the main line of effort which has been so energetically repudiated by the current management. It's possible, of course, that there could be a change; a man who can change Paul Nitze's name to Ed might

McGeorge Bundy *is Professor of History at New York University, New York, N.Y.*

change his position on other matters. But I don't see any evidence of it in the morning papers. The contrary is the impression that I get—that the President is determined to follow a course in which he does not move quickly to explore what may be acceptable to others that is also acceptable to us, which appears to me to be the right way to proceed.

I believe that we ought to go this way because we have to recognize that any freeze is hard to get; that it is, in fact, not simple to negotiate with the leaders of the Soviet Union; that there is great difficulty in getting agreements sufficiently precise to endure and to hold confidence. While we do indeed have many building blocks left to us from the process of SALT and some more may be in the making in terms of definition and clarification in the current discussions in Geneva, nonetheless it is not simple, and I don't think that I heard anyone claim that it is. The concept of any given freeze may be simple, but the language of a freeze agreement will not be. And it will take time to negotiate, and we have to realize that the more you put in, the harder it is to negotiate. A freeze on the production of fissionable material, for example, is going to be very hard to negotiate on a bilateral basis, for obvious reasons relating to the Soviet Union's concern about third, fourth, and fifth powers, and very difficult to negotiate on a multilateral basis because of the attitude of the third, fourth, and fifth powers. It seems to me only honest to recognize that. And that kind of difficulty is what accounts for my own reservations about the language of the Kennedy/Hatfield freeze. I do not believe that it is quite right to propose and seem to believe in an immediate, bilateral, and verifiable freeze on testing, deployment, and production. There is no such animal, and either the people who propose this are naive or they are incompletely candid.

So I think the question you have to ask is: if you can't get it all at once, what do you do? And my line of approach would be, as I say, to go after the question by finding out what you can get and what you can get will determine, of course, what you give. This process is quite hard enough, demanding enough, to require the full attention of very strong and effective executive branch leadership. That brings me to another point: along with a good deal of interesting analysis and effective reference to history, we have had some not very good history in the last day or two. It really isn't true that the limited test ban, for example, was negotiated in 13 days. What happened was that a very important Presidential decision was made, that we would sign an atmospheric test ban treaty and would not test again if others did not. And that decision, in turn, rested upon an increase of confidence on the part of the President himself in his ability to make that proposal. And it's worth recalling that the history of atmospheric testing included a moratorium, begun in the late 1950s in the Eisenhower Administration and broken to the tune of fifty-eight megatons by the Soviet Union late in 1961, and that the shock of that broken moratorium was, in itself, a factor in further delay. So one needs to be careful in thinking that the way you get agreements is simply by stirring public concern. That is essential, but that is not all that is needed. What happened was that after the moratorium was broken, the Soviets tested, we tested, then the Soviets had a second series of tests. And, in effect, what the President did was to reach the conclusion that that two-to-one ballgame didn't matter, that that score was unimportant, and he imposed that view on his administration and then persuaded the country—not, incidentally, by consulting his administration before he did so, but by announcing his position in a speech.

Now, I think the history of arms control agreements is that you don't get them without strong and determined Presidential leadership. Of course the job is not always done by the President himself; it can be done by the delegation of powers of negotiation to a trusted individual. That could happen in the Reagan Administration if, in fact, the President intends that Secretary Shultz should truly be his deputy in these matters. We don't know whether that's true or not, nor do we know whether the premises on which the President seems to be basing his policies can be changed. I would predict, without much hesitation, that unless there is a change in premises, there will not be an agreement in this administration.

Nonetheless, the proposition holds, I think, that you cannot go past the President to an international agreement. The White House has enormous superiority of visibility, when it is used—and it certainly is used in this Administration. More than that, the process of coordinating a naturally rambling and discordant government, full of divergent views, and especially on this subject, is hard to manage unless the President's direct interest or his delegation of authority is clear. That being so, my own view about freezes is that most of our effort should go into ways and means of making changes in our own positions and thinking in the United States during these next two years so that there will be a wider and deeper base for effective negotiation when we have an administration that truly is determined to get the best obtainable agreement. And I think in that sense that I would differ from a number of those who spoke to issues of understanding, perception, and public opinion in the last day or two.

I think it's a mistake to accept the proposition that attitudes toward particular problems of arms control are immutable. It is certainly true, as Lou Harris reminded us, that the American people don't trust the Russians. It is probably true that that is a sound instinct. But it is also true, as others said, that on balance the record of the Soviet Union is that, while it is unconstrained by the "spirit" of agreements, it will keep to their letter—a fact which makes the text and meaning of agreements in the most literal sense of the words a matter of great importance. But we can, I think, make progress in getting people to understand that it is possible to have workable agreements with people who, in the ordinary sense of the words are not very trustworthy and not particularly addicted to the truth. That change is an important change. There has been change of this kind already. If you think about the way we thought about these matters in the '50s, before we got on serious arms control, and the reasons often given in those days for not having serious arms control negotiations, you will see how much our attitude has changed, and I think it can change further.

The same thing, I believe, is true about the problem of verifiability, and the relative value of the intelligence process and the more visible process of on-site inspection—a matter which was debated in the last day or two. I think it is possible, as both Colby and Scoville suggested, to increase public confidence in the process by which we do verify, within tolerable limits, many kinds of things that are harder to verify than the essential elements of most freezes. I am persuaded that the central problem is not verifiability, with nearly any freeze that has been proposed, but negotiability. And I believe it is possible to get that point clearly across. It should be possible—and I think this is very important and again that we have made progress in it—to get wider and deeper public understanding of the fact that although all nuclear weapons are terrible, if ever used, some systems are much worse than others from the point of view of the danger they create to stability, the risk they present of making the world even more dangerous than it inescapably is and would be under the best of freezes. I think that the difference between MX and Minuteman II is a very important difference in terms of what it means to an adversary, and that survivability is increasingly understood as the most important single element in any weapons system. There is, moreover, a lot of value in focusing on the worst weapons, both in discussions of the present situation and in thinking about what needs to be negotiated first, because in the end, even if our objective is the most sweeping of freezes, we will find ourselves necessarily proceeding step by step unless we prefer to do nothing until we do everything, which would not be my own preference.

I believe that we need to work still harder for increased national understanding of relatively basic questions which are, I think, in less debate among us that I would have expected before I came; not only that verifiability is attainable, but that the balance is essentially insensitive to marginal changes. It really is not a very hard proposition that when you are working in the range of ten thousand strategic weapons on each side, you really don't care about the marginal five hundred or one thousand. I believe that the concept of overkill can be persuasively explained to and accepted by the Americal public. And I don't believe that we need to be caught forever in Senator Jackson's or Richard Perle's definition of essential equivalence. I think it's possible to make it plain that essential equivalence came in sight in August 1949 when the first Soviet explosion went off and was regarded as inescapable and close by such realistic and sober men as Eisenhower and Churchill by the middle of the 1950s. In terms of what would really happen if these things were ever used, and in terms of what they are good for, we have not moved that much in the succeeding thirty years and cannot expect to move that much even under the best of freezes, which would leave thousands in place.

I obviously believe, and I think most of us believe, that even the best of freezes is no panacea, that the thermonuclear age is with us and with us to stay. But I believe that this kind of deeper understanding and perception can help us with that reality too. And I will close by saying that that is the reason that I have a particular interest, which Henry Kendall and I share in this meeting, in emphasizing the need to reduce and presently to eliminate any reliance on any first use of these weapons for any purpose. Because if you do that, you recognize and respect the basic reality that the only ultimate value of these weapons is to prevent their use by anyone.

Deterrence, as our panel on ethics reminded us, is not the most clearly moral of policies. It is only the least bad one available to us in the range of time over which we can realistically plan and think. It is not a pleasant requirement. It is, I believe, an essential one, but it is also of the highest importance that our reliance upon it be as limited as possible. I thought that Leon Sloss was correct to remind us that this reality raises questions about the validity of a policy of so-called extended deterrence. My own position on that matter is that we will come to terms with ourselves, with our fears and our allies only when we redefine extended deterrence. It will still be very broad in historic terms to mean that within the alliance we will be ready to use weapons in the event of their use by others, although even that poses very grave questions. But not that we will be ready for their first use.

Let me here add one quite different final thought. In this conference, addressed as it was to questions that have arisen between freezers and arms-controllers, we gave little attention to a different but very important area of poor communication and frequent misunderstanding: the relation between believers in arms control and those who have direct responsibility for the design, deployment, targeting, and operation of these systems. The record shows all sorts of difficulties in these relations, although it also shows plenty of cases where men in uniform have understood the need for arms control better than civilians, and conversely cases where civilians have been more alert than military men to the real military implications of particular developments (most notably MIRV).

I think the freeze in its broad form—the freezers' freeze, if you will—presents special difficulties here. One purpose in some of the thinking behind the comprehensive freeze is quite simply to reduce the effectiveness and reliability of all nuclear systems. Such a purpose is seen as genuinely threatening by many military men who are in no sense believers in any unrestrained arms build-up. The notion that a less reliable weapon, or a less modern aircraft, or a less accurate guidance system is somehow better for peace, is not one that comes naturally to a professional who has been taught by precept and experience to hold exactly opposite convictions. On this sort of question, I believe, the instinctive reaction of most Americans (to say nothing of the relevant Russians) will be more like that of the military men than that of the ardent freezer.

I note this difficulty not because I think it undermines the case for the freeze—I'm not convinced that it does—but rather because it illuminates, by a particularly sharp example, the difficulty of working for arms control in ways that can win and hold the broad and steady support of the American public. If there is one proposition that Americans have been agreed on over the years, it is that our fighting men deserve the best. It will be necessary for all of us who believe in arms restraint to be ready to meet the questions that can be asked, from this starting point, about old aircraft, old missiles, old submarines, and old warheads. To put it more technically, sooner or later freezers must face up to the pros and cons of particular kinds of modernization much more clearly and completely than they have so far. And to put it more broadly, the present movement for the reduction of nuclear danger, if it is not to be just one more upswing in a sine curve of rising and waning public concern, will have to address the ways and means of getting beyond the simple posture of perceiving those who have the direct responsibility for effective nuclear deterrence as automatic opponents. The temptations of polarization are great; its consequences are shriveling to the prospect of durable action. The real hope is in the identification and the persuasive exposition of a doctrine of restrained and controlled deterrence—of limits and reductions, of unilateral moderation and reliable bilateral constraints—which can have the sustained support of an effective coalition of men and women, expert and nonexpert, in and out of uniform. Incomplete as its work has been, I think this conference has been conducted in a spirit that can help us also in this still wider and more difficult task of inquiry, communication, and understanding.

* * *

Stopping the Nuclear Arms Race: Defining the Possible

Randall Forsberg

I would like to thank the Organizing Committee, Paul Doty, and the Center for Science and International Affairs for arranging an excellent conference. A conference of this kind, a real dialogue with people listening to each other make points that they have not agreed to before, is very rare. It is particularly rare among people who have as widely divergent initial views as those at this conference. From my own point of view, this may be the single most important meeting that I will attend this year; for it is the beginning of a discussion within the arms control community and between the arms control community and the activists about how much is possible in nuclear arms control.

The freeze campaign is not at all dogmatic or uninterested in listening to reason, looking at evidence, looking at possible tradeoffs among timing, verifiability, and coverage. However, the activist members of the campaign—those who have gone out and gathered the petition signatures, who have done the leafletting, who have manned the offices—are skeptical. They are skeptical when they see arms control experts dismiss a new idea with a hand wave at infeasibility, without any apparent effort to investigate feasibility or consider the possibility of a new approach. The attitude of the activist community toward the arms control community is definitely one of interest, but interest combined with a desire to see openness in addressing the issues. From that point of view, this morning's session is certainly not going to bring us any conclusions which will be accepted as final by the activists about what sort of freeze might be achievable in the near future and by what means. Rather, what we can accomplish here is to sketch out some possibilities and, more importantly, to raise and define issues which need to be investigated further before we can decide what kind of freeze might be achievable over what period of time.

Randall Forsberg is President and Executive Director of the Institute for Defense and Disarmament Studies, Brookline, Massachusetts.

I should like to look at this issue from the point of view of three time periods. First of all, the medium term: by that I mean around 1985 or 1986. The reason I choose this period is, first, that there is a possibility of a change in administration. Second, 1986 still lies within the "window of opportunity" for stopping the majority of the new generation of nuclear weapons to be produced on the U.S. side; and it lies well on this side of the time when the Soviet Union might feel compelled by the new generation of U.S. nuclear weapons to engage in a corresponding new buildup. Finally, it seems clear to me that 1985 is far enough away so that we *do* have time to look seriously, with detailed research, into the definitions, the verifiability, the intrusiveness, the tradeoffs, the feasibility from the point of view of Soviet politics and Soviet internal bureaucracy, of different types of freezes. Even if we cannot answer all the questions by next week, that does not mean that we cannot make a lot of progress on them by, say, June 1985, nor that we cannot do that unilaterally. That sort of progress—looking at the obstacles and the solutions within the research community in this country and then making the results available to the Soviet Union—in the past has accomplished a lot of what one might expect to go on in secret negotiations.

Looking over the period to 1986, then, this conference has *not* shown me that the sort of comprehensive freeze outlined in the Call to Halt the Nuclear Arms Race is impossible. There are, however, a variety of legitimate issues about such a freeze which have been raised at this conference. I should like to give my assessment of what we can tell about them so far.

First of all, on the matter of verification, the single most important issue from some points of view: I think that there is a wide consensus at this point that we can adequately verify things that have essentially already been negotiated or shown to be verifiable in the past, specifically, the testing and deployment of strategic and intermediate-range missiles. Exactly where the cutoff line would go, in terms of size, is unclear. Franklin Long suggested thousand-kilometer-range missiles; Roger Molander suggested six-hundred-kilometer range. In addition, most experts think we would stop testing nuclear warheads. In other words, there is a broad consensus that we could verify by national means and agreed cooperative means a quick moratorium between the two countries on testing and deployment of strategic and intermediate-range missiles and testing of nuclear warheads.

At the other end of the spectrum, I think there is a wide measure of consensus that, from satellites, we cannot tell whether the Soviet Union is producing nuclear-equipped torpedoes. The production of small tactical nuclear weapons, the numbers of those weapons, whether or not they are being stored, cannot be detected, most would agree, by current satellites and other national means of detection. However, the poor monitoring capability applies to the *production of small* nuclear weapon systems as one activity, taken in isolation, within an ongoing nuclear arms race. If *all* nuclear weapon production and deployment were suspended, as is proposed in the freeze, there would be many junctures at which we could detect continued production of small tactical nuclear systems.

For any nuclear weapon system there is a long production and deployment process which starts with the production of the warheads themselves and concludes with not merely the production of a particular delivery system, but also the production of all the ancillary equipment, the delivery to forces, the training of those forces in use of that weapon system, the provision for security and for command and control which is unique to nuclear weapons within the panoply of armed forces, and, finally, the chain of command which is unique to nuclear weapons. In other words, even in the case of small tactical nuclear weapons, there are highly visible signs of their existence, at least insofar as they are deployed in a way in which they can actually be used.

What about the special case of breakout, when weapons are produced but not deployed? I do not have time to review that in detail, even though many people think that it is the decisive case. Let me just outline the principal response. The purpose of nuclear weapons is to deter war. If the weapons are not deployed, if the troops have not been trained, if the opponent is not even aware of their existence, then they do not serve any function in our world. So, the prima facie case, even for small tactical nuclear weapons, is that if there were a comprehensive test ban on production, testing, and new deployment of all nuclear weapons there would be many junctures at which a country attempting to secretly get a usable or meaningful capability could be detected by national technical means.

Between the two extremes—the area where we have broad consensus on verifiability, that is, large weapons and their highly visible deployment and testing, and the least verifiable area of very small nuclear weapon sysetms and their concealed production—there are a range of other activities and a range of views on their verifiability. One of the most verifiable of such activities is the cutoff of the production of fissionable material. In reference to this activity, I must disagree with Mr. Bundy. The continued production of fissionable material by France, China, and England is not an obstacle to the cutoff of production of fissionable material by the Soviet Union and the United States, given the enormous disparity—a couple of orders of magnitude—between the existing stocks of fissionable materials in the United States and the Soviet Union and those in China and France. In addition, the small numbers of delivery vehicles of France and China, their lack of sophistication and range, the lack of a comprehensive, superpower-type nuclear panoply mean that even if the United States and the Soviet Union stopped making nuclear weapons today, the two superpowers would still be far in advance of where France or China could be not just in ten years, but in twenty years, or even thirty years. The freeze proposal for the United States not to produce twenty thousand new warheads over the next decade and for the Soviets not to produce what is probably a smaller number—five-to-ten thousand warheads—cannot be vitiated by the fact that France and China might produce two or three hundred new warheads, each over the next decade. It represents a lack of a sense of proportion about the role of nuclear weapons in world politics to see the Chinese as an obstacle to a U.S.-Soviet halt. Now, I have heard some Soviet experts refer to China as a potential obstacle, so they may use references to France and China as a political ploy to avoid a halt. Nevertheless, I think the point is entirely inappropriate and should be dismissed.

The production of large nuclear delivery vehicles—intercontinental ballistic missiles, intermediate-range ballistic missiles, and long-range cruise missiles—is an area where, in my view, there has been a lot of loose talk about non-verifiability. If we did not in fact have a very good degree of national intelligence capability in this area, we would not have strategic nuclear arms control on deployment, of the type represented by SALT I and SALT II. So I urge those who have stated flatly that "we cannot verify production" to reconsider the boundaries here. At issue is not whether or not we can monitor Soviet production of ballistic missiles, but with what margin of error. This is confirmed in the last two years' presentations of the Defense Intelligence Agency before the Joint Economic Committee on Soviet Defense Production. The DIA lists *annual* totals of Soviet *production* of ballistic missiles, both strategic and intermediate-range. These production totals each differ several hundred from what the Soviet Union was deploying during the same year. In fact, there is an apparent inconsistency among (1) the SALT limits on Soviet deployment of ballistic missiles, (2) the DIA-estimated numbers of missiles produced by the U.S.S.R., and (3) the statements by the Secretary of Defense that the Soviet Union has not produced more missiles than roughly the number that they are permitted to deploy. I imagine the disparity represents missiles produced for testing, in the case of strategic missiles, and for future deployment, in the case of IRBMs. In any event, the commonly held arms control objection that "production cannot be verified" clearly needs serious rethinking for large delivery vehicles.

Finally, in the case of medium-range systems, there is probably an inverse relationship between the size of the object and our ability to monitor the production of that object. Roger Molander claims in his survey that SALT-type monitoring can detect the production of planes as small as the FB-111. In addition, the DIA reports on Soviet production cover not merely large items, like submarines and ICBMs, but also tanks, fighter airplanes, and even artillery pieces. This suggests that the United States has a considerable capability to monitor Soviet production of these smaller items. Of course, this standard monitoring of Soviet military production does not rely on any cooperation on the part of the Soviet Union with consultative committees or other special arrangements. U.S. monitoring of production occurs despite the full effort of the Soviet Union to conceal their production of these items. Yet the United States seems to be doing a pretty good job. So, again, I would like to urge the arms control community to drop the facile statements that we cannot monitor production and to assess U.S. capability much more carefully.

Going beyond verification, the next most important issue for a comprehensive freeze is the durability of existing nuclear systems. This is both a technical question and an issue of political choice. How long would we want a freeze to last? Would we be able to maintain the weapons we have now until we decided to dismantle them? Could we maintain them indefinitely through maintenance procedures if we spent a little more and reopened production lines for the replacement of parts? Or is that not possible for some reason? Would it be desirable at some point to open whole production lines for replacements? Is it possible to have replacement rather than just maintenance with spare parts without technical innovation? Is this politically possible? Is it technically possible? As far as I know, these questions have not been investigated. It has been argued that it would be impossible to reopen, say, a B-52 production line or a Minuteman II production line because the parts and the technology are obsolete. Who would want to reproduce an old computer when there are new ones sitting on the shelf? In summary, I tend to believe that maintenance without innovation, through replacement of parts, would be technically possible but politically difficult.

In the final analysis, the durability of existing forces is not so much an obstacle to a freeze on new production as it is a question for the post-freeze program of reductions. Which forces would we want to maintain for how long after new production stopped? Maintenance over a period of five or ten years would not be a real problem. Twenty or thirty years might also be manageable, but then one must ask: What sort of reductions might we hope for at the end of thirty years? Could we in that time create conditions that would make it possible to abolish nuclear weapons? Or are we going to continue manufacturing more nuclear weapons now, and maintaining the confrontation that perpetuates the arms race, simply because we are already convinced that it will prove impossible to abolish nuclear weapons within the next two or three decades—and thereby seal our own fate with a self-fulfilling prophecy?

Overlapping with durability in the sense that it is a question of definition—that is a question of political choice more than a technical problem, at least in the first instance—is the question of what to do about dual-capable systems. Dual-capable systems, for example, could be allowed to be manufactured, but without a nuclear capability. This would require probably very intrusive on-site inspection; it would be one of the aspects of a comprehensive freeze least verifiable by national technical means, though not totally unverifiable. Dual-capable aircraft are deployed near warhead storage depots which are possible to observe. Equally important, the aircraft are trained in nuclear delivery bombing runs, which can be observed.

Another way to treat dual-capable systems, somewhat less demanding on verification capabilities, would be to ban any increase in the *numbers* of dual-capable systems to permit replacement of existing systems with new ones. This would allow the technological arms race to go on in dual-capable aircraft and howitzers, but with controls on payload and range, there would be no increase in the nuclear threat.

Thus, we could provide a reassuring answer to a question that is bound to be raised when the freeze is taken more seriously; that is, if we freeze dedicated nuclear delivery vehicles, don't we risk an increase in dual-capable systems or systems which would quickly be converted to nuclear capability? A freeze on numbers would preclude such an increase. Finally, the least demanding way of dealing with dual-capable systems would be not to limit them directly, but simply to rely on a cutoff of the production of fissionable material and nuclear warheads to prevent any net increase in the nuclear threat.

A last set of issues about a comprehensive freeze has to do with Soviet interests and the negotiability of a freeze with the Soviet Union. What seems likely to me is that there is not one consistent Soviet point of view, but at least two main conflicting tendencies. On the one hand, as Stephen Meyer's analysis indicates, Soviet military interests, narrowly defined, should tend to support a freeze. The Soviet Union has recently modernized its nuclear forces. It has achieved parity with the United States.

And it faces the U.S. deployment during the next decade of many new counterforce systems that will threaten Soviet forces and increase the risk of war. From the point of view of the overarching Soviet national interests in the military area, a comprehensive freeze on new nuclear production should be welcome.

On the other hand, the Soviet Union, like the United States, has an entrenched military and foreign policy bureaucracy that feels comfortable managing a permanent technological arms race and threatened by the idea of making a fundamental change.

Probably not much serious thought has been given to the freeze proposal by Soviet government agencies, just as little thought has been given to it by the appropriate bureaucracies here. That means, at the very least, that in the tug of war among competing Soviet interests, the freeze proposal will take some time to work its way through. But we need not wait until 1985 to start that process: we can get it going now by initiating research studies and scholarly dialogue now.

Difficult areas of verification, durability of existing systems, dual-capable systems, Soviet interests: these are my propositions for what needs to be studied and debated in a far more sophisticated and detailed way over the medium term, the next two years, than has even begun to be done. Let me conclude with some comments on the very short term and on the longer term.

On the very short term, I think that we, the freeze campaign, face a problem in Congress and with the people in the sense that from now until 1985 is a long time to keep motivation up and to keep people active. From that point of view, I am enthusiastic about Jeremy Stone's proposal for interim reciprocal restraints on testing of new missiles, bombers, and warheads, to be introduced in Congress as amendments to the appropriation bills. It is clear that the freeze resolution will occupy the campaign's attention in the spring of 1983. I expect that the reciprocal restraints amendments will occupy our attention in the fall of 1983. From that time on we will be moving into the 1984 elections. The freeze campaign will attempt to influence the outcome of the elections in many ways: in terms of House and Senate races, in terms of presidential candidates, and in terms of the party platforms and the issues that differentiate among candidates.

Looking at the long term, beyond 1985, beyond whatever is the broadest freeze we can achieve, both internally in our own domestic "negotiation" and in negotiations with the Soviet Union, I would like to state my own position, which should be clearly distinguished from that of the freeze campaign. The freeze campaign is a single-issue campaign. It is a coalescing of people around one idea. The reason that it is so large is that it is not complicated by longer-term questions of where you go from there.

My view is that the nuclear arms race cannot be locked off from conventional warfare and world politics. Control of the nuclear arms race is not something that can be, has been, or will be treated separately from the influence of the nuclear balance on the outbreak and outcome of conventional warfare and, indeed, its influence on lesser foreign policy choices. Like a no-first-use policy, the freeze represents an effort to weaken the inevitable link between conventional warfare and the possiblity of escalation to nuclear warfare; but that link can never be entirely broken, in my view. Thus nuclear weapons, to my mind, cannot be abolished unless and until we have brought conventional warfare under control. This is a far more difficult proposition than nuclear arms control. As I often say to popular audiences: "If you think it is difficult to stop the nuclear arms race, wait until you see what it is like to stop Soviet and U.S. intervention in developing countries." That, I believe is where arms control must go in the longer term.

A nuclear freeze would stop a further evolution of stages in the ladder of escalation between conventional warfare and nuclear holocaust, an elaboration of escalation capabilities which will otherwise take place over the next ten years. But because it would leave in place fifty thousand nuclear weapons, a nuclear freeze would do little to widen the firebreak between nuclear and conventional war. Reducing the strategic arsenals, which account for less than half of U.S. and Soviet nuclear weapons, by a couple of thousand warheads is not going to do very much to weaken the link either. And, in conclusion, I do not believe that we will get much beyond that in nuclear arms control—much beyond stopping and maybe reducing a few thousand warheads—before we will find that we must turn our attention to the use of conventional force in international politics. For that reason, I think we must be extremely cautious about concepts of building up conventional forces or allowing and supporting the development of rapid deployment forces for unilateral intervention as though that were something that was completely unrelated to the danger of nuclear war. Conventional intervention and nuclear escalation are interrelated. With the freeze we must stop the increased propensity to escalation. Then we can turn to the provocation most likely to lead to escalation: unilateral intervention by the superpowers in their own self-interest.

* * *

Avoiding Nuclear Sectarianism: Toward a Compromise Freeze Proposal

Joseph S. Nye

I would also like to start with a comment about the last day in particular of this conference. I think it's worth noticing some nice moments that occurred. One was at a point when there was a good deal of skepticism being expressed from this panel, and then a question was put to which the answer was: "Well, let's face the fact that we arms controllers owe an awful lot to the freeze movement." I think that's absolutely true and we don't want to lose sight of the fact that the freeze has provided support for arms control that it hasn't had in a long time. Compare the debate today to the debate of 1980 and the rhetoric of 1981, and you can quickly see what I mean. That was admitted by freezers and non-freezers alike. Another point I thought was particularly interesting was the statement by one of the members of my ethics panel to the effect that the freeze movement has expressed a high ethical standard in terms of dealing with profound issues in a very responsible way, without a great deal of posturing, without deafness, but with an effort to really listen and to respond seriously. I think that the fact that we may disagree on some particular points has to be seen in that larger context.

On the other hand, there is a certain difficulty that I have as somebody who supports the freeze movement for what it has accomplished as a movement, but who is not yet convinced by all the particulars of the device of a comprehensive nuclear freeze. And basically, there are three choices that somebody in that position could take. One would be to oppose it, which would be mistaken because it would merely give comfort to those with whom I disagree much more. Another would be to accept it, and I'll say in a minute why I can't accept a comprehensive freeze pure and simple. The third is to try to seek a compromise, to try to essentially look for some way to bridge the gap, and I gather that that is the purpose of this conference. So, I will suggest such a compromise in my remarks.

But first, why don't I just shut up and go along? Well, the answer is that I'm not honestly convinced by all the arguments about a comprehensive freeze. I think there's been some progress at this conference in answering some of my concerns, but not all of them. And there are several on the verification level that we did discuss at some length yesterday. Verification is obviously a political judgment. I thought yesterday's discussion was particularly useful in making sure that people who were skeptical about the freeze not use the shorthand that's been used all too often in the past of saying a freeze is not verifiable. There are many things that are verifiable that would be frozen. And I think that the important things are not so simple. I also thought yesterday's panel was particularly useful in getting away from some of the shibboleths in

Joseph S. Nye is Professor of Government at the John F. Kennedy School of Government, Harvard University, Cambridge, Massachusetts.

this area, particularly some of the intrusive on-site inspection ideas, and pointing out that what really matters are cooperative measures which enhance the value of national technical means. Things like counting rules, limitations on types of platforms on which to deploy things, efforts to provide data can make sure that national technical means can extend the range of verification within the kinds of confidence standards that McGeorge Bundy was referring to.

So, in that sense I thought the panel was very helpful. But I thought the panel was not helpful in one other way, which is the way it focused on the easy problems, the things we know we can verify. And there are some things that are harder—in gray areas if you like—that we didn't adequately discuss. I remain somewhat concerned with the cutoff of fissile material in a country which has a major breeder reactor program, as the Soviets intend to have in the future. You could say that the problem is not a current one, and the numbers that could be covered in such a program might be only 50 to 500 bombs a year, so why should we worry about that? Well, if we also have deep cuts and it goes on for ten years, presumably that would make some difference. I think that one should also be concerned about the problem of warhead dismantlement and reassembly, in other words mining the fissile material from existing warheads, many of which would be withdrawn anyway. I'm not at all convinced that we know how to monitor that as well as has been asserted. There are other areas that we didn't discuss such as anti-submarine warfare and air defense. If we freeze a measure and not a countermeasure, particularly when we're talking about the assured destruction components of the forces—the sea and air components—what does the world look like ten years from now? And if you say, well, I don't want to freeze submarines or their new longer range missiles without freezing anti-submarine warfare, or freeze aircraft without freezing air defenses, how do you verify limits on changes? What is a permitted replacement and what is an illegal modernization? Should the limits be unrelated to the progress in the countermeasures?

That gets me to the second question that I'm still not convinced about: the effects of a comprehensive freeze on crisis stability. When one looks ahead in any defense area, one is looking at decisions taken today that will affect the world eight to ten years from now. That's simply the nature of the lead times we have to work with in these systems. The question is not whether one feels terribly uncomfortable with the balane today—obviously there's been a lot of scare language about today's balance, but it's not something that I am currently scared about—but if one looks ahead ten years and thinks of what it could look like, the situation could be different. Soviet submarines are not very quiet and American progress in anti-submarine warfare could make the Soviets in the 1990s fear for the reliability of their second strike deterrent. They might wish not only for new subs, but for longer range submarine-launched missiles. Or look at American aircraft and the ability to penetrate Soviet air defenses and imagine that we're frozen with B-52s and Stealth technology cannot be developed and cannot be applied to cruise missiles. Then one asks what do you think is the prospect of penetration of these slow forces in the '90s? Those strike me as points with which we have to be concerned. What are the net effects of freezing measures but not countermeasures upon crisis stability, and upon that sense of security that one would need that there would not be any kinds of sudden breakthroughs?

It strikes me that these are issues that we haven't discussed enough. In the ICBM area which we have discussed, if one believes that there still is an important deterrent role for land-based missiles because of their reliable communications and because of the difficulty of simultaneous attacks on both bombers and ICBMs, then one could want to have at least some ICBMs, but not the kind we're developing now. One might indeed prefer to have a better solution, which I believe would be a small, single-warhead missile, preferably mobile. If one has these types of concerns about stability in the '90s, then one has to ask why should we freeze all things now?

Well, one of the answers we've heard is an assumption about the effect of technological change. The assumption is that technological change is destabilizing per se. But I don't think that's necessarily true. Some technological changes are, indeed, destabilizing; a freeze in 1969 which would have prevented MIRVing would have left us a lot better off today than we are. On the other hand, a freeze in 1959 that would have prohibited the deployment of the sea-based Polaris force would, I think, have left us far worse off at the time of the Cuban missile crisis. So, in that sense, I think one has to ask not can we stop all technology or is all technology destabilizing, but more specifically, what should we target within that range? So, that's a second area where my concerns are still not totally put to rest by the conference.

And the third is the area of negotiability that Randy Forsberg mentioned. When one has a very broad list, as in the comprehensive freeze, there are many gray areas, and verifiability problems in many of these gray areas can be solved if you have cooperative measures. But cooperative measures mean a great deal of negotiation. And I guess as Walt Slocombe put it yesterday, verification tends to be an American problem more than a Soviet problem. That means those negotiations are not as simple as they might first appear. So, in that sense, one has concern about the breadth of the list and the time that it takes to negotiate an agreement.

The other point is the problem of incentive to negotiate. I also felt that Steve Meyer's presentation about particular systems was very useful, but I think his evidence cuts both ways as to where the incentives are for negotiation. There is a danger shared by arms controllers and freezers of referring in shorthand to "the discredited bargaining chip argument." Unfortunately, I don't think the argument is totally discredited. There may be many instances where the reason that the Soviets might have an interest in freezing is because of the systems they see coming. That is the other half of Steve Meyer's argument. Those systems that they see coming are on the American side. We can ignore that, but we ignore it at our peril. Of course it doesn't follow that one should build everything that one sees on the wish list as a result of "bargaining chip" arguments. I think one has to ask oneself the hard question: if this is a bargaining chip and I don't get the bargain, do I still want the chip? And if you're clear in your mind that you don't, then you'd better not play that game. But there are some other instances where there may be some ambiguity, where in fact there is a benefit from the bargaining chip argument. It is difficult to be definite about

Soviet incentives, but I don't think we as freezers or arms controllers serve our own interests by denying that the argument has something in it. Otherwise, I think we're not really looking at some of the details of Soviet behavior in the past. So, I think there's a lot more to be studied and thought through in the area of negotiability. And these three points relating to details of verification, crisis stability, and negotiability are why I still find it hard to accept a comprehensive freeze in the Kennedy/Hatfield type formulation. But I am interested in looking for a compromise because the danger I see is that the freezers and arms controllers may cross purposes and discover only too late that sectarianism has destroyed their common effort to try to get some serious control on nuclear arms.

Moreover, I think there are areas where one could imagine a compromise. For example, you could imagine splitting the difference between the comprehensive freeze people and the arms control people, both in terms of how much is on the list—one dimension—and in terms of time, or stages—another dimension. And it might be possible, if not to agree on a full program, to at least agree on what should be the first stage and what should be priorities on the list.

In that sense I think you can imagine a partial freeze as a first step. It would have three components. One would be what Jan Lodal and I have written about, which is the idea of a freeze on the number of deployed strategic warheads with ranges over a thousand miles. That is easily verifiable by the existing national technical means we have now, plus the already negotiated SALT counting rules and procedures. Because the numbers come out about the same, it may not be all that hard to negotiate. That is an assumption which may be wrong, but at least one is starting from an area where the numbers are about the same on both sides.

The second item in a partial freeze would be a freeze on new MIRVed ICBMs. This would stop MX, but that's a price I'm willing to pay. The third part would be to freeze deployment of sea-launched cruise missiles, which are likely to damage verification. If you had wide deployment of sea-launched cruise missiles on both subs and surface ships, it would be extraordinarily difficult to know anything about numbers. Such a freeze could be a prelude to a negotiated ban or to an agreement on cooperative measures to assure verification.

Along with these three steps, you have to combine a fourth step of negotiations with the Soviets which would focus on reductions and on cooperative measures. Such negotiations would include how to handle problems of mobility and how to handle difficult-to-verify systems like cruise missiles generically. If you're working with cooperative measures to back up national technical means, there are things you could do to get a reasonable handle on the verification of small, mobile missiles. There are also things you can do to get reasonable standards on verification of cruise missiles, limiting the numbers to a particular type of platform. It can be done, but it can only be done in the context of those cooperative measures.

So, the fourth step in this proposal is particularly about destabilizing forces. In that sense, I'm attracted to some of the points that Albert Gore has presented in terms of an alternative to the arms control proposals of the Reagan Administration.

Now, let me answer my good friend Jeremy Stone who complains that my approach is too narrow. Well, I've expanded my proposal to meet Jeremy's criticism, but let's not duck the point. It's a much more limited proposal than the proposal for a comprehensive freeze. Although it is a freeze in the sense that it responds to the public concern that enough is enough, it is not the same as a comprehensive freeze.

On the other hand, what I propose is a compromise which can help, I think, to pull together for political action people whose general interests run in the same direction. And I suspect, although I don't know this, that that may be the way the politics work out in terms of getting broader appeal in the body politic and in the Congress. But politics might not work out that way if we get into sectarian fights, if we get into "you're not a pure freezer; you are an impure freezer" and so forth. That would be unfortunate. In that sense, I think it's very beneficial for the freeze movement to keep the symbolism of the word "freeze" relatively vague.

Say that we're interested in a broad range of freezes, and that we're still studying many of the problems as to how comprehensive or inclusive they can be. If you keep to a broad symbolism, then you can incorporate all and excommunicate none, and you have a much more effective political movement. If, on the other hand, one gets into fights about who's a pure or impure freezer, a unilateralist or a multilateralist and so forth, I think we run the danger of weakening our own positions. As just a little example of this, even though I have written some things expressing skepticism about the Kennedy/Hatfield Resolution, I was pleased to be able to vote for the freeze resolution on the Massachusetts ballot last November. A lot of freeze people said, "Well, that Massachusetts resolution doesn't have exactly the right wording, it's too vague, it has loopholes in it and so forth." But it recruited at least one other person to your coalition; that's not to be neglected as 1984 approaches.

*　*　*

Avoiding Nuclear War: Can the Freeze Help?

Graham T. Allison

I regret that I have not been able to be present at all of the sessions of the conference. Unfortunately for a good portion of the last two days I have been preoccupied with another freeze, namely an attempt to negotiate a freeze on Governor Dukakis' raids on our faculty and central management. It does seem from what I have heard from participants who attended all of the sessions that this has been one of those rare meetings in which individuals not only talked to each other, but listened and maybe even learned.

Most of the recent public discussion of issues like this, particularly of nuclear strategy, including freezes, arms control, and the defense build-up, remind one of the comment that Alfred North Whitehead once made after a lecture by Bertrand Russell. Russell had given a lecture on the cosmos. Whitehead believed that Russell was ignorant of the cosmos. So at the conclusion of the lecture, he complimented him for the brilliance with which he left the vast darkness of the subject unobscured.

Fortunately, I gather that here, at least some of the darkness may have been dispelled. That this has occurred under the auspices of the Academy and the Center for Science and International Affairs of Harvard's John F. Kennedy School of Government, I am most pleased. The process of mutual education is a major purpose of this University, but one we too often neglect.

I find myself in substantial agreement with most of the comments in the panel. I will resist my inclination to comment on my disagreement with this or that particular item. Rather, I will try to raise and address three questions that take us perhaps a little further back to first principles as well as to what we agree on and where we may disagree.

My three questions briefly stated are:

1) What are we trying to do? Most mornings I remind myself of Nietzsche's observation that the most common form of human stupidity is forgetting what one is trying to do.

2) In that cause, whatever it is, what is our vision of the likely evolution of the U.S.–Soviet relationship over the next decade or two or three? Do we judge nuclear arms and changes in nuclear forces as a primary cause, or principally a symptom of the problem?

3) Politically, at the margins, where should one invest?

Let me address each in turn.

What are we trying to do? I have been impressed by the extent to which this conference has mostly remembered what we are about. Our objective is avoiding nuclear war, avoiding a major nuclear war. The goal is not to "stop the arms race," or to

Graham T. Allison is Dean of the John F. Kennedy School of Government, Harvard University, Cambridge, Massachusetts.

"save money," or to "insist that enough is enough." These may be instruments towards a longer-run objective. But the longer-run objective is to avoid nuclear war.

How is this problem to be approached? Let me outline a framework that several of us at Harvard have been trying to develop—a framework for thinking about actions that have the objective of reducing risks of nuclear war. As a first approximation, let me sketch three dimensions of the issue.

First, there are first *paths* to nuclear war—generic paths by which a nuclear war might plausibly occur. There is a large number of such paths. Most of us here could readily agree on a list of several, from a bolt out of the blue (that we prepare for, but which is least likely) to an escalation from a conventional conflict, to an accidental or unauthorized use, or even a catalytic or terroristic use of nuclear weapons that escalates to a major nuclear war.

The second column identifies *factors* that *increase* the risks of nuclear war. For each of the paths to nuclear war we can list a cluster of factors that increase risks of war along that path. For example, particular imbalances in force structure might, under certain circumstances, make it likely that there would, in some crisis situation, be a first use of nuclear weapons that would lead to nuclear war. So the second column identifies factors leading to nuclear war.

The third column consists of *actions* that, if taken, would *diminish* risks of nuclear war.

Let me offer an example. One generic path to war is a catalytic use of nuclear weapons by a third party against the U.S. or the Soviet Union—perhaps the People's Republic of China, perhaps Israel, which was, during the '73 war, rumored to have considered attempting to destroy Moscow if it was in jeopardy. Factors that increase risks that a catalytic use could lead to war between superpowers include the proliferation of nuclear weapons, the technical capabilities in delivery systems of those who have nuclear weapons, and the intelligence capabilities of both the U.S. and the Soviet Union to identify who might have launched a nuclear weapon from where and with what effect.

We can identify a number of actions that might diminish the risks of nuclear war down that path—for example, proposals for an expanded U.S.-Soviet hotline. I believe it possible to identify a half dozen or even dozen other actions which, if taken, would reduce the risks of nuclear war. Developing such an agenda of action would seem to me to be an appropriate aspiration for those of us who remember, in the first instance, what we are trying to do.

The second question: in this cause of avoiding nuclear war, what is our vision, our expectation about the way the U.S. and the Soviet Union may relate to each other over the next ten or twenty or thirty years? My starting point for this is an observation made by a wise man some one hundred and fifty years ago. If you will permit me a paragraph, he says: "There are now two great nations in the world which, starting from different points, seem to be advancing towards the same goal. Their point of departure is different and their paths diverge. Nevertheless, each seems called by some secret design of Providence one day to hold in its hands the destiny of half the world." The two nations that de Tocqueville identified were the Soviet Union (Russia at the time) and the United States (or the Anglo-Americans as he called them). What then is our vision for this U.S.-Soviet relationship? What is our expectation of how this relationship is likely to evolve over the next decade or two or three?

My answer consists of three points. First, the relationship is essentially competitive for the geopolitical and historical reasons that de Tocqueville understood a hundred and fifty years ago. This is not likely to change in our lifetime, ideology aside. And ideology makes it even more so. It is a competition grounded deeply in all the forces of history as usual. While there is no benefit in the competition that would be worth a major nuclear war from which all of us or even the species would be threatened, there are, nonetheless, some benefits for which it is worth accepting some risk of nuclear war.

Second, as a function of technology the U.S. and the Soviet Union have the ability to destroy each other's society. This fact will not change over the next decade or two or three. This creates, therefore, between the U.S. and the Soviet Union a rather unlikely partnership, grounded in a fundamental interest, a fundamental common interest, and a necessity to work on behalf of that common interest—namely avoiding nuclear war. This provides a solid foundation on which to build.

Third, strategic arms are inevitably one dimension of the competition. By competing, the parties can win advantages that would, in fact, in some scenarios constitute disadvantages. Arms control agreements, as in the case of a freeze, therefore, can only restrain and channel, but not eliminate, this competitive element or a relationship consisting of some combination of a fundamental common interest (if we are smart enough to remember it) and competition (that is grounded in all the forces of history as usual). So, my answer to the second question is: no radical change from the pattern we have observed in the last ten or twenty or thirty years.

Which brings me then to my third question. At the margin, where should one invest? Where should folks here spend their limited time and energy in attempting to promote actions that would have the effect of reducing the risks of nuclear war?

I have been struck by the modesty of the pronouncements by the arms control experts at the conference. We have much to be modest about. The arms control community's record in this arena, in comparison, for example, with that of the Committee on the Present Danger, is one of the striking differences in recent national policy. Who would have forecast that the theoretical vulnerability of the land-based Minuteman could become a major issue in a campaign and, indeed, become a focus of national policy? Certainly this prospect appeared less likely than does the success of the freeze today.

Given the extraordinary success of freeze advocates in mobilizing public concern about the issue of nuclear war, I hesitate to offer a judgment. Nonetheless, when I consider the long-term competition between the U.S. and the Soviet Union I wonder: Would we prefer the comprehensive freeze currently proposed, or the current Soviet proposals on the table in START? Why might the Soviet Union be proposing equal numbers of launchers at 1800 as against a freeze at a level of 2400 Soviet and 2000 American missiles? While bargaining chips have been substantially discredited, and well so, what about incentives to negotiate? Is it likely that the Soviet Union would have made its current proposal—remarkably similar to President Carter's starting proposal that the Soviets rejected out of hand in 1979—without the Reagan Administration's demonstrated determination to compete?

Analyzing the American side of this long-term, dynamic competition between the U.S. and the Soviet Union, I conclude that there are two objectives that constitute operational constraints on the kinds of programs and proposals that will prove viable over any length of time. These two objectives or constraints seem to me to be *strength*, on the one hand, and *peace*, on the other. Immediate pressures and preoccupations aside, over any period of a decade, a posture that is not strong—which I suspect has to be defined as strength second to none—will not be viable. People who want something more than equality will join those in the middle ground to change the situation. The first constraint is thus strength second to none.

This system has an upper as well as a lower bound, as I think President Reagan has recently discovered. The second constraint requires a real commitment to peace-seeking and justification of U.S. strategic forces in terms of contributions to the avoidance of, not success in, nuclear war.

There is also, I infer, a third constraint: verifiability. Neglect of this concern, or too much infringement, will undermine any negotiated constraint on the competition.

Viable initiatives to reduce risks of nuclear war must meet these three criteria. While the freeze has been extremely successful in mobilizing public concern, I must confess I am doubtful that a comprehensive freeze will, over time, meet the test. I am more sanguine about Jeremy Stone's improved SALT II and Al Gore's proposals. I have been interested for some time in de-MIRVing and a single RV launcher. I also judge the range of options on the table in START today very interesting. Some may turn out to be negotiable; some would, if accepted, have the desired effect.

To conclude on a point with which I take it most participants will disagree, I am betting that over the next two years an agreement between the U.S. and the Soviet Union in START to limit strategic nuclear weapons will emerge. If so, this will be in no small part a result of the energy, enthusiasm, and political momentum of the freeze.

*　　*　　*

Legislating Bilateral Freeze Restraints and Mandating Negotiations on the Freeze

Jeremy J. Stone

Although a nuclear freeze was proposed by President Johnson in 1964, and by the U.S. Senate in 1970, the main precondition for a freeze—essential equivalence—has existed only recently. Some other important preconditions of a freeze that are falling into place are listed below:

a) There are economic conditions in both superpowers which, for perhaps the first time in decades, provide serious political motivation to try to lower weapon costs;

b) On the Western side, there now exists a much higher level of public sophistication about arms procurement and irritation with it;

c) On the Soviet side, there is much greater sophistication in designing and proposing arms control than ever before—backed by the successful experience of negotiating the very complicated SALT II treaty;

d) There is a popular movement in the United States seeking a freeze and much Soviet declaratory policy saying that a freeze would be worth pursuing;

e) There are Western unilateral verification capabilities that continue to improve steadily, but which are already fantastically better than any imagined to be possible when the freeze was first proposed in 1964;

f) There are so many weapons around on both sides that further deployment in the absence of agreement—much less cheating *under* an agreement—is unlikely to have any significant impact on the strategic balance.

Under these circumstances, it is politically feasible for arms controllers to do more than pursue such marginal formulas as "managing the arms race." On the contrary, it is becoming politically sensible to think in terms of achieving in the 1980s some kind of comprehensive agreement worthy of the name "freeze."

Indeed, relatively simple adjustments to the SALT II treaty—adjustments universally admitted to be every bit as verifiable as the SALT II treaty itself—would constitute such a freeze. In particular, the two sides could:

a) Eliminate the one-new-type of land-based missile permitted under SALT II.

b) Eliminate the right of both sides to new types of sea-based missiles under SALT II.

c) Solve the problem of alleged land-based missile vulnerability by reducing the SALT II limits by 50 percent, thereby permitting each side to reduce the emphasis on land-based missiles through "freedom to choose" what is thrown away.[1] (This was proposed by President Carter at the Vienna Summit.)

Jeremy J. Stone *is Director of the Federation of American Scientists, Washington, D.C.*

In short, one strategic freeze *does* exist—unquestionably verifiable and wholly feasible. Other freezes are negotiable, and would go still further. But the point is that *one* does exist and hence the notion of a freeze is not a fantasy.[2] (This proposal was the subject of hearings held by the Federation of American Scientists [FAS] and summarized in its January FAS Public Interest Report.)

Other "interim" freeze proposals which have been mentioned include:

a) A general ban on testing of warheads and flight-testing of new missiles of all kinds (Randy Forsberg).

b) A ban on flight-testing and further deployment of all weapons covered by either the START talks, the SALT II talks, or the INF talks (Roger Molander).

Sentiment will shift, I believe, away from denouncing "the" freeze as unworkable and infeasible toward designing acceptable freezes as steps toward ever more complete freezes. As a part of this shift some conference participants opposed to a freeze will announce that these more acceptable freezes are "not really" freezes. But this is only part of the adjustment process toward acceptance of the freeze notion.

Legislating Arms Control

For the next two years, the Reagan Administration may be unwilling to negotiate seriously about *any* arms control much less about a freeze. There is, however, an alternative to waiting for a new administration. The alternative is to design congressional amendments to military authorization bills that prohibit spending for specific weapon programs contingent on the Soviet Union's halting comparable spending. This can only be done, obviously, in cases where the proposal is easily defined and highly verifiable. But examples exist:

a) No funds shall be spent in fiscal 1984 to flight-test the one new ICBM permitted by SALT II whether it be the MX or any substitute unless the Soviet Union flight-tests the one new ICBM permitted it under SALT II in that fiscal year. (This interruption of flight-testing prevents deployment.)

b) No funds shall be spent to flight-test, in fiscal 1984, SLBMs which, under the SALT II rules applied to ICBMs, would be considered "new types" unless the Soviet Union conducts such tests in fiscal 1984.

c) No funds shall be spent to conduct underground nuclear weapons tests in fiscal 1984 unless and until the Soviet Union engages in underground nuclear weapons tests in that fiscal year.

d) No funds shall be spent in fiscal 1984 to deploy the 572 ground-launchd cruise and Pershing missiles if the Soviet Union announces, and begins to carry out, on a three-year schedule, a program of dismantlement of an equal number of warheads on SS-4s, SS-5s, and SS-20s (capable of striking Western Europe from their present deployments).

Over and above their value as "pieces" of a freeze, these interim restraints can be justified as methods of maintaining the preconditions of a freeze by forestalling developments that would make a freeze more difficult to attain. Taken together, they even constitute a freeze. In sum, such amendments constitute a method by which Congress could legislate bilateral, mutual, verifiable arms control leaving to the executive branch only the obligation and right to certify whether or not the contingency has been met by the Soviets.

Congressional Injunctions to Propose a Freeze

In addition to legislating arms control, Congress could attempt to legislate the tabling of proposals by the Administration. While it is not, obviously, possible for the legislature to enforce the good-faith bargaining of the executive branch on proposals which the executive branch does not wish to entertain, a congressional campaign of this kind could at least expose the isolation of the President on the issue of the freeze—isolation which wholly deserves being exposed—and might change the Administration's mind.[3]

For example, the Congress could cut off funding for one program or another until such time as the Administration made a freeze proposal to the Soviet Union. Programs which would be candidates for such cutoffs include: the program for weapons-grade fissionable material; the President's salary; the funding for the START negotiators; etc.

European Freezes

A main reason that the Reagan Administration does not want even a freeze related to strategic weapons—and a major reason why the Soviet Union might agree to one—is that such a freeze would have, as a corollary, some kind of halt to the U.S. deployment of Pershing and cruise missiles in Europe. Thus it is fair to say that a freeze of strategic forces would, almost necessarily, bring with it some kind of negotiated halt to major elements of the intermediate range forces in Europe.

Comprehensive Freeze

From a strictly technical point of view, it is not true that verification is the overwhelming obstacle to freezes that go beyond halts to new types of ICBMs and SLBMs and move on to halts in the production of nuclear warheads or the production of weapons grade fissionable material, etc. All depends, really, on how one defines verification, and relates it to national security.

For example, anything which the Soviet Union might do secretly under a treaty, it could do secretly in the absence of a treaty. Indeed, the treaties give rights of observation that make secrecy harder! As a consequence, as far as Soviet procurement is concerned, a comprehensive freeze agreement *strengthens* U.S. security against Soviet buildups. The "cost" in the agreement is its prohibitions on *U.S.* buildups. But since the *major* components precluded (ICBMs, SLBMs, etc.) are clearly verifiable, the only elements that have a potential cost are our agreement not to do such subsidiary things as testing new warheads, etc. And none of this is of much importance to our national security in the short and medium run. Moreover, since any significant Soviet cheating would eventually surface, there is not only little cost but an adequate degree of deterrence of Soviet cheating. Why would they risk the whole treaty for such minor advantage?

In particular, the flat statement of some arms controllers that a comprehensive freeze is not feasible, because unverifiable, hides a large number of political presumptions about what Congress might accept in a treaty and/or what the public wants.

And in the face of an aroused public, Congressmen will quickly shift from narrower to more enlightened definitions of verification.

The Role of Public Support

The arms control community discussing this subject is not sufficiently aware of the rising possibility of having real live public support for its goals. All past agreements of value (the Atmospheric Test Ban treaty and the ABM treaty) were the results of such support. Moreover, no meaningful proposals came about without such public support (e.g., note the failure of SALT II to be ratified). Accordingly, a major component of the thinking of all arms controllers should be to design proposals which capture the imagination of the public and harness the energies of the citizenry. For this reason, if no other, proposals which need not be more complete freezes, for one strategic reason or another, may do better when expanded to the point where they can be advanced under the flag of a halt to the arms race. And if there is serious popular support for a proposal it will be found to do surprisingly well politically; again, Congressmen with aroused constituents are not going to be pushovers for the kind of nit-picking objections to arms control agreements which are, at present, the main obstacles.

By the same token, arms control proposals which require more arms procurement are not going to be accepted as arms control; in particular, schemes to solve hypothetical vulnerability problems by building thousands of new single-warheaded missiles are entirely out of step with the times. They represent a misguided effort to solve an unreal problem. The argument that the Reagan Administration is not about to negotiate a freeze is quite short-sighted since the campaign for a freeze, like the campaign against the ABM, will take a few years anyway. Indeed, the decade or more necessary to produce and deploy the new single-warheaded missile will also extend beyond the Reagan Administration's tenure.

Timeliness

We are at a point in time in which a freeze would be especially appropriate. Once the two sides begin to deploy new ICBMs, especially if these turn out to be mobile and numerous, there will be new problems of verification, both political and substantive, and in any case, the ICBM deployment patterns will be in motion well into the 1990s. Modern cruise missiles will be beyond halting also. As a consequence, the first real chance to secure a freeze comes at a time when such a freeze has real value.

In sum, the times demand, and make possible, an effort to secure agreements that are more than scaffolding surrounding the arms race. Such comprehensive agreements, with a minimum of loopholes, are far more feasible than is generally considered, both technically and politically.

Further, if the administration refuses to table such proposals, Congress might legislate pieces of such agreements in a holding action. And if Congress wished, it could even mandate the tabling of some kind of freeze proposal.

Administrations easily forget that the executive branch is the servant of the people, through the Congress, and that the President is simply the executive officer of the

Government. As may be happening with budget policy generally, the President is risking a popular revolt on the freeze.

FAS Public Interest Report, April, 1982

Some Freeze Precursors
Lyndon Johnson and Secretary McNamara Proposed Freeze in 1964

The freeze was first proposed 18 years ago when the U.S. strategic buildup of 1,000 Minuteman missiles and 41 Polaris submarines was nearing completion and the Soviet buildup was not yet underway. At Geneva, U.S. representative Adrian Fisher proposed that:

The U.S., the Soviet Union, and the respective Allies should agree to explore a verified freeze of the number and characteristics of strategic nuclear offensive and defensive vehicles.

Here is what was said about it on January 31, 1964, at Geneva by ACDA Director William Foster:

First, the freeze should, we believe, include strategic missiles and aircraft. The categories of weapons affected should be defined along lines of range and weight. For this measure, the categories suggested in stage I of the United States outline of 18 April 1962, should be adjusted, we think, for several reasons. For instance, there have been changes in technology since those earlier categories were proposed. Moreover, the freeze would include only strategic categories; and it could be implemented before agreement on general and complete disarmament.

Secondly, the United States believes the freeze should also include antiballistic missile systems. A freeze on strategic delivery systems without a freeze on anti-missile systems would be destabilizing and therefore unacceptable.

Thirdly, the immediate objective of the freeze on numbers should be to maintain the quantities of strategic nuclear vehicles held by the East and the West at constant levels. As we see it, the agreement should provide for a suitable number of missile tests without warheads to ensure that missile systems continue to be reliable over a period of time. For this and related purposes, it should also provide for production of replacements on a one-for-one basis: one missile produced for one destroyed. This should not, of course, permit any increase by either side in the constant level which it is the purpose of the agreement to maintain.

Fourthly, the objective of the freeze on characteristics should be, the United States believes, to prevent the development and deployment of strategic vehicles of a significantly new type. Like the freeze on numbers, this should apply to defensive as well as offensive vehicles. The significance of this provision might well be greater than that of the freeze on numbers. It would halt the race to produce better strategic vehicles to carry bigger warheads. It would mean an end to the qualitative as well as to the quantitative strategic arms race.

Fifthly, as I have already indicated, we have singled out strategic vehicles partly because we believe that the verification requirements would be less onerous than for a production freeze on the entire range of major armaments included within our general and complete disarmament plan. One possible means of verifying the freeze would be to monitor significant existing production and testing facilities which each side would declare, and to provide for a special number of spot checks to guard against possible undeclared facilities. That is an example of the kind of verification requirement we have in mind. Additional problems would remain. However, we believe verification can be effective without being burdensome. We hope that a system acceptable to all concerned could be worked out.

Freeze Resolution Passed by Senate 73-6 in 1970

On June 17, 1969, Senator Brooke and 39 co-sponsors introduced a resolution urging the U.S. to refrain from additional flight tests of multiple independently targetable reentry vehicles so long as the Soviet Union did also. The Nixon Administration being reluctant to make such an initiative and the Foreign Relations Commitee being unsure whether the resolution should pinpoint this particular aspect of the arms race, it substituted a broader version at the initiative of Senator John Sherman Cooper which read:

Resolved: That it is the sense of the Senate that the President should urgently propose to the government of the Union of Soviet Socialist Republics an immediate suspension by the United States and by the Union of Soviet Socialist Republics of the further deployment of all offensive and defensive nuclear strategic weapons systems, subject to national verification or such other measures of observation and inspection as may be appropriate.

This resolution actually passed the Senate by a vote of 73-6 on April 9, 1970.[4]

ACDA Director Gerard C. Smith Considered Freeze in 1969

It appears likely that Senator John Sherman Cooper had been, at the least, encouraged by Gerard C. Smith, Director of ACDA under President Nixon. Smith had met, in classified session, with the Foreign Relations Committee on February 2, 1970, to discuss the Brooke resolution and it was subsequently, on March 20, 1970, that Senator Cooper proposed his "substitution." We see in Gerard Smith's book on arms control, *Doubletalk*, that Mr. Smith was also moving in 1969 from considering flight-test bans of the kind Brooke wanted to considering a general freeze, at the instigation of Sidney Graybeal. He says there:

My MIRV ban proposals soon merged into a broader position called SWWA, "Stop Where We Are," which involved not only stopping MIRV testing but cessation of Soviet ICBM and SLBM launcher construction programs. This proposal stemmed from a suggestion made by an Arms Control Agency official, Sidney Graybeal, who was a member of the SALT delegation and later the U.S. commissioner on the Soviet–American Standing Consultative Commission set up by the 1972 agreements. SWWA was based on a simple concept that the way to stop arms competition was to stop strategic construction programs on both sides. Both now had sufficient strategic forces to deter nuclear war. Instead of trying to elaborate agreed levels for strategic forces and other complex arrangements, why not just freeze things at the 1969 level? At the suggestion of Henry Owen, a former colleague on the Policy Planning Staff of the State Department and later its director, I recalled for the President the worldwide support which the United States received when Charles Evans Hughes proposed such a plan for strategic naval forces at the Washington Naval Conference in 1921. It was not at all clear that the U.S.S.R. would accept such a proposal, but by proposing it we could take the "high ground" psychologically and, if necessary later, move to something more modest if that was the most the Soviets would accept. I considered SWWA the best way to start the negotiation.

SOVIET FREEZE-RELATED PROPOSALS

The U.S.S.R. proposed a prohibition on the development and manufacture of nuclear weapons and new types and new systems of weapons of mass destruction on September 28, 1976 (in conjunction with a ban on nuclear weapons tests, and reductions of warhead stockpiles and their means of delivery). A call to halt production of nuclear weapons and a ban on nuclear weapon testing was repeated by President Leonid Brezhnev on November 2, 1977, to the 25th Party Congress.

A halt to production of all types of nuclear weapons was repeated on May 26, 1978 to the U.N. General Assembly, and was effectively repeated, with a call also for reductions on February 6, 1979 to the Geneva Committee on Disarmament.

In April, 1980, a letter from Andrei Gromyko to the U.N. Secretary General called for the same goals including qualitative limitations, and quantitative reductions of ICBMs and SLBMs.

FAS WINS RELEASE OF FREEZE ANALYSIS, OCTOBER 1982

Responding to an ACLU lawsuit initiated by FAS, the Government released, on October 29, declassified portions of a 1969 analysis prepared by the Arms Control and Disarmament Agency (ACDA) in support of a freeze. Initiated by Gerard Smith, then the ACDA Director, the paper was the basis of an ACDA appeal to President Nixon to propose a freeze to the Soviet Union under the rubric "Stop Where We Are."

To secure the document, the Federation had turned to its Council Member Morton Halperin, now Director of the Center for National Security Studies, which specializes, among other things, in Freedom of Information Act (FOIA) suits. Halperin's Center, which is affiliated with the ACLU, was doubly well suited to pursue the suit since, at the time of the paper, Halperin had been a key staff member of the Nixon White House National Security Council and had lived through the period when Nixon refused this appeal.

The Government first refused any release both on initial request (March 12, 1982) and on appeal. But after the suit was filed in District court, and pursued by ACLU attorney Susan Shaffer, who works with Halperin, the Defense Department decided to release such portions as might placate Judge Richey in subsequent hearings.

Although the paper appears to have at least 14 pages, only about 2 pages worth of text were released. But as Halperin readily spotted, the first two lines of the introduction carried the key conclusions. The paper began:

This paper examined the implications of a quantitative and qualitative freeze on all aspects of strategic offense and defensive forces that are subject to adequate verification by national means. In view of the extent of our present and projected national intelligence resources, this essentially amounts to a proposal to "Stop Where We Are" (SWWA) with respect to strategic forces.

In short, there was, even in 1969, enough in the way of intelligence resources to monitor a freeze on strategic forces.

The paper noted that the SWWA proposal would:

1. "preserve the present stable strategic balance in which both sides have a confident second-strike capability and are far from achieving a first-strike capability";

2. "virtually eliminate the potential Soviet counterforce threat against U.S. Minuteman force";

3. "improve our confidence that the Soviets were not developing MIRV's";

4. "would provide the U.S. with far greater budgetary savings, both short-term and long-term, than any alternative which permits substantial new strategic weapons programs."

The sections of the paper on "verification," "strategic analysis," "safeguards," "negotiability" and "economic implications" were completely blank. But the analysis ends by seeming to encourage a moratorium during negotiations:

some of the advantages of a SWWA agreement to the U.S. would be reduced if the Soviets continued to build ICBM silos and SLBM submarines and carry on MRV or MIRV flight testing during the SALT negotiations.

The paper was precisely what we desired: concrete proof that a freeze could be conceived. Speaking for the Federation, Director Stone said:

"We had to sue to secure this document because we knew and the Administration knew, that it would show the freeze was not a pipedream."

The paper was turned over to an AP reporter and, because it had been released only four days before the election, seemed important news at least in those nine states where the freeze was on the ballot. Some of the media with larger audiences played the story down or ignored it because it was too close to the election; they prefer not to print news that seems to require a response too near an election. But after the election, the *Washington Post* printed a 2,000 word piece by Stone entitled: "The Experts Can't Ignore Demands for a Nuclear Freeze Forever" which included reference to it. Only the *New York Times* appears to have ignored the issue. Its editorials have not only opposed the freeze but done so with real venom.

A few days later, the Defense Department released further information in response to our suit: the first public description of the SWWA proposal, still highly relevant! It follows:

Description of SWWA Proposal

A. *Basic Proposal*

1. The number of operational ICBM, IRBM, MRBM, SLBM, SLCM, and ABM

launchers on each side shall be limited respectively to the number in each category which are operational at the time the agreement is negotiated.[5]

2. There shall be a complete prohibition of flight testing or deployment of MIRV's and mobile land-based strategic offensive and ABM missiles.

3. Changing or improving the characteristics of deployed strategic missiles and missile launchers shall be prohibited, except for minor internal changes, such as those designed to improve missile reliability or RV hardening, or to provide exoatmospheric penetration aids. Prohibited changes shall include those involving throw-weight, accuracy, range, and external launcher, missile, and RV characteristics.

4. Flight tests of strategic offensive missiles and ABM missiles shall be limited to an agreed number of pre-announced confidence firings of only previously tested types of strategic missiles on agreed ranges. Both sides shall agree to announce two weeks in advance all firings of both military and non-military rockets which are intended to exit the atmosphere (achieve altitudes exceeding 200 kilometers). There shall be a complete prohibition of further flight testing of multiple reentry vehicles (MRV's), maneuvering reentry vehicles MaRV's), post-boost maneuvering, fractional and multiple orbital weapon systems (FOBS and MOBS), ICBM's which reenter the atmosphere at elevation angles less than 10 degrees, and endo-atmospheric penetration aids.

5. The introduction of new types of missile-firing submarines, or changes in the size or external configuration of existing types, shall be prohibited. However, one-for-one replacement of such submarines with new units of the same type, under agreed procedures for verification of submarine destruction, shall be permitted.

6. The number of ABM-associated radars shall be limited to those which are operational at the time the agreement is negotiated.

7. The number of strategic bombers and SAM launchers on each side shall be limited to those operational at the time the agreement is negotiated. The introduction of new types of strategic bombers or air defense systems, or changes in the size or external configuration of existing types or systems, shall be prohibited. However, one-for-one replacement of aircraft with new units of the same type, under agreement procedures for verification of aircraft destruction, shall be permitted.

---

1. Such an agreement would, by mathematical coincidence (and with simple and natural side conditions) force the Soviet Union to most of what the Reagan plan requires (850 ICBMs and SLBMs on a side, 5,000 warheads on such missiles and 2,500 warheads on ICBMs—the last is the only condition not quite achieved and here the result would be 3,500, down from 5,500).

2. What is a freeze agreement? I start from the assumption that the freeze proposal historically, and today as well, has not been designed to eliminate nuclear deterrents by letting them rust away without replacement. On the contrary, "reductions" rather than "rust" are the implied method of diminishing the nuclear threat.

Accordingly, replacement of worn-out missiles by missiles of this same type is assumed. As a consequence, what is at issue in a freeze agreement is precluding "new types" of missiles. Therefore an agreement that precludes such new types of strategic missiles is, insofar as missiles are concerned, a strategic force freeze.

With the same reasoning, bombers and submarines carrying nuclear warheads could be replaced when they wore out; indeed, they are considered by some leading freeze personalities to be the "trucks" which carry the missiles around, and are not restricted to replacement only when worn out.

In effect, a strategic nuclear freeze is an agreement not to expand in number or modernize strategic missiles or warheads. Strictly speaking, by this definition, the Comprehensive Test Ban should be added to the above, and we would indeed consider this wholly verifiable especially when conjoined with the other measures, as argued below under "Comprehensive Freeze."

For the record, President Johnson's freeze was a "verified freeze of the number and characteristics of strategic nuclear offensive and defensive vehicles" whose "immediate objective" was to "maintain the quantities of strategic nuclear vehicles . . . at constant levels" and, in its freeze on characteristics, to prevent the "development and deployment of strategic vehicles of a significantly new type."

Both it and the circa 1979 freeze worked out in ACDA under Gerard Smith looked toward "one-for-one" replacement of weapons. Information on these two freezes is attached from past FAS newsletters for the reader's convenience.

3. The Administration recently answered the request of the National Campaign for a Freeze for an appointment with the President to discuss the meaning of the November 2, 1982 referendums with a form letter. And the President has falsely stated, as part of the Administration's effort to smear the freeze, the Mr. Brezhnev was the first to propose it—this despite earlier proposals by Presidents Johnson (1964) and Carter (1979) and the U.S. Senate (1970).

4. The Senate Committee Report commented on verification in a way that could have been written today:

The question naturally arises whether a suspension of the deployment of all offensive and defensive strategic weapons systems, which the resolution as reported urges, can be verified. The committee is inclined to the view that a general halt in the deployment of all strategic weapons is more secure against significant evasion than a more limited suspension would be. First of all, it is easier to monitor the strategic activity of an adversary in the context of a general freeze on the deployment of all new weapons than it is to monitor a situation characterized by constant change in the types and numbers of strategic weapons systems involved. Second, given the rough parity which now prevails between the United States and the Soviet Union, far more evasion would be required to provide one party with a significant advantage within the context of a general suspension of the further deployment of all weapons than would be required in the case of a more limited suspension.

5. Launchers are deemed operational when their external appearance indicates that they could be operational.

* * *

Executive Summary

A Nuclear Freeze Reprise

Steven E. Miller

The nuclear freeze issue that has burst upon the public scene in the United States in the past two years is important in two interrelated ways. First, as a political force, it is a movement to be reckoned with in American politics; its electoral power and influence on the behavior of Congress and even the Reagan Administration have become increasingly significant. Second, as an arms control proposal, it represents the revival of a broad and bold approach to the problem of limiting nuclear arms, one whose essential simplicity and comprehensiveness have made it appealing to the wider public, but one whose ambitious inclusiveness raises a number of important substantive issues pertaining to verification and negotiability.

Public Opinion and the Freeze

Public support for the freeze is very strong and presently shows no sign of abating. Opinion polls taken at the end of 1982 and early in 1983 indicate that three-fourths or more of the electorate favors a nuclear freeze and that as many as 90 percent of those polled back an end to the production and testing of nuclear weapons by the superpowers. The depth and intensity of current public support for nuclear arms control are unusual, if not unprecedented, and contrast notably with the experience of the recent past, as when SALT II failed to rouse public enthusiasm. In mobilizing public sentiment behind the freeze proposal, the freeze movement has succeeded in creating a political environment in the United States highly favorable to arms control. This is something that the traditional community of arms control experts has rarely been able to do. It creates an opportunity for measurable progress in arms control.

The Reagan Administration, however, has firmly resisted the notion of a nuclear freeze and has sought to rebuff and discredit the freeze movement. Nevertheless, many feel that the freeze movement (and its European counterpart) has played a significant role in pushing the Reagan Administration to overcome its reservations about Soviet–American arms control and that the administration's pursuit of nuclear arms negotiations in Geneva and its continued adherence to SALT limits even in the absence of formal ratification of the SALT II treaty are indirect, if not direct, consequences of public pressure. And, of course, should the Reagan Administration's own arms control efforts bear fruit, the political atmosphere would be supportive of that result.

Steven E. Miller *is Assistant Director of the Center for Science and International Affairs at Harvard University, Cambridge, Massachusetts, and Managing Editor of* International Security.

Congress, an even more sensitive barometer of public opinion, has been quite responsive to the stimulus provided by the freeze movement; several outspoken champions of the freeze have emerged in the House and Senate, for example. And a congressional freeze resolution seems likely to pass the House in 1983 and will attract considerable support in the Senate as well. The political strategy of the freeze movement is to focus its efforts on Congress in 1983 while working to ensure that the freeze is a major issue in the 1984 presidential campaign.

The Conceptual Foundations of the Freeze

The freeze movement is obviously a potent political force, but what are the ideas and attitudes that lie behind it? There are several central notions which constitute the foundation on which the freeze proposal is based. The most basic of these is the belief that it is no longer adequate simply to manage the arms race, as past arms control efforts have attempted to do. Rather, it is time to halt and then reverse the arms race. A comprehensive freeze which stops all deployments is seen as a first significant step in this process.

This belief is derived from several closely related conclusions: that the superpowers have advanced to the point in the development of their nuclear forces that no new improvements are needed, even if they might be stabilizing; that the arsenals on both sides are so large that the deployment of additional warheads is no longer a source of added stability; and, moreover, that most of the impending deployments represent the acquisition of warfighting—that is, destabilizing—capabilities. The size and diversity embodied in the current nuclear balance have led, in this view, to a highly durable deterrent situation, even by prudent definitions of deterrence. More expansive definitions of deterrence, which require significant warfighting capabilities and options, are seen as both unnecessary and dangerous. At base, then, this perspective flows from confidence in the stability of the nuclear balance and its relative insensitivity to quantitative or qualitative changes.

But the partisans of the freeze believe not only that the requirements of deterrence have been satisfied and that it is senseless to attempt more; beyond this, they feel that the continuation of the arms race is itself a source of danger and instability. The ongoing accumulation of nuclear arms is felt to poison Soviet–American relations, creating mutual mistrust and friction, and to contribute to the militarization of world politics, thus increasing the risk of nuclear war in two ways. Hence, it is imperative to stop the nuclear arms race because it is both wasteful and hazardous. This line of reasoning, which much of the American public seems to find persuasive, has led to the articulation of the proposal for a comprehensive nuclear freeze.

The Content of the Comprehensive Freeze Proposal

The comprehensive freeze proposal calls for a mutual and verifiable halt to the production, testing, and deployment of nuclear weapons and their means of delivery. The general idea of a freeze is not really new. Indeed, President Johnson advanced a nuclear freeze proposal in 1964; the Senate passed a resolution in 1970 calling for a freeze; and President Carter offered a freeze to Soviet leader Leonid Brezhnev in 1979.

Nor is the comprehensive freeze a complete departure from the agenda of arms control in the past decade or two. In fact, there is a substantial overlap between the freeze and the major nuclear arms control endeavors pursued in the past. Much of what is contained in the comprehensive freeze proposal, for example, is encompassed by the SALT II treaty and the comprehensive test ban (CTB) negotiations. This element of continuity has often not been sufficiently appreciated even by traditional supporters of arms control, at least some of whom have been dubious about the freeze because they feared it was too abrupt, too radical, and too ambitious a break with the past.

But in two significant respects, the freeze is different. First, and most important, it is intended to prevent further modernization of nuclear forces. Previous agreements placed limits on numbers of nuclear delivery systems and nuclear warheads, and, through constraints on testing, even attempted to control the pace of modernization, but nevertheless still permitted wide latitude to the superpowers in the acquisition of new systems. This is true, for example, of the Reagan Administration's START proposal, which would reduce the number of systems possessed by the two sides but would not prevent continued modernization. The freeze would bring modernization to a complete stop (save for a small number of carefully defined exceptions—such as the replacement of aging strategic submarines—which would be made in order to ensure that the superpowers' deterrent retaliatory capability would not erode over time). In this sense, the freeze exceeds in scope all past and current official arms control efforts. And it is this feature of the freeze, proponents feel, that curtails the arms race, that prevents the next twist in the arms spiral, and that strongly appeals to a public that feels that "enough is enough."

Second, and more narrowly, the freeze would include a ban on the production of nuclear warheads. This, too, is a genuinely new proposition, one that goes beyond anything seriously proposed in the past. Its virtue is that it attacks the problem of the nuclear arms competition at its source: the creation of nuclear weapons. It is also, however, one of the more controversial aspects of the comprehensive freeze proposal, since critics contend that such a ban could not be verified except by highly intrusive means of inspection. Advocates of the ban argue that it is adequately verifiable, if only because cheating on a scale that would make a strategic difference in the current era of nuclear plenty is extremely unlikely to go undetected, and that it constitutes an integral part of the effort to confront the nuclear arms race directly and to bring it under meaningful control.

Thus, the comprehensive freeze proposal combines the essential elements of the SALT, START, and CTB negotiations with these two more ambitious constraints. Hence, while much of what would be included in the freeze has already been the subject of negotiation and in many instances has been included in agreements, full acceptance of the comprehensive proposal would require the breaking of new and unprecedentedly constraining ground in arms control.

Critiques of the Freeze

This approach has not been without its critics. Some of these are basically sympathetic to the freeze but fear that its reach will exceed its grasp, that in seeking to achieve everything it will achieve nothing. Other sympathizers differ on questions of priority, and worry, for example, that the freeze campaign ought to focus first on the most destabilizing weapons.

But there are also those who reject the freeze as a fundamentally flawed approach to nuclear arms control. These critics voice several central concerns. First, to impose a freeze now would be to preserve the present high numbers of nuclear forces and would perpetuate the instabilities that presently exist in the strategic balance. In addition, it would condemn the United States to the possession of an aging and, in some respects at least, vulnerable strategic posture. Moreover, and worse, it would preserve current Soviet strategic advantages or, put differently, would lock the United States into a position of inferiority. This, in turn, would weaken Soviet incentives for moving toward reductions since a freeze would better preserve their advantages. It is also argued that a comprehensive freeze is not fully verifiable and consequently might jeopardize America's national security if the Soviets were to cheat successfully. And finally, it is suggested that the current proposals for reductions tabled by both the United States and the Soviet Union in the START talks have already gone beyond the freeze to substantial cuts in nuclear forces. Many, including the Reagan Administration, find the sum of these points to be a compelling case against the freeze.

Freeze proponents, of course, have answers to these criticisms. The freeze, they say, is not meant to perpetuate high numbers or to be an alternative to reductions, but rather is a prelude to cuts in the nuclear arsenals of the superpowers. They point out that it is possible to remedy instabilities by eliminating systems as well as by adding them. They dispute the notion that such vulnerabilities as exist in the U.S. strategic force are of a combined magnitude sufficient to jeopardize the fundamental deterrent relationship. They comment, as noted above, that the START proposals do not go beyond the freeze proposal in prohibiting modernization. And most supporters of the freeze would simply disagree with the assertions of their critics about the status of the nuclear balance and the structure of Soviet arms control incentives.

Indeed, proponents and opponents of the freeze tend to divide along several major fault-lines with respect to their perceptions of the current strategic situation. Whereas critics feel that America's nuclear inferiority makes the freeze a bad idea, advocates believe that the present existence of nuclear parity makes this an opportune moment to pursue a freeze. Whereas opponents fear that nuclear stability is fragile and presently jeopardized by present or emerging vulnerabilities, freeze supporters believe that mutual deterrence is extremely durable given the enormous nuclear forces on both sides. And while critics see technological modernization as a way of *solving* vulnerability problems, proponents see that modernization as the *cause* of vulnerability. Finally, while skeptics fear the political and military consequences of marginal changes in the strategic balance, enthusiasts believe that such changes are insignificant. Thus the disagreement between supporters and critics of the freeze boils down to several fundamental (and in some cases, theological) differences of perception and interpretation. Where these differences are questions of fact, they can and ought to be resolved. Where they are matters not of fact but of instinct, the existence of disagreement should not be taken as proof that the freeze is flawed.

Partial Freezes

Although it is the comprehensive freeze proposal that has attracted the most attention, caught the public imagination, and garnered the most political support, the rise of the freeze movement has also generated considerable interest in various partial freezes. Those who advocate the pursuit of a partial freeze are motivated by one or the other of two concerns. There are, first, those who more or less wholeheartedly support the comprehensive freeze but see the need for quick, easily negotiable interim steps. In the second category are those who are sympathetic to arms control but continue to harbor doubts about the feasibility and/or desirability of the comprehensive freeze. To this group, a partial freeze represents a way to capitalize on current public interest and support while avoiding some of the difficulties that might be raised by the more ambitious proposal. As a result of these two sorts of concerns, there has arisen a modest but growing menu of partial freezes.

One of the simplest of these is the idea of freezing numbers of warheads deployed on delivery systems with ranges in excess of 1000 kilometers. By a stroke of good fortune, both the United States and the Soviet Union possess approximately 11,000 nuclear warheads deployed on such systems, which lends a nice symmetry to this proposal. This freeze would, its proponents argue, break the psychology of the arms race by ending the heretofore ceaseless accumulation of warheads and by creating a situation in which new deployments would require the dismantling of old systems. By forcing tradeoffs among strategic deployments, it would contribute to more rational force planning. Last, but far from least, this approach has the virtue that it would be simple to negotiate, to understand, and to explain to the public.

A related scheme calls for a freeze on the testing and deployment of all nuclear weapons systems with a range greater than 1000 kilometers. This would have the effect of indirectly limiting numbers of warheads while preventing deployment of new strategic delivery systems. Like the former proposal, this has the virtue of simplicity, and is thought to be rapidly negotiable and easily verifiable.

Some go a step further and urge that a freeze on ballistic missiles be combined with a comprehensive test ban so that the development of new nuclear weapons is prevented also. Still others see in SALT II the core of a substantial freeze, one that is demonstrably negotiable and verifiable. And, of course, it is possible to develop partial freezes that combine elements of these approaches with other specific restraints. One way to expand the warhead freeze, for example, would be to couple it with a ban on new multiple warhead missiles, thus constraining the most destabilizing form of modernization while limiting warhead numbers.

The common feature of the partial freezes is that they do not include the two most distinctive features of the comprehensive freeze: the complete halt to nuclear modernization and the ban on production of warheads. In addition, they tend to exclude tactical nuclear weapons, of which there are many thousands. For these reasons, proponents of the comprehensive freeze tend to feel that partial freezes fall short of truly bringing the arms race under control and they worry that talking of freezes in the plural may dilute the political attractiveness of the freeze campaign.

The Feasibility of a Comprehensive Freeze

But is a comprehensive freeze really feasible? In the end, that is the crucial question, for it will not matter how desirable it is if it is not attainable. The answer depends primarily on judgments about three substantive issues: verification; the tradeoffs between timing, coverage, verification, and negotiability; and Soviet interests and incentives.

Of these, the one which has inspired the most skepticism about the freeze is verification. It seems clear, however, that it is misleading simply to dismiss the comprehensive freeze as unverifiable. In many of its dimensions—for example, the ban on testing and deployment of ballistic missiles or the limit on numbers of warheads and delivery systems—the comprehensive freeze has requirements for verification that are identical with those of SALT I, SALT II, and the Reagan START proposal, which are generally considered to be verifiable. It is evident, therefore, that there is much within the comprehensive freeze proposal that *is* verifiable.

This point many critics will concede. But they will then ask: Is a comprehensive freeze *fully* verifiable? Answering this question leads to a contemplation of some of the aspects of the comprehensive freeze that are difficult to monitor and less certainly verifiable. The ban on the production of new fissionable material and new warheads falls into this category, as does the prohibition on production of new delivery systems; and constraints on dual-capable systems raise ticklish verification problems as well. Issues such as these have not been fully addressed in past negotiations, nor have they been extensively studied by the academic arms control community. Hence, the definitive word on the verifiability of these more challenging aspects of the freeze has not yet been produced. Proponents of the freeze ask, not unfairly, that the absence of final answers on some of these questions not lead to the conclusion that the freeze is unverifiable and thus infeasible, that the freeze not be assumed guilty until proven innocent.

Furthermore, there are reasons why these measures may be more verifiable than the skeptics believe possible. For one thing, because the freeze would involve a comprehensive ban on production, testing, and deployment, *any* detected nuclear weapons-related activity would constitute an unambiguous violation of the agreement. A second and related point is that the production of, say, a nuclear warhead is not simply an isolated act but part of a process of manufacture, testing, deployment, storage, and training leading to incorporation into the force in an operationally usable manner. While some phases of this overall process are harder to track than others, there are points in the process which are highly visible, which makes it very difficult to operationally augment one's force unobserved even if it is possible to fabricate nuclear weapons covertly.

Third, the levels of forces on the two sides are so high that cheating would have to be on a very large scale for it to make much difference in the strategic balance; cheating of that magnitude, it is suggested, is extremely unlikely to go undetected. This line of reasoning leads to a more fundamental point about the nature of verification: its purpose is not to catch every conceivable violation (indeed, if we ask for perfection in verification there can be no arms control) but to safeguard America's security against threatening breaches of agreement. Consequently, the important question is not whether violations could occur, but rather whether undetected violations would be important and whether important violations could go undetected. By these standards, freeze advocates argue, the comprehensive freeze is verifiable because any substantial covert Soviet program of strategic significance would surely be detected before it reached the operational stage.

The argument over verification is not finished, and there remain issues in need of further detailed investigation. But the lines of debate so far are not such as to discredit the freeze. And further study seems as likely to vindicate supporters of the freeze as it is to give comfort to their opponents.

A second major dispute relating to the feasibility of the freeze has to do with the possible tradeoffs between the comprehensiveness, the verifiability, the negotiability, and the timing of a freeze. The freeze resolutions call for an immediate, bilateral, verifiable freeze. Critics charge that this is a contradiction in terms, that it is impossible to achieve all that simultaneously. According to this logic, the more inclusive an agreement is, the more difficult it is to verify, the more complicated it is to negotiate, the less likely it is to be acceptable to the Soviet Union, and the longer it will take to complete the negotiation. If this be true, ask the skeptics, what is sacrificed? How do we establish priorities among these several considerations? And it is because they fear that the foremost concern of the freeze campaign is to stop new American deployments (thereby sacrificing the mutuality of the freeze) or to rapidly reach agreement (while compromising standards of verification if necessary) that opponents of the freeze find it so alarming.

In response to these concerns, freeze advocates deny that the tradeoffs are so stark. For one thing, they point out that haste is not essential to the freeze; indeed, given the slow pace of deployment, the freeze could stop the next round of the arms race even if conceived of as a medium-term goal. For another, they do not accept the proposition that the inclusiveness of the freeze necessarily detracts from its verifiability or its negotiability. Rather, they suggest that the freeze is more verifiable (because of the arguments noted above) and may well be easier to negotiate than many less ambitious arms control schemes.

The issue of negotiability raises the third main area of controversy about the feasibility of the freeze: Soviet interests and incentives. Obviously, the freeze cannot be bilateral if the Soviet Union will have no part of it. On this subject the evidence is mixed. While Soviet commentary has generally been favorable toward the freeze proposal and while it clearly views the emergence of the freeze movement as a favorable development, it has almost without exception avoided official endorsement of the bilateral freeze proposal. Moreover, Moscow's own arms control agenda (as evidenced in official statements as well as behavior in the Geneva talks) differs in essential respects from the Western freeze proposal. In particular, the Soviets show few signs of interest in precluding modernization and may in fact have an incentive to preserve the possibility of modernization so that they may deal with the vulnerability of their ICBM force and deploy their new MIRVed submarine-launched ballistic missiles.

On the other hand, Moscow has just completed a cycle of modernization that substantially increased the operational capability of their force and the programs now in the pipeline will not radically augment their force. Meanwhile, the United States is now moving ahead rapidly with a broad strategic modernization program that will measurably improve its operational capabilities. Under these circumstances, the Soviets could well conclude that they are better off if neither side deploys new weapons than if both do. If so, the freeze could seem quite attractive to them.

In sum, then, is the comprehensive freeze feasible? Short of actually reaching an agreement, of course, it is impossible to prove that it is. At this stage of the game, however, it may be more significant that no one yet has demonstrated conclusively that it is not. In order to fully assess the prospects for a comprehensive freeze, several contentious issues will need to be clarified:

- By what criteria are we to judge whether or not a freeze would lock the United States into a disadvantageous position in the strategic balance?
- What are the detailed, technical considerations that bear on the verifiability of a ban on the production of warheads and delivery systems and of constraints on dual-capable systems?
- How will the timing of the implementation of a freeze affect its utility?
- If a freeze is implemented, can existing deterrent systems be properly maintained without violating the ban on modernization?
- How will a freeze be related to various possible schemes for reduction? And would a freeze diminish incentives to reduce?
- What are Soviet interests relative to a comprehensive freeze, and how might it affect Soviet policies and politics?

These questions deserve careful, detailed answers. For the moment, what we need to do is get to work providing them. Only thus can we move beyond the political frictions that divide us to some common understanding about what arms control paths best tame the nuclear danger without jeopardizing American security.

* * *